**Student Study Guide
to Accompany**

# EDUCATIONAL PSYCHOLOGY
## Classroom Connections

**Paul D. Eggen**
University of North Florida

**Don Kauchak**
University of Utah

Merrill, an imprint of
Macmillan Publishing Company
*New York*

Maxwell Macmillan Canada
*Toronto*

Maxwell Macmillan International
*New York  Oxford  Signapore  Sydney*

Cover art: Paul Klee, <u>Child and Aunt</u>, 1937, Courtesy Galerie Beyeler, Basel

Macmillan Publishing Company
113 Sylvan Avenue, Englewood Cliffs, NJ 07632

ISBN 0-02-331705-1

Printing    3 4 5 6 7 8 9  Year    5 6

# TABLE OF CONTENTS

INTRODUCTION

# INTRODUCTION TO THE STUDENT STUDY GUIDE
## TO ACCOMPANY EGGEN AND KAUCHAK'S
## *EDUCATIONAL PSYCHOLOGY: CLASSROOM CONNECTIONS*

## TO THE STUDENT

As with our revision of the text, we have prepared this guide to *Educational Psychology: Classroom Connections* (2nd ed.) with you, the student, in mind. This review is intended to complement and reinforce the content in the text. If you use the guide in concert with your study of the text, it should help give you a more thorough and deeper understanding of the nature of learning, and how factors such as student development and individual differences, motivation, classroom management, instruction, and assessment all affect student learning. Our goal is for this guide to contribute to your success as you study educational psychology--a critical foundation for understanding teaching and learning.

## USING THE GUIDE

In preparing the guide we have attempted to use concepts from the content of the text. For example, the guide is organized according to the chapters of the text, and each chapter is divided into seven sections: 1) A detailed Chapter Outline, 2) Chapter Objectives, 3) A Chapter Overview that summarizes the content, 4) A Chapter-At-A-Glance matrix, 5) A Guided Review that has you put chapter content into your own words, 6) Application Exercises that ask you to apply chapter content to new situations, and 7) A Self-Check Quiz that gives you some additional feedback about your understanding of the chapter.

Each section is summarized below.

## CHAPTER OUTLINE

The Chapter Outline presents the organization of each chapter. All section headings are identified in the outline.

## CHAPTER OBJECTIVES

The Chapter Objectives specify what you are expected to achieve as you study each chapter.

## CHAPTER OVERVIEW

The Chapter Overview summarizes the content of each chapter. You can use the overview in different ways. You may want to read it before you begin your detailed study of the chapter in the text to provide you with a frame of reference, you may want to read it after completing your study to help you identify the most important elements of each chapter, or you may combine the two.

## CHAPTER-AT-A-GLANCE _____

This section provides a quick reference to each of the chapter's main sections, the most important ideas presented in the sections, and the key concepts for each section identified by page number. As with the Chapter Overview, the Chapter-At-A-Glance can be used to provide a frame of reference, review, or both.

## GUIDED REVIEW

The Guided Review requires that you carefully reexamine the content of the chapter and respond in writing to specific questions. In this way you are actively involved in processing the information in each chapter. This interaction with the text content, together with your responses to the Connections in the margins of the text, and the Application Exercises in this guide should help you acquire a thorough understanding of the content of each chapter.

## APPLICATION EXERCISES _____

The Application Exercises ask you to apply the content of each chapter to an authentic classroom situation. As with the Guided Review, the Application Exercises place you in an active role.

Since specific answers to the exercises cannot be taken directly from the text, feedback is provided for each. The feedback is at the end of the guide. Your study will be much more effective if you first try to answer the exercises in writing before referring to the feedback, and we strongly recommend this as a study strategy.

## SELF-HELP QUIZ _____

Each chapter concludes with a quiz. As with other sections of the guide, you can use the quiz in different ways. You may choose to respond before you begin your study, to pretest your background with the chapter content, your may wait until you've completed your study, or you can combine the two. Answers to all the items are provided at the end of the guide.

# CHAPTER ONE
# TEACHING IN THE REAL WORLD

## CHAPTER OUTLINE _____

## CHAPTER OBJECTIVES _____

- Identify implications of studying educational psychology for classroom practice.
- Explain how research in educational psychology is applied to classroom practice.
- Describe the relationship between research and theory.
- Explain what "professional decision making" means.
- Describe ways that knowledge of educational psychology contributes to the professional decision-making process.
- Summarize the major points in the teaching--art or science--controversy
- Explain how reflective teaching uses educational psychology to improve professional decision making.

# CHAPTER OVERVIEW

This chapter introduces you to educational psychology, which is an analysis of learning and the influences on it. As you examine the contents of your text, you will study--in addition to the nature of learning itself--learner development, individual differences, and motivation, together with the impact that teachers have on learning as a result of their skills in instruction, management, and assessment.

In order to best promote learning in their students, teachers must have a thorough understanding of research on teaching and learning, the principles of important theories, and the wisdom derived from veteran teachers' experiences. The same is true for professionals in every field.

To be practical, this knowledge must be applicable to real-world classrooms. The use of case studies--common in the education of students in business and law--is one way of helping you understand how the principles of educational psychology are used in the everyday world of the practicing teacher.

Knowledge cannot be applied as a set of rules to be administered without thinking, however. To be effective, teachers must use careful decision making in applying their understanding of teaching and learning to their own situations. True professionals have both--a thorough background on which judgments are based, and the ability to make the judgments when the situation warrants them.

Teaching is a combination of art and science. Teachers as artists operate with such facility that their management and instruction appear relatively effortless. This doesn't happen by chance. The decisions that make everything work so smoothly are based on a thorough understanding of learning, learners, and teaching together with consistent self examination. This is the science of teaching combined with reflective practice.

To be most effective, teachers must consider their learners' personal needs, must feel good about themselves, and honestly care for their students as people; teaching is at its core a human activity. Some people argue that the human dimension is the most important aspect of all teaching.

Caucasians now make up three fourths of our country's population; by the middle of the next century, they will be about half. More than 30,000,000 million people in this country are not native English speakers. Language and culture, socioeconomic status, gender and intelligence are all aspects of student diversity that will challenge teachers in the future. Effective teachers genuinely accept and care for all students, have expectations of success for each one, and value the differences in their learners.

As you study your text, you will grow in all of these areas. You will acquire a background of research, theory, and the "wisdom of practice." This background will be combined with experiences that will require your analysis, judgment and reflection. In the process you will be moved toward expertise in teaching--the most noble profession that exists.

# CHAPTER ONE
# TEACHING IN THE REAL WORLD

## CHAPTER-AT-A-GLANCE

| MAIN TOPICS | KEY POINTS | KEY TERMS |
|---|---|---|
| Educational Psychology Teaching in the Real World | • People learn to teach by drawing from a variety of sources; experience, research, and their own reflection. | |
| Research in Teaching | • All professions are developed on a base of knowledge, which is the content of the profession.<br>• Some research results confirm what we informally observe to be true; other results are counterintuitive.<br>• The body of knowledge in education, as with other professions is incomplete.<br>• When a number of research based patterns are related, they are gradually combined into theories. | • Body of Knowledge, 7<br>• Theory, 10 |
| Applying Educational Psychology in the Classroom | • To be effective, the principles of educational psychology must be applicable in the real world of classrooms.<br>• Case studies illustrate teachers applying educational psychology in their work. | • Application, 11<br>• Case studies, 11 |
| Teacher Decision Making | • To be effective teachers must combine their understanding of research with careful decisions about what works best with their students.<br>• Teachers examine research critically, they consider its practicality, and they apply it with artistry in their teaching.<br>• Effective teachers are both artists and scientists; they make decisions based on the best available information.<br>• Reflective teachers analyze their own instruction in an effort to constantly improve. | • Art, 16<br>• Reflective teaching, 18 |
| Teaching, The Human Dimension | • Effective teachers respond to their students' personal needs, and they genuinely care about their students as people. | • Human dimension, 19 |

| Learner Diversity | • Differences in intelligence, culture and language, socioeconomic status, and gender are all aspects of learner diversity that can impact the amount students learn<br>• Effective teachers accept and care for all their students, expect each one to succeed, and value the differences in learners. | |

## CHAPTER ONE
## TEACHING IN THE REAL WORLD

GUIDED REVIEW _____

EDUCATIONAL PSYCHOLOGY: TEACHING IN THE REAL WORLD _____

Educational psychology can help us identify the relationships between teachers' practices and student learning. In addition, it can us explain many common events that we encounter in our daily living.

(1-1) Identify each of the five themes that organize your text. (p. 7)

_____

_____

_____

_____

RESEARCH IN TEACHING _____

The body of knowledge we use as a basis for making our professional decisions is based on the results of research gathered over a period of years.

(1-2) Identify two examples of research results that are intuitively sensible and two others that are not intuitively sensible. (pp. 7-9)

_____

_____

_____

_____

(1-3) Identify one common criticism of educational research. (p. 9)

_____

_____

_____

_____

(1-4) Explain how research results may eventually become theories. Identify two important functions that theories serve  (pp. 10-11)

_____

_____

_____

_____


## APPLYING EDUCATIONAL PSYCHOLOGY IN THE CLASSROOM

If the content of educational psychology is to be practical, teachers must be able to apply it in the real world of their day-to-day teaching.

(1-5)  What is a *case study*? How do case studies make the content of educational psychology practical? (pp. 11-13)

_____

_____

_____


## TEACHER DECISION MAKING

To be effective, teachers combine their knowledge of research and theory with careful judgments.

(1-6) Give a classroom example of critical decision making, practical decision making, and artistic decision making. (pp. 14-16)

_____

_____

_____

_____


(1-7) Give an example of art and another example of science in the case study that is used to introduce the chapter. (pp. 16-17)

_____

_____

_____

_____

1-8) What is meant by reflective teaching?  Give an example that illustrates reflection in the case study used to introduce the chapter. (pp. 17-19)

_____

_____

_____

## TEACHING: THE HUMAN DIMENSION

Teaching at its most basic level is an activity in which people's personal needs and desires must be accommodated in order for learning to be the most effective.

(1-9) Describe at least two characteristics of "human" teachers. (pp. 19-20)

_____

_____

_____

_____

## LEARNER DIVERSITY

The backgrounds of our students vary dramatically. Students differ in their intelligence, language and culture, socioeconomic status and gender. Effective teachers both accommodate and value these differences as they teach.

(1-10) Identify three general strategies effective teachers use for dealing with diversity. (p. 22)

_____

_____

_____

# CHAPTER ONE
# TEACHING IN THE REAL WORLD

## SELF-CHECK QUIZ

TRUE/FALSE QUESTIONS. Write T in the blank if the statement is true and write F if the statement is false.

_____ 1. Professions, such as medicine, are based on theory, while education is developed primarily on the basis of classroom experience.

_____ 2. Research is of no value if the results of different studies are conflicting.

_____ 3. A body of knowledge is of little value unless it is complete.

_____ 4. Research results and theories are essentially unrelated to each other.

_____ 5. Education is essentially the only profession that has conflicting research results.

MULTIPLE-CHOICE ITEMS. Circle the best response in each case.

6. Of the following, the best description of a theory is:
   a.   the information known about a particular field of study.
   b.   the knowledge and facts that people in professions know.
   c.   classroom applications of principles in the real world of teaching.
   d.   combinations of related patterns.

7. Which of the following statements are true of theories.
   1.   They are based on the results of patterns identified by research.
   2.   They serve as a basis for predicting the outcome of future events.
   3.   They serve as a basis for explaining events.
   4.   Once developed, they are not modified.

a. 1,2,3,4   b. 1,2,3   c. 1,2,4   d. 2,3,4   e. 1,4

Use the following description for items 8-10.

Mrs. Adcox, was having a difficult time getting her students involved in her lessons. She would begin by telling them that the content they were studying was important, but the students were unresponsive.

She thought a lot about the problem, asking colleagues and looking for ideas. In reading an article in one of her professional journals one evening, she saw a report indicating that students are often curious when teachers begin their lessons with a question or problem that doesn't have an apparent solution. It sounded like it might help her in her frustration with her students, but she asked herself, "How am I going to do this in language arts? That's where the students are the most listless."

Then she hit on an idea. She began her next class by telling the students, "Look, kids, when we have one baby we spell it b  a  b  y, but when we have more than one we spell it b  a  b  i  e  s. On the other hand, we spell boy, b  o  y, but when we have more than one we spell it b  o  y  s rather than b  o  i  e  s. Why do you suppose we have the difference?"

She was pleased to discover that her students were much more interested in what she was doing, so much so that whenever possible, she began her lessons with a problem or question.

8. Of the following, the above description best illustrates a:
   a.   theory
   b.   body of knowledge
   c.   research result
   d.   case study

9. Mrs. Adcox read her professional journal and learned about the effects of beginning lessons with a question

or problem.  This process best illustrates:
- a.  the scientific dimension of teaching.
- b.  the artistic dimension of teaching.
- c.  reflective teaching.
- d.  the development of a theory of teaching.

10. Mrs. Adcox's thinking about her difficulty with her students and search for solutions best illustrates:
- a.  the scientific dimension of teaching.
- b.  the artistic dimension of teaching.
- c.  reflective teaching.
- d.  the development of a theory of teaching.

# CHAPTER TWO
# STUDENT DEVELOPMENT

## CHAPTER OUTLINE

I. Development: A Definition
II. Piaget's Theory of Intellectual Development
    A. The Drive for Equilibrium
    B. Organization and Adaptation
        1. Adapting schemata
    C. Causes of Development
        1. Maturation
        2. Experience with the physical world
        3. Background experience: A source of diversity
            a. Dealing with student diversity
        4. Social interaction
        5. Social origins of learning: Vygotsky's work
            a. Social support and language
            b. The zone of proximal development
            c. Scaffolding: Interactive instructional support
    D. Stages of Development
        1. Sensorimotor stage (0 - 2 years)
        2. Preoperational stage ( 2 - 7 years)
            a. Egocentrism
            b. Centration
            c. Nontransformation
            d. Irreversibility
            e. Reasoning
            f. Conservation
            g. Preoperational characteristics in adult behavior
        3. Concrete operations stage (7 - 11 years)
            a. Seriation and classification
         4. Formal operations (Adolescence to adult)
    E. Development: Research and Classroom Application
        1. Influence on curriculum and instruction
            a. Impact on curriculum development
        2. Classroom applications: Research results
            a. Thinking in the junior high school
            b. Thinking in the high school and beyond
    F. Designing and Sequencing Instruction: Constructivism
        1. Concrete examples
        2. Personalization
        3. Intellectual empathy
        4. Interaction
    G. Piaget in the Classroom: A Teaching Strategy
III. Information Processing: An Alternative View of Cognitive Development
    A. The Strategic Learner
    B. What Develops: An Information-Processing View of Memory Development
IV. The Development of Morality, Social Responsibility, and Self-Control
    A. Issues of Morality in School and Society
    B. The Growth of Internalization: Piaget's Description of Moral Development

1. Level I: Preconventional reasoning
   a. Stage 1: Punishment-obedience
   b. Stage 2: Market exchange
2. Level II: Conventional ethics
   a. Stage 3: Interpersonal harmony
   b. Stage 4: Law and order
3. Level III: Postconventional ethics
   a. Stage 5: Social contract
   b. Stage 6: Universal principles
E. Kohlberg's Theory: Research and Analysis
   1. Criticism of Kohlberg's work
      a. Gender differences: Kohlberg revisited
   2. Moral development and classroom structure
   3. Moral development through peer interaction
   4. The moral framework of schools
V. Personal and Social Development
   A. Erikson's Theory of Personal and Social Development
      1. Trust vs. mistrust (Birth - 1 year)
      2. Autonomy vs. shame and doubt (Ages 1 - 3)
      3. Initiative vs. guilt (Ages 3 - 6)
      4. Industry vs. inferiority (Ages 6 - 12)
      5. Identity vs. confusion (Adolescence)
      6. Intimacy vs. isolation (Young adulthood)
      7. Generativity vs. stagnation (Middle adulthood)
      8. Integrity vs. despair (Old age)
   B. Erikson's Work: A Further Look

# CHAPTER OBJECTIVES

- Describe the process of intellectual development using concepts from Piaget's theory.
- Classify student behavior into Piaget's stages of development based on the characteristics of each stage.
- Give an example of an individual's behavior and explain why the behavior occurs using concepts from intellectual development.
- Explain the outcomes of teaching practices using concepts from intellectual development.
- Classify ethical reasoning into one of Kohlberg's six stages of moral development.
- Classify individual behavior into one of Erikson's eight stages of psychosocial development.

# CHAPTER OVERVIEW

As students progress through our schools development exerts a subtle but powerful influence on learning. Development refers to the orderly, durable changes in a learner resulting from learning, maturation, and experience. As our students develop they not only acquire new abilities but also come to view the world in different ways.

Jean Piaget, a Swiss psychologist, described cognitive development in terms of an individual's drive for equilibrium. As we organize our experiences into schemata or patterns we use these to interpret our environment. When we encounter new events we assimilate these into existing schemata. When new events don't fit into existing schemata disequilibrium causes us to adapt these, reorganizing or accommodating them to fit reality. With this cycle of experience-assimilation, experience-accommodation, development occurs.

As Piaget observed young children, he found that the way they responded to the world fell into stages or patterns. During the sensorimotor stage (0-2 years) children concentrate on their own bodies and its relation to the physical world. In the preoperational stage (2-7 years) children learn language and begin the development of symbolic thought. During the concrete operational period (7-11 years) children begin to perform logical operations (e.g. classifying and ordering) on concrete objects. In the final stage, formal operations (11 years to adult) students can perform logical operations abstractly, in the absence of concrete objects. These stages help teachers adapt their instruction to the developmental capabilities of their students.

Information processing theory provides another view of cognitive development. Information processing theory views learners as active organisms that take in, organize, store and use information. As learners develop they become more efficient in these processes through the use of strategies that allow them to encode information efficiently. For example, as students develop they become more efficient at remembering things through the use of strategies that help them encode and retrieve information.

As second area of development contained in this chapter describes the growth of moral and ethical reasoning. Piaget's work in this area suggests that moral development relates to a shift from external to internal control. As this shift occurs students approach issues of right and wrong from a more logical, rational perspective and come to view justice as a reciprocal process of treating others as they would want to be treated.

Another researcher who has studied moral development is Lawrence Kohlberg. Like the other theories, Kohlberg's describes development in terms of orderly development in response to the environment. As children progress through these stages, they first think of right and wrong in terms of punishment and obedience or doing what's right in terms of how it will benefit themselves. This is called the Preconventional Level. During the Conventional Stage, morality is defined in terms of rules and laws. At the Postconventional Level students come to view ethics as a matter of social contract and acting in accordance with universal principles of right and wrong. As with the other developmental theories schools and teachers influence development through the experiences they provide students.

Eric Erikson, another developmental psychologist, focused on students' psychosocial development. Like Piaget, he also believed that development occurs in stages and that these stages influence how the individual interprets and interacts with the world. Unlike Piaget, Erikson's theory focuses on social or emotional development and describes how people use problems or crises to grow and develop.

The three major crises/stages that students face during the school years are initiative versus guilt, industry versus inferiority and identity versus confusion. In the first of these young students (3 to 6 years) wrestle with newly developing independence and develop a positive, can-do attitude in meeting new challenges. During the elementary grades students work to achieve mastery and competence to resolve the industry versus inferiority crisis. Adolescents in junior and senior high school struggle to define themselves both as developing teenagers and young adults during the identity versus confusion stage. Teachers powerfully influence psychosocial development directly through their interactions with students and indirectly through the academic tasks they ask them to perform.

12

# CHAPTER TWO
# STUDENT DEVELOPMENT

## CHAPTER-AT-A-GLANCE

| MAIN TOPICS | KEY POINTS | KEY TERMS |
|---|---|---|
| Development: A Definition | • Development, which begins at birth and continues until death, occurs when learning, experience, and maturation combine to make durable changes in an individual.<br>• Cognitive development is characterized by the emergence of more complex strategies that allow students to deal with increasingly abstract ideas. | • Development, 33 |
| Piaget's Theory of Intellectual Development | • There is a human tendency, instinctive or innate, for people to find order, structure, and predictability in their existence.<br>• As we gain experience, we are constantly adjusting our existing schemata in order to maintain our equilibrium.<br>• Development is influenced by maturation, social interaction, and experience with the physical world.<br>• Vygotsky stressed the importance of social support and language in developmental growth.<br>• Although development is continuous, it can be described in ordered stages with identifiable characteristics.<br>• Sensorimotor children's processing strategies are physical and motor; preoperational children are dominated by perception; concrete operational youngsters perform logical operations on tangible materials; and formal operational thinkers perform logical operations on abstract and hypothetical problems.<br>• People pass through the stages at different rates, and some, who lack direct experience in a specific field, may fail to reach formal operations and remain dominated by perception.<br>• Renewed interest in Piaget's philosophy calls for learning through direct experience using concrete materials, personalization of examples, and active participation on the part of students. | • Equilibrium, 34<br>• Equilibration, 34<br>• Organization, 35<br>• Schemata, 35<br>• Adaptation, 35<br>• Accommodation, 35<br>• Assimilation, 35<br>• Inner speech, 42<br>• Social interaction, 41<br>• Zone of proximal development, 42<br>• Scaffolding, 43<br>• Maturation, 38<br>• Sensorimotor stage, 44<br>• Preoperations stage, 44<br>• Egocentrism, 45<br>• Centration, 46<br>• Nontransformation, 45<br>• Irreversibility, 46<br>• Conservation, 47<br>• Perspective-taking, 48<br>• Concrete operational stage, 49<br>• Seriation, 50<br>• Classification, 50<br>• Formal operations stage, 50<br>• Constructivism, 54<br>• Misconception, 55<br>• Intellectual empathy, 56 |

| Information Processing: An Alternative View of Cognitive Development | • Information processing views development as the acquisition of new strategies that allow learners to encode and use information more efficiently.<br>• The information processing approach allows researchers to identify specific content areas and describe developmental differences in learners' use of strategies.<br>• Teachers can use this view of development to assess strategies students are using and to provide them with more efficient ones. | • Information processing, 58<br>• Strategies, 59<br>• Encoding, 59<br>• Generalization, 59 |
|---|---|---|
| The Development of Morality, Social Responsibility, and Self-Control | • Piaget views moral development as a process of internalization where external control gradually proceeds to internal or autonomous control.<br>• Moral development results in reduced egocentric ethics in favor of concerns for others, society, and principles.<br>• Preconventional ethics focuses on the self, conventional ethics on laws and rules, and postconventional ethics on principle.<br>• Students can learn about and evaluate their own moral thinking by examining it in relation to others in classroom discussions. | • External morality, 63<br>• Autonomous morality, 63<br>• Moral dilemma, 63<br>• Punishment-obedience stage, 65<br>• Market exchange stage, 65<br>• Interpersonal harmony stage, 65<br>• Law and order stage, 66<br>• Social contract, 66<br>• Universal principles, 67 |
| Personal and Social Development | • Psychosocial development occurs in response to learning, maturation, and experience.<br>• Psychosocial development occurs in stages, each stage marking a point of vulnerability to a psychosocial challenge which, when resolved, prepares the individual for the next stage.<br>• Resolution of school-age crises or challenges results in a feeling of competence and sense of identity.<br>• Imperfect resolutions of crises results in personality imperfections that detract from effectively functioning. | • Psychosocial theory, 72<br>• Crisis, 72<br>• Trust, 73<br>• Autonomy, 73<br>• Initiative, 73<br>• Industry, 73<br>• Identity, 74<br>• Identity crisis, 74<br>• Intimacy, 75<br>• Generativity, 76<br>• Integrity, 76 |

# CHAPTER TWO
# STUDENT DEVELOPMENT

## GUIDED REVIEW

### DEVELOPMENT: A DEFINITION

Students' ability to handle content presented in the classroom is influenced by their development whether it be intellectual, social and personal, or moral and ethical. Developmental changes result from a combination of learning, experience, and maturation.

(2-1) Using the following developmental changes as a basis for your examples, explain how each could be influenced by learning, experience and maturation. The first example has been done for you. (pp. 33-34)

Keith develops an ethical stance towards recycling: He **learns** in class that resources are not limited and should not be wasted; he participates in the **experience** of actually recycling aluminum cans at home; he decides that he, even as one person, can make a difference versus when he was younger (less **mature**) and thought that what he did had no effect on the world around him.

Mary decides that she will not use drugs recreationally:

_____

_____

_____

Dora is able to teach a younger student how to add fractions:

_____

_____

_____

Jacob, a kindergartner, can tie his own shoes:

_____

_____

_____

Piaget's theory of intellectual development is based on his research using his own children as subjects and the careful observation of small numbers of subjects. Although it took a long time for his work to accepted, his influence on current educational practices is substantial.

(2-2)  Match the following terms with their definitions. (pp. 34-36)

| | |
|---|---|
| ____ development | A. coherent patterns based on life's experiences |
| ____ equilibrium | B. the process of adjusting schemata to experiences in order to maintain equilibrium |
| ____ equilibration | |
| ____ schemata | C. orderly durable changes in a learner resulting from learning, experience, and maturation |
| ____ organization | D. a form of adaptation in which an experience in the environment is modified to fit an existing schema |
| ____ adaptation | |
| ____ accommodation | E. an instinctive or innate need in people to find order, structure and predictability in their existence |
| ____ assimilation | F. the process of using language to describe the steps needed to reach a goal |
| | G. a form of adaptation in which an existing schema is changed in response to new experiences |
| | H. the product of the process of equilibrium |
| | I. the drive for order |

(2-3)  Give an original example of adapting a schema in response to new information or experiences.  (pp. 35-36)

_____

_____

(2-4)  Explain the relationship between development and inner speech.  Why is inner speech important?  (p. 42)

_____

_____

_____

(2-5)  How can a teacher tell whether a child is in, beyond, or not yet to the zone of proximal development?  Why is it important for a teacher to know this?  (pp. 42-43)

_____

_____

_____

16

(2-6) Briefly describe below each of the following stages of development, its main characteristics and its implications for teachers. (pp.44-51)

I. Sensorimotor stage

_____

  A. Object permanence

_____

  B. Teaching implications

_____

II. Preoperations stage

_____

  A. Egocentrism

_____

  B. Centration

_____

  C. Nontransformation

_____

  D. Irreversibility

_____

  E. Reasoning

_____

  F. Conservation

_____

  G. Teaching implications

_____

_____

III. Concrete operations stage

_____

_____

  A. Logical operations (concrete)

_____

_____

  B. Seriation and classification

_____

_____

17

C. Teaching implications (pp. 51- 54)

_____

_____

IV. Formal operations

_____

_____

A. Abstract problem solving_____

B. Isolation and control of variables_____

_____  _____

C. Teaching implications (pp. 53-54)_____

_____

The *constructivist* approach stresses the importance of direct experience through use of concrete examples, personalization, intellectual empathy and classroom interaction.

(2-7)  Classify each of the following as demonstrating use of CE (concrete examples), P (personalization), IE (intellectual empathy), or IA (interaction).  (pp. 54-57)

_____  An elementary math teacher understands students' initial apprehension and frustration when faced with long division for the first time.

_____  A social studies teacher has students make a map of their own bedrooms to begin a study of map skills.

_____  A health teacher demonstrates several first aid techniques and then divides students into groups of three to practice them, give each other feedback, and report back to the class.

_____  A kindergarten teacher brings in food samples for students to taste when studying the four basic food groups.

_____  A junior high English teacher has students keep a journal in which they write to her about their reactions to the class.  She reads them weekly and responds with written comments.

_____  When high school students question the "don't smoke" adage while being aware that teachers smoke in the lounge, a health teacher listens and sympathizes.

18

(2-8) List and describe the four phases of the teaching model based on Piaget's work. (p. 57)

1. _____

2. _____

3. _____

4. _____

(2-9) Identify where each of the stages occurs in the lesson on "plain" on pp. 38-39 in the text. Identify any stage that has been left out and describe how it could be included. (pp. 57-58)

1. _____

2. _____

3. _____

4. _____

## INFORMATION PROCESSING: AN ALTERNATIVE VIEW OF COGNITIVE DEVELOPMENT

An information processing theory of development describes developmental changes in terms of specific new capabilities that learners acquire through their interactions with the environment.

(2-10) Provide a definition and example of the three characteristics of strategic learners. (pp. 58-59)

_____

_____

_____

_____

_____

_____

(2-11) What are three memory strategies that develop in young children? (p.59)

_____

_____

_____

## THE DEVELOPMENT OF MORALITY, SOCIAL RESPONSIBILITY, AND SELF CONTROL

Concern about the moral development of America's youth has become increasingly prominent in our schools. Educators agree that moral dilemmas and issues cannot be avoided in school and, in some cases, need to be directly dealt with in class.

(2-12)  What are some possible moral or ethical issues that students might encounter today?  (p. 61-63)

●Elementary level

_____

Junior high level

_____

●High school level

_____


(2-13)  Select one of the issues you listed in exercise 2-12 and describe what reason a child might give for adhering to the moral side of the issue at the following stages.  (pp. 64-67)

●Punishment and obedience

_____

●Market exchange

_____

●Interpersonal harmony

_____

●Law and order

_____

●Social contract

_____

●Universal principles

_____

(2-14) What are some of the criticisms of Kohlberg's work?  (p. 67-68)

_____

_____

(2-15) What are some ways to make discussions of moral dilemmas effective in the classroom?  (pp. 68-70)

_____

_____

_____

## PERSONAL AND SOCIAL DEVELOPMENT

Erikson's theory of personal and social development is the result of his interest in how people acquire a personal identity and how they relate to society in general.  In each of his eight stages of psychosocial development, a crisis or challenge needs to be met.  Positive resolution of the crisis leads to a fully functioning personality while negative resolution can retard development at later stages.

(2-16)  Complete the following chart describing the possible results of positive and negative resolutions of each of Erikson's stages.  (pp. 71-76)

| Stage | Positive Resolution | Negative Resolution |
|---|---|---|
| Trust vs. Mistrust | | |
| Autonomy vs. Shame and Doubt | | |
| Initiative vs. Guilt | | |
| Industry vs. Inferiority | | |
| Identity vs. Confusion | | |
| Intimacy vs. Isolation | | |
| Generativity vs. Stagnation | | |
| Integrity vs. Despair | | |

21

# CHAPTER TWO
## STUDENT DEVELOPMENT

APPLICATION EXERCISES _____

EXERCISE 2.1

Exercise 2.1 measures your understanding of topics covered on pages 31-37 of your text.

Examine each of the examples that follow and explain the individual's behavior or reaction by using one or more of the concepts: *equilibrium, schema, accommodation, assimilation, and development*. The person you focus on is the one whose name is underlined. In each case, use as many of the concepts as necessary to form a full and complete explanation.

1. Andre's class has completed a unit on the multiplication of fractions and is now working on division. Tim, when faced with the problem

$2/3 \div 1/3 = $    , gets 2/9 as an answer.

_____

_____

_____

_____

2. Celena commented to her friend Jane in the teachers' lounge one morning, "Susan really puzzles me. You never know how to take her. One day she's your best friend, and the next she barely squeaks out a hello.

_____

_____

_____

_____

3. Kathy's English class has been assigned to write a paper making a persuasive argument. "I was initially confused, but I think I know how to do it now," she commented to her dad, who was helping her with it. "It's like making and defending a position, except you have to include a suggestion or a plan of action."

_____

_____

_____

_____

4. "Malivai's spelling has improved dramatically since the beginning of the year," Mrs. Stone enthusiastically told Dan's mother in a conference in May. "At first he approached spelling as if every new word were completely new. Then he started seeing patterns in the words and his spelling performance took a jump."

_____

_____

_____

EXERCISE 2.2

Exercise 2.2 measures your understanding of topics covered on pages 38-51 of your text.

Classify the behavior of the person whose name is underlined in the following examples into one of the four stages of development. Then explain your classification based on information from the example.

1. Conchita Martinez is discussing the causes of World War I in her junior high American history class. "It started with the assassination of the archduke," Brad suggested. "But," Karen added, "there was also a rising spirit of nationalism all over Europe at the time."

_____

_____

_____

2. Cher knows that the word *horse* represents horses.

_____

_____

_____

3. Tim is 5 minutes late for class and jokingly says,"I have minus 5 minutes to get there."

_____

_____

_____

_____

4. Susan didn't understand the fulcrum of a simple lever until the teacher used a meterstick to pry up a stack of books.

_____

_____

_____

5. Luis is playing somewhat roughly with the family cat, and his mother, concerned that he might be scratched, puts the cat around the corner. Luis's attention quickly turns to something else.

_____

_____

_____

6. Ann's teacher is working on numbers in base 6. She shows the students bundles of six sticks and individual sticks. After a series of examples, she displays two bundles of six sticks each and three more sticks and asks the class to write the number in base 6 that represents the 15 sticks. Ann correctly responds with the numeral 23. She can't do this without stick bundles.

_____

_____

_____

## EXERCISE 2.3

Exercise 2.3 measures your understanding of topics covered on pages 51-58 of your text.

1. Karin Dunlop is a ninth-grade English teacher. She knew that students take the PSAT (Preliminary Scholastic Aptitude Test) as tenth graders, and she wanted to prepare them as well as possible, so she did extensive work with antonyms and analogies. She gave her students the following words with brief definitions.

relic--keepsake
ordain--officially appoint
acuteness--sharpness
dawdle--waste time
superfluous--more than needed

She directed students to learn the words, and the next day she gave them an exercise involving antonyms for the words in the left column. Even through students vigorously claimed that they had studied the words carefully, the results were disappointing.

Using Piaget's work as a basis, provide a specific explanation for why the students did so poorly, and then specifically suggest what Karin might have done differently to get better results.

_____

_____

_____

_____


2. James Washington has been working with his fifth graders on a unit involving air and air pressure. He has discussed air and air pressure in detail, and the children read about it in their books. In a demonstration, he adds a cup of water to an empty ditto fluid can, heats the can to drive out some of the air inside, caps the can, and watches while the atmospheric pressure crushes the cooling can. To speed up the cooking, however, he pours cold water on the can. To his dismay, students suggest that the water crushed the can.

  Based on the research results discussed in this section, explain specifically why students would conclude what they did.

_____

_____

_____

_____


_____

EXERCISE 2.4

Exercise 2.4 measures your understanding of topics covered on pages 59-70 of your text.

For items 1 through 8, consider each of the stated reasons for not using drugs. Classify each description into one of Kohlberg's first five stages.

1. If I'm caught using drugs, my reputation will be ruined.

_____

2. If everyone used drugs, our society would disintegrate.

_____

3. It's expensive, and I don't get that much out of it.

_____

4. If I get caught, I could go to jail.

_____

5. If my parents found out I used drugs, they would be crushed.

_____

6. My dad drinks, and alcohol is a drug, so who are they to tell me not to use them.

_____

7. If my parents knew I used drugs, I'd be grounded.

_____

8. Freedom to choose is critical, and drug use results in the loss of that freedom.

_____

For items 9 through 14, consider a teenager who is out with her friends. She has been directed by her parents to be in by midnight. She complies. Classify the following reasons into one of Stages 1 through 5.

9. If I stay out, I'll be in big trouble with my parents.

_____

10. Nobody's doing anything anyway, so I won't be missing anything.

_____

11. I agreed to do it, and you can't go back on your agreements.

_____

12. If I stay out, my parents will be worried.

_____

13. Midnight is the curfew, so I'll be in by midnight.

_____

14. My friends have curfews, too, and they're going home then.

_____

## EXERCISE 2.5

Exercise 2.5 measures your understanding of topics covered on pages 71-77 of your text.

In items 1 through 6, classify the person whose name is underlined into one of Erikson's eight stages of psychosocial development.

1. Carmella washes her hair every day. Her mother says she is going to wash it out of her head. "But, Mom," Susan protest, "I'll look so gross if I don't wash it."

_____

2. Deon is small for his age, and schoolwork isn't quite his "thing." He loves sports, though, and puts a lot of his energy into competition. He's the fastest runner in his grade. He pitches for his Little League team, even though he's a year younger than most of the other kids, and he set a team record by striking out 10 batters in one five-inning game.

_____

3. "Guess what happened today?" Kathy's dad asked her mother as she walked in the door from work. He laughed. "Kathy scratched some stuff on some papers--she called them pictures--and glued them to the wall of her bedroom. It ruined the wallpaper."
  "Did you get after her?"
  "I thought about it, but then she said, 'Look at the pictures I made for you, Daddy.' That did it. I told her that the pictures were very nice. We'll talk to her later and push the dresser in front of the marks."

_____

4. Mr. Thomas is raving to his wife about the present national administration's apparent lack of concern about the environment. "Those S.O.B.'s are trying to ruin the parks," he yells. "If there isn't a policy change, there will be nothing left for our kids or anyone else's kids to see and enjoy when they grow up."

_____

5. "Are you getting serious about Joyce?" Tom was asked. "I could be, but I'm not going to allow myself to," he answered. "I've been through two relationships that didn't work out, and I've hurt two people. I'm beginning to wonder about my ability to feel strongly about someone else. I was fascinated with Sheri's great looks, and it was nice having Jan chase me like that, but now I don't know what to think."

_____

6. "Guess what I found under Mike's mattress," his mother said somewhat uneasily to her friend as they were jogging. "*Playboy* magazine opened to the centerfold."

Her friend laughed. "Not to worry. He's a boy. He isn't even sure himself what he's feeling. Relax. He's normal," she said with an unconcerned wave of her hand.

_____

7. <u>Emmitt</u> is an eighth grader whom you can't seem to "get going." He never volunteers answers in class and does only the minimum required on homework assignments and projects. However, the work he turns in is always acceptable, and he has been an above-average student throughout his schooling. In other ways, he seems to be a typical, "normal" youngster for his age.

Analyze the boy's behavior using Erikson's theory as a frame of reference. Then suggest what you might do to help change his behavior.

_____

_____

_____

# CHAPTER TWO
# STUDENT DEVELOPMENT

## SELF-HELP QUIZ _____

TRUE-FALSE QUESTIONS:  Write T in the blank if the statement is true, and F if the statement is false.

_____ 1.  Development and learning are coordinate concepts, both describing similar types of changes in a learner.

_____ 2.  When a child modifies his idea of a football and a tennis ball so that both fit into his previously formed concept of "ball", this is an example of assimilation.

_____ 3.  A major theme in Vygotsky's work is that children frequently use language to describe problem solving or goal-reaching steps to themselves, especially on difficult tasks.

_____ 4.  Children pass through Piaget's stages of development in distinct steps, although some may skip a stage if they are intellectually mature.

_____ 5.  Junior high students have usually reached the formal operational level and are able to reason abstractly and logically without the need for concrete materials to manipulate.

_____ 6.  An elementary music teacher who helps students understand the concept of rhythm by having them chant their names while tapping on drums made from oatmeal boxes is using a constructivist approach.

_____ 7.  Teachers can help children overcome severe obstacles later in life by challenging them and giving them opportunities in which they can succeed in the elementary grades.

_____ 8.  The industry versus inferiority stage of psychosocial development is characterized by exploration of personal, social, sexual, and occupational identity and a preoccupation with peer approval.

_____ 9.  According to Kohlberg, an effective way to teach moral behavior is to explain ethical laws and principles.

_____10.  One of the main criticisms of Kohlberg's work on moral development is that moral behavior cannot be predicted from his descriptions.

MULTIPLE CHOICE QUESTIONS:  Circle the best response in each case.

11.  Which of the following is true about Piaget's theory of intellectual development?
   a.  Piaget's theory was initially well accepted in the U.S. because of his background and training in natural science.
   b.  The drive for equilibrium is the basis for Piaget's theory, in that we are always trying to order and categorize experiences to relate to what we know.
   c.  According to Piaget, adaptation and accommodation are reciprocal processes, one describing changing a schema to fit new experience and the other changing new input to fit an existing schema.
   d.  Piaget found that social interaction plays a minor part in development since a child's rate of development is already determined by the time he is three--long before he becomes very interested in socializing.

12. The phase in learning in which a student can profit from assistance or help is called:
   a. inner speech.
   b. scaffolding.
   c. preoperations stage.
   d. zone of proximal development.

13. The stage in which children develop the ability to remember physical objects when they are no longer visible is called:
   a. sensorimotor stage.
   b. preoperations stage.
   c. concrete operations stage.
   d. formal operations stage.

14. A child is shown two sponges and identifies them as identical. One sponge is then cut up while the child watches so that it is now in ten or twelve little pieces. When asked which is more, the child says the two groups are still identical. This is called:
   a. egocentrism.
   b. centration.
   c. transformation.
   d. conservation.

15. Erikson's work is based on which of the following ideas?
   a. People from different cultures have different basic needs.
   b. A person must resolve every crisis at each stage of development in order to function in society.
   c. A person has different motivations at each different stage of personal and social development.
   d. All of the above.

16. The psychosocial stage of development characterized by cognitive growth and exploration in all areas of life is called:
   a. autonomy versus shame and doubt.
   b. initiative versus guilt.
   c. industry versus inferiority.
   d. identity versus confusion.

17. People who remain in the identity-confusion crisis can be typified as:
   a. adolescents who feel competent to overcome questions about who they are.
   b. teenagers who are doomed to a period of distress and uncertainty.
   c. individuals who retain behavioral traits characteristics of adolescence later in life.
   d. people who have a basic sense of trust, can function on their own, and can take initiative.

18. Kohlberg's work in moral development is closely related to the work of Piaget in that:
   a. both developed theories of psychosocial development that can be used to educate children.
   b. both advocate teaching morals and ethics through presentation and discussion of moral dilemmas.
   c. both based their research on the observation of large groups of children from all over the world.
   d. both based their theories on the idea that there are stages of development through which people must pass in a certain order.

19. If an individual decides not do so something because his father and his mother will be disappointed in him, he would be at the:
   a. interpersonal harmony stage.
   b. law and order stage.
   c. social contract stage.
   d. universal principles stage.

20. One way to teach ethics and morals is for teachers to:
    a.  give students opportunities to discuss moral dilemmas with each other which provides opportunities to hear other points of view.
    b.  emphasize topics that involve values encouraged by the school and avoid those that don't.
    c.  state explicit guidelines for school behavior and strictly enforce them.
    d.  reinforce positive behaviors and punish negative ones.

*CHAPTER THREE*
*STUDENT DEVELOPMENT: APPLICATIONS*

CHAPTER OUTLINE_____

I.   Early Childhood and Primary Grades
     A.   Physical Development of Young Children
          1. Energy and attention span
          2. Gender differences
     B.   Cognitive Growth of Young Children
          1. Implications for instruction
     C.   Language Development in Young Children
          1. Theories of language acquisition
               a. Behaviorist theories
               b. Social learning theory
               c. Psycholinguistic theories
          2. Stages of language acquisition
               a. Early language: Building the foundation
               b. Fine-tuning language
               c. Advancing development
               d. Increasing language complexity
     D.   Student Diversity: English Dialects
          1. English dialects: Research results
          2. Dialects in the classroom: Implications for teachers
     E.   Student Diversity: English as a Second Language
          1. Types of bilingual programs
               a. Maintenance programs
               b. Transitional programs
               c. Immersion programs
               d. Submersion programs
               e. English as a Second Language programs
          2. Evaluating bilingual programs
     F.   Teaching Bilingual Students
          1. Awareness
          2. Language development
               a. Whole language
               b. Whole language and student diversity
          3. Concept development
     G.   Socioemotional Growth of Young Children
          1. Initiative-guilt: Erikson revisited
          2. Sexual identity
          3. Play
               a. Types of play
               b. Play and conflicts
          4. Fostering socialization
          5. Parenting and teaching styles that promote initiative
     H.   Programs for Preschool and Primary-Age Children
          1. Head Start
          2. Structure and focus: Is more or less better?
               a. Open education
          3. Selecting the appropriate approach

II. The Elementary Grades
    A.     Physical Growth of Elementary-Age Children
    B.     Cognitive Growth of Elementary-Age Children
          1.  Teaching with concrete materials
             a.  Concrete materials and language
    C.     Socioemotional Growth of Elementary-Age Children
          1.  Self-concept
             a.  The development of self-concept
             b.  Academic self-concept
             c.  Self-concept and achievement
             d.  Subject-matter specificity
             e.  Improving self-concept
          2.  Coregulation:  A step toward independence
          3.  The family and socioemotional development
             a.  Implications of the changing American family
             b.  Child abuse and neglect
III. Adolescence
    A.     Physical Development of Adolescents
          1.  Early and late development:  Effects on students
          2.  Health issues in adolescence
          3.  Adolescent suicide
    B.     Cognitive Growth of Adolescents
          1.  Characteristics of formal thought
          2.  Variations in development:  Implications for teaching
    C.     Social and Emotional Development of Adolescents
          1.  Social development
          2.  Emotional development
              a.  Different views of identity resolution
             b.  Different states of identity development
             c.  Identity formation:  Research results
          3.  Effective parenting and teaching styles
    D.     Middle Schools:  Intermediate Schools for Early Adolescents

CHAPTER OBJECTIVES_____

- Describe the physical characteristics of children at different stages of development and discuss their implications for teaching.
- Explain different theories of language acquisition.
- Identify different stages of language acquisition.
- Discuss the relationship between self-concept and academic achievement.
- Describe the influence of different family patterns on students' growth and development.
- Explain how physical development in adolescence affects social and emotional development.
- Describe the characteristics of formal operational thought.
- Discuss different views of conflict and how they explain the child's struggle for independence.

# CHAPTER OVERVIEW

This chapter examines the process of development from several perspectives--physical, cognitive, and socioemotional--and asks how schools can help children develop in healthy ways. These different dimensions of development interact to help determine both student growth and learning.

Preschool and early elementary development is characterized by rapid and diverse physical growth. Young children grow at different rates, and these different rates have implications for psychomotor development and attention. These years also see huge strides in language growth, with increased vocabulary and increasingly complex sentence structures. Teachers can further this growth by encouraging students to use existing language patterns as the basis for future growth.

A number of students bring English dialects with them when they enter our schools. English dialects are a variation of standard English that are distinct in vocabulary, grammar, or pronunciation. Teachers should treat these dialects as functional language systems that are used and accepted in students' home cultures.

In addition to dialects, a number of students enter schools speaking English as their second language. Bilingual programs designed to teach English as a Second Language (ESL) students range from maintenance programs that teach both languages and attempt to develop both, to submersion programs that place non-English speaking students into classrooms where only English is spoken. Effective instruction for ESL students emphasizes language development based upon experiential learning and the use of language across the curriculum.

Successful programs for young children present them with tasks that encourage initiative, promote social interaction, and develop language competence. Effective patterns of teacher interaction emphasize authoritative structure that promotes personal initiative while providing high expectations and limits. Programs using a more direct instructional approach target basic skills and teach these through teacher explanation and modeling; open education, by contrast, places heavy emphasis on student choice and initiative.

During the middle elementary grades physical growth is more gradual, and cognitive growth occurs through maturation and students' interaction with their environments. Effective teaching for elementary students emphasizes concrete experiences as the foundation for abstract concepts.

These elementary years are also important for the development of self-concept, the sum total of the perceptions about a student's academic, social and physical self. Research shows that self-concept is multi-faceted, with academic, social and physical components. Successful experiences in instructional tasks help build a healthy academic self-concept, which in turn has a positive influence on subsequent achievement.

Adolescence, the period spanning the junior and senior high school years, brings with it dramatic physical, cognitive and emotional changes. Physically, the onset of puberty can have powerful effects on students' self-concepts. Early maturation in boys tends to have positive psychological effects while the opposite is true for girls. Late maturation for boys can have the opposite effect with decreases in self-confidence.

The teenage years also mark the onset of the development of formal thought in which students can think abstractly, systematically and hypothetically. Though the onset of formal thought is uneven across students, teachers can help by providing opportunities for these thought processes to occur and by encouraging think-alouds by students.

During adolescence students also wrestle with identity formation in which they attempt to determine who they are and what they want to become as adults. This process is complicated by the diversity found in our modern society as well as uneven rates of development in students. Middle schools are schools specially designed to help early adolescents deal with these issues.

# CHAPTER THREE
# STUDENT DEVELOPMENT:
# APPLICATIONS

## CHAPTER-AT-A-GLANCE

| MAIN TOPICS | KEY POINTS | KEY TERMS |
|---|---|---|
| Early Childhood and Primary Grades | • There is a wide range of physical, cognitive and socioemotional development in young children.<br>• Learning activities for young children should be active in nature due to the high energy levels of these children.<br>• Preoperational children need a wide variety of concrete experiences.<br>• Three theories of language acquisition stress different aspects of learning: behaviorism emphasizes reinforcement; social learning theory stresses modeling and imitation; and psycholinguistic theory views language learning as an innate process activated by exposure to language.<br>• Although English dialects differ from standard English in some ways, they are legitimate and complex languages to be accepted, valued and built upon.<br>• Effective teaching of English as a second language first builds on the linguistic strengths of the native language and then gradually introduces English.<br>• Bilingual programs differ in the extent to which they use the student's native language.<br>• Whole language approaches stress the child's natural language and integrate it into the curriculum.<br>• Although young children try to take initiative and be independent, they are still heavily dependent on adult/parent assessment and guidance.<br>• Effective programs for young children try to match the amount of focus and structure to the learning needs of children. | • Behaviorist position, 90<br>• Social learning theory, 90<br>• Psycholinguistic theories, 90<br>• LAD (language acquisition device), 92<br>• Holophrases, 92<br>• Overgeneralization, 93<br>• Undergeneralization, 93<br>• Dialect, 94<br>• Bilingual programs, 96<br>• Maintenance programs, 97<br>• Transitional programs, 98<br>• Immersion programs, 98<br>• Submersion programs, 98<br>• English as a Second Language Programs (ESL), 98<br>• Whole language, 101<br>• Gender stereotyping, 104<br>• Authoritarian style, 107<br>• Permissive style, 107<br>• Authoritative style, 107<br>• Head Start, 107<br>• Open education, 110 |

| | | |
|---|---|---|
| The Elementary Grades | • Physical development at this age is gradual and constant, with a growth spurt for girls in the upper grades.<br>• Concrete operational students still need concrete examples to make sense of abstractions, but use these abstractions more strategically to understand and solve problems.<br>• Children at this age develop different dimensions of self-concept: academic, social and physical, the first of which is directly tied to success at school.<br>• The type of family pattern is not as important to social and emotional health as the quality of supervision and interaction within the family.<br>• Teachers have a professional and legal responsibility to report child abuse and neglect. | • Self-concept, 116<br>• Co-regulation, 119<br>• Child abuse, 122<br>• Child neglect, 122 |
| Adolescence | • Physical changes at this age are often dramatic and rapid, coming at a time when conformity is very important.<br>• While girls typically mature 2 years earlier than boys, the social and emotional effects of early maturation is usually beneficial for boys and the opposite for girls.<br>• The transition to formal thinking increases abilities to think abstractly, use hypothetico-deductive reasoning, and attack problems systematically.<br>• Not all high school and even college-age students make the complete transition to formal thinking.<br>• Peers assume a major role in influencing the adolescent.<br>• Different views of the tensions involved in identity-seeking in adolescents vary from inevitable to culturally influenced to healthy growth-related.<br>• Teachers can help adolescents accomplish identity achievement by listening, talking, and helping students understand the choices that confront them. | • Pubescence, 125<br>• Identity diffusion, 133<br>• Identity foreclosure, 133<br>• Identity moratorium, 133<br>• Identity achievement, 133 |

# CHAPTER THREE
# STUDENT DEVELOPMENT:
# APPLICATIONS

## GUIDED REVIEW

### EARLY CHILDHOOD AND PRIMARY GRADES

Children of this age probably undergo more dramatic changes in terms of physical, cognitive and socioemotional growth than any other age group. During this time period, students make impressive gains in physical, mental and social growth that lay the foundation for future growth.

(3-1) Suppose you are a first grade teacher planning an introductory science unit on plants. What specific activities could you provide which would help to develop the following characteristics typical of this age children? (pp. 88-90)

• Refinement of gross motor skills

_____

_____

• Development of fine motor skills

_____

_____

• High energy/short attention span

_____

_____

(3-2) Classify each of the following as to whether it most closely represents a statement made by an advocate of the behaviorist theory of language acquisition (B), the social learning theory (SL), or a psycholinguistic theory (PL). (pp. 90-92)

_____ Children are programmed genetically to search for patterns and rules when they are exposed to language.
_____ Children learn language by hearing it used, by trying it out, and by the responses or feedback they receive when they attempt language.
_____ Children are reinforced for using the sounds that belong to their particular language and therefore use those sounds more and more until language develops.
_____ The parent models, the child imitates the parent, and the parent reinforces and corrects the child.
_____ Language learning is an increase in discrete behaviors resulting from reinforcement.
_____ Exposure to language triggers the genetic tendency to learn language.

(3-3) Complete the chart below naming the stages of language acquisition, listing their characteristics, and giving an original example of each.  (pp. 92-94)

| STAGE | CHARACTERISTICS | ORIGINAL EXAMPLE |
|---|---|---|
|  |  |  |
|  |  |  |
|  |  |  |

(3-4) Describe guidelines for teaching students who speak nonstandard English dialects.  (pp. 94-95)

_____

_____

_____

_____

(3-5)  What arguments are used to defend the use of bilingual programs in lieu of English-only instruction for speakers of languages other than English?  (pp. 96-99)

_____

_____

_____

(3-6) Explain how each of the following activities can be used to foster language development in children.  (p. 100-103)

•Ask "who," "what," and "where" questions

_____

_____

•Take field trips

_____

•Have students keep a journal

_____

_____

•Have students dictate descriptions of experiences

_____

_____

(3-7)  Match the following terms and definition.  (pp.92-93, 101-107)

_____ holophrases

_____ overgeneralization

_____ undergeneralization

_____ whole language approach

_____ gender stereotyping

_____ parallel play

_____ associative play

_____ cooperative play

_____ authoritarian

_____ permissive

_____ authoritative

A. An interaction style that gives children total freedom and makes few demands.

B. Children play using the same materials but use them in different ways.

C. Use of a word too narrowly.

D. Use of children's own language to teach reading and writing.

E. A one- or two- word utterance that conveys the meaning of a sentence.

F. Children play alongside each other without any significant interaction.

G. Use of a word too broadly.

H. A variation of nonstandard English

I. An interaction style that values conformity and lacks give-and-take.

J. Distorted or limited male or female roles.

K. An interaction style that is firm but caring, and has high expectations.

L. Children coordinate activities toward a common goal or theme.

(3-8)  Fill in the following chart comparing the advantages and disadvantages of the developmental and direct instruction approaches (pp. 109-111)

| Instructional Approaches | Advantages | Disadvantages |
| --- | --- | --- |
| Developmental Approach | | |
| Direct Instruction Approach | | |

## THE ELEMENTARY GRADES

The elementary grades are a period of change, some dramatic and some gradual.  While cognitive growth is quite impressive, physical growth is much less noticeable.  Attitudes towards school are formed and greatly influence self-concept.

(3-9)  What factors are likely to influence the physical fitness of elementary-age children?  (p. 112-113)

_____

_____

(3-10)  How could you as a teacher use a lesson about dinosaurs to develop a positive self-concept in your students in the following subcomponents?  (p. 116-119)

•Academic self-concept_____

_____

•Social self-concept_____

_____

•Physical self-concept_____

_____

(3-11) What can adults do to promote the development of independence in their children while still exercising general control (coregulation)? (pp. 119-120)

_____

_____

_____

(3-12) What is a teacher's legal responsibility in cases of child abuse or neglect? (p. 122-123)

_____

What is included in the term "abuse?"

_____

## ADOLESCENCE

Teachers, as significant adults, play an important role in guiding students through the process of identity searching that is typical of students this age. Understanding the dramatic physical and cognitive changes that occur at this stage is essential to teachers.

(3-13) Describe the typical effect of development in the situations below. (pp.125-126)

•Early development (girls)

_____

•Early development (boys)

_____

•Late development (girls)

_____

•Late development (boys)

_____

(3-14) What does the need for concrete problems and experiences tell you about junior high and high school students' thinking? (pp. 128-130)

_____

_____

List two ways in which Maria Cortez (p. 128) carried this out in her science class.

_____

_____


(3-15) Describe in your own words the contributions of each of the following researchers to the question of identity resolution in adolescents (pp. 131-134)

• Faw and Belkin_____

_____

• Margaret Mead_____

_____

•
Erikson_____

_____

•Waterman_____

_____

•Montemayor_____

_____

(3-16) What is the rationale behind the creation of the middle school concept? (pp. 134-135)

_____

_____


(3-17) What are three ways that middle schools are different from junior high schools? (pp. 134-135)

_____

_____

_____

# CHAPTER THREE
# STUDENT DEVELOPMENT:
# APPLICATIONS

## APPLICATION EXERCISES

Exercise 3.1 measures your understanding of topics covered on pages 85-92 of your text.

Exercise 3.1

Look at the following episodes involving parents trying to teach their children language and identify the theory of language acquisition best illustrated by each.

1. "Me toy," says 2-year-old Tanya, holding out her hand.

"Oh, Tanya wants the toy. Say, 'I want the toy.' "

"Want toy," replies Tanya.

"Good girl!"

_____

_____


2. An eager dad was playing with his daughter and working on her vocabulary. He had a small box of toy animals. As he held each one up, he asked, "What is it?"
   When the child responded correctly, he replied, "Good, here's a lion." When the response was incorrect, he'd say, "No, that's not a rhino. That's a hippo. You say it."

_____

_____


3. Mom was walking through the park with her 1-year-old on her back. People looked at her a little strangely as she carried on the following monologue: "Look at the dog. What a funny-looking dog. Look at his legs. They're so short.
   "Oh, there's some water ahead. It looks like a pond. See the ducks swimming in the pond. The one with the green head is the daddy. Should we go feel the water?"
   The child listened with wide-eyed detachment.

_____

_____

_____

Exercise 3.2 measures your understanding of topics covered on pages 92-103 of your text.

Exercise 3.2

1. Read the following sentences/phrases, and classify them as reflecting early (E) or later stages (L) in language development. Explain why in each case.

a. He was there.

_____

_____

b. Was he there?

_____

_____

c. The boy brought the toy because he thought he would be bored.

_____

_____

d. Me go.

_____

_____

e. The car that was skidding slid off the icy road.

_____

_____

2. Classify each of the following as maintenance, transitional, or ESL bilingual programs.
a. Pablo Suarez spends his day in a self-contained fifth-grade classroom. In that class he learns primarily in English. When he has a problem or doesn't understand something he can raise his hand and an aide will come over and talk to him in Spanish, explaining the content or directions he doesn't understand.

_____

b. Jacinta Escobar is a first-grade student at Woodrow Wilson Elementary School. When she arrives in the morning her teacher greets her in Spanish. Jacinta is learning to read and write in both Spanish and English, and many of the songs the class sings are in Spanish.

_____     _____

c.  Abdul Hakeem has recently moved to New York from his old home in the Middle East. He is in the seventh grade and attends most of the regular classes like the other students. Though his speaking skills in English are limited, he can read enough to get by in most classes. During fourth period every day he goes to a special class that focuses on English vocabulary and oral communication skills.

_____

3.  You are a fourth-grade teacher with 8 non-native English-speaking students in your class of 26.  You're beginning a unit on *adjectives* and *adverbs* with your students in language arts.  Based on the information in this section, describe *specifically* how you would teach the topic, taking into account the special needs of your non-native English speakers and capitalizing on the information in this section.

_____

_____

_____

┌───────────────────────────────────────────────────────────────────────────────┐
│  ┌─────────────────────────────────────────────────────────────────────────┐  │
│  └─────────────────────────────────────────────────────────────────────────┘  │
└───────────────────────────────────────────────────────────────────────────────┘

Exercise 3.3 measures your understanding of topics covered on pages 103-107 of your text.

Exercise 3.3

Examine the following teaching episodes, and decide whether the teacher's response was Authoritative (A), Authoritarian (An) or Permissive (P).

1.  A fifth-grade teacher finds two students arguing in the back of the room. She says,
    a.  "Stop that fighting and return to your seats immediately. You know the rules about fighting."
    b.  "What's the problem here? You both know what we do when we disagree. You two need to work this out quietly and return to your seats or I'll have to settle it for you."

_____

2.  A high school social studies teacher is assigning topics for reports on a unit on World War II.
    a.  "Who wants to report on the Lend-Lease Act? No One? Well, I guess we won't have a report on that topic."
    b.  "Class, who wants to report on the Lend-Lease Act? No one? Hmm. I know all of these aren't equally interesting, but we need to know about each of these topics. Any volunteers? Seth, good."

_____

3.  A third-grade teacher looks away from the blackboard and sees Adam sharpening his pencil.
    a.  "Adam, sit down! How many times do I have to remind you?"
    b.  "Adam, sit down. When you sharpen your pencil in the middle of a math activity, it distracts the class and me."

_____

4.  A teacher is working with her class at the beginning of the school year on grades and grading.
    a.  "Well, what about extra credit? Should you be allowed to hand in as much as you want? Let's see a show of hands. OK, unlimited extra credit."
    b.  "Well, what about extra credit? What are the advantages and disadvantages? Let's talk about these, and I'll share my perspective with you. Then I'll make a decision."

Exercise 3.4 measures your understanding of topics covered on pages 107-111 of your text.

Exercise 3.4

Suppose you want to teach word problems involving subtraction to your second graders. The problems will ask questions, such as "How many more?" and "How many are left?" Describe specifically how you would teach the topic using a *direct instruction* approach, and then describe specifically what you would do to teach the topic using a *developmental* approach. Include anything you would do with the students, such as pretesting, before you begin teaching the topic.

_____

_____

_____

_____

_____

_____

Exercise 3.5 measures your understanding of topics covered on pages 111-123 of your text.

Exercise 3.5

You're a fourth-grade teacher teaching your students the functions of different parts of the skeletal system (e.g., the leg bones are thick and strong because they propel our bodies, the ribs protect our internal organs). Describe in detail how you would teach this topic based on the information in this section. Include the specific examples and materials you would use and specific questions you would ask.

_____

_____

_____

_____

Exercise 3.6 measures your understanding of topics covered on pages 123-135 of your text.

Exercise 3.6

l. Analyze the following statements about adolescents' identity crisis and determine whether they reflect Hall's, Mead's, or Erikson's perspective on tension and conflict in adolescence. In each case, explain your choice.

a. "Kids today have too many choices. Back in my day, we either worked on the farm or got a job in the factory. Now teenagers don't know what they're doing."

_____

_____

_____

b. "Things are okay now that I'm a junior, but it was rough when I was in the seventh and eighth grades. I thought I was unattractive, dumb, and clumsy. Now, I see that a lot of kids felt the same way."

_____

_____

_____

c. "I know it's not easy being a teenager. A couple of years ago, a kid's parents told him what to eat and what to wear. Now it's decisions, decisions, decisions. I guess it's all part of growing up."

_____

_____

_____

2. Look at the statements Sandy, Ramon, Nancy, and Taylor made at the beginning of the section discussing routes to identity formation (p.132-133). Classify each statement as *identity diffusion, identity foreclosure, identity moratorium,* or *identity achievement.*

_____

_____

_____

_____

_____

# CHAPTER THREE
## STUDENT DEVELOPMENT: APPLICATIONS

### SELF-CHECK QUIZ_____

TRUE-FALSE QUESTIONS: Write T in the blank if the statement is true, and write F if the statement is false.

_____ 1. Sex differences in early childhood are more due to the influences of society than any actual physical differences between boys and girls.

_____ 2. Although they differ on exactly how language is acquired, behaviorists and social learning theorists both agree that language learning occurs when children try out language and get feedback from others around them.

_____ 3. "He goed outside" is an example of a child undergeneralizing the use of -ed to form the past tense of a word.

_____ 4. Teachers can effectively help students who speak nonstandard English by maintaining high expectations and correcting students when improper grammar or pronunciation is used.

_____ 5. Students who participate in Head Start generally perform better academically in the lower grades than those who don't, but lose gains in upper grades unless they participate in follow-through programs.

_____ 6. Bilingual programs vary in terms of their attitudes toward the native language and how much emphasis they place on English acquisition.

_____ 7. In the elementary grades, teachers have more influence on children's self-concepts than their peers.

_____ 8. Children of elementary age who are given opportunities to make some decisions for themselves and to be held accountable for their responsibilities have been found to be higher achievers than those who have no such opportunities.

_____ 9. One of the main traits of formal operational thinkers is the ability to store more experience and domain specific knowledge in long-term memory than concrete operational thinkers.

_____10. Generally students' self-concepts begin low in the elementary grades and gradually increase and strengthen through junior high and on into high school.

MULTIPLE CHOICE QUESTIONS: Select the best answer for each question.

11. Which of the following is <u>NOT</u> true of the physical development of a child in early childhood?
    a. Growth spurts account for a wide range of sizes and shapes among children of the same age.
    b. Fine motor coordination is well developed while gross motor skills are just being acquired.
    c. Energy levels are high and sometimes difficult to control.
    d. Boys and girls grow at about the same rate.

12. An innate, genetic drive that predisposes children to understand the rules of language in others and to use them in their own speech is called:
    a. a social learning theory.
    b. an overgeneralization.
    c. an undergeneralization.
    d. a language acquisition device.

13. A true bilingual approach to teaching English:
    a. builds on language skills that children already bring with them to class through their native language.
    b. can be used effectively when several different languages are spoken in a classroom or school.
    c. maximizes language development, although studies show initial losses in math and reading due to the catch-up time involved in learning English.
    d. will be needed less and less in the future as the influx of non-English-speaking students decreases.

14. A teacher who says, "Teresa, did you <u>ask</u> Marcos if you could use the book? You know we have all agreed to respect other people's property. I would expect the same from Marcos if he wanted to look at <u>your</u> book," would be exhibiting:
    a. an authoritarian interaction style.
    b. a permissive interaction style.
    c. an authoritative interaction style.
    d. verbal conflict.

15. A preschool teacher begins a unit on plants by having an aide take one group of children for a walk around the school to notice different plants, having another group sort different kinds of seeds to plant, and having a third group hear a listening tape with a read-along book about plants in the forest, at the seashore, and in the desert. This is an example of:
    a. a developmental approach.
    b. a psycholinguistic approach.
    c. a direct instruction approach.
    d. a behaviorist approach.

16. Initiative-guilt is to the preschool child as _____ is to the elementary-aged child.
    a. identity-confusion
    b. autonomy-shame
    c. trust-mistrust
    d. industry-inferiority

17. A bilingual program that has as its goal the development of competence in two languages and that teaches in both of these is called a(n):
    a. Maintenance Program.
    b. Transitional Program.
    c. Immersion Program.
    d. Submersion Program.

18. In examining the results of research on the American family and its effect on children and their development, it can be concluded that:
    a. preschoolers are more insecure and have lowered achievement if their mothers work.
    b. children of divorced parents are more poorly adjusted in school than children of two-parent families.
    c. a teacher's role in terms of the social and emotional needs of students is minimized as children grow older.
    d. the structure of the family is not as important as the quality of the interaction within it.

19. Which of the following is true of the effects of differences in physical development in adolescence?
    a. Early-maturing girls tend to be poised and out-going.
    b. Early-maturing boys are often socially shy and introverted.
    c. Later-maturing boys tend to be insecure and rebellious.
    d. Later-maturing girls are often intellectual overachievers.

20. Which of the following is NOT considered an element of identity resolution in adolescence?
    a. The struggle for independence from family and parents.
    b. The effort to decide upon a career.
    c. The conflict between conforming to peer pressure and maintaining independence.
    d. The struggle to develop cognitively into a formal operational thinker.

# CHAPTER FOUR
# INDIVIDUAL DIFFERENCES

## CHAPTER OUTLINE

I. Intelligence
   A. Intelligence: What Does It Mean?
   B. Measuring Intelligence
   C. Intelligence: One Trait or Many?
      1. Guilford's Structure of the Intellect (SOI)
         a. Guilford's model: Curriculum contrasts
      2. Gardner's Theory of Multiple Intelligences
         a. Gardner's theory: Educational applications
      3. Sternberg's Triarchic Theory of Intelligence
         a. The processing components
         b. Intelligence and the environment
         c. Intelligence: Modification through experience
         d. Sternberg's work: Educational implications
   D. Intelligence: Nature vs. Nurture
   E. Instructional adaptations for differences in ability
      1. Flexible time requirements
      2. Increased instructional support
      3. Strategy instruction
      4. Peer tutoring and cooperative learning
      5. Ability grouping
   F. Ability Grouping
      1. Types of ability grouping
      2. Ability grouping: Research results
      3. The negative effects of grouping: Possible explanations
         a. Instructional effects
         b. Effects of student self-esteem
      4. Grouping: Implications for teachers
II. Socioeconomic Status (SES)
   A. The Influence of SES on Learning
      1. Physical needs and experience
      2. Interaction patterns in the home
      3. Attitudes and values
III. Culture
   A. Ethnicity
   B. Cultural and Schooling
      1. Attitudes and values
      2. Cultural differences in adult-child interactions
      3. Classroom organization
      4. School communication
      5. Cultural matches with school learning
      6. Culture and Learning: Deficit or Difference?
   C. Culturally Responsive Teaching
      1. Accepting and valuing differences
      2. Accommodating different learning styles
      3. Building on cultural background learners

IV. Gender Differences
    A. Different Treatment of Boys and Girls
       1. Societal and family influences
       2. Treatment in schools
          a. Differences in reading
          b. Intervention studies in reading
          c. Title IX: Federal attacks on sex discrimination
       3. Gender bias in the schools: Progress and caution
V. Learning Styles
    A. Field Dependence/Independence
    B. Impulsive and Reflective Learners
    C. Learning Styles: Research Results
    D. Learning Styles: Implications for Teachers
VI. At-Risk Students
    A. At-Risk Students: A Definition
    B. At-Risk Students: What Works
       1. Schools for at-risk students
       2. Programs for at-risk students
       3. Effective teachers for at-risk students
       4. Effective instruction for at-risk students: Structure and support
       5. Effective instruction for at-risk students: The need for challenge

## CHAPTER OBJECTIVES

- Define the concept of intelligence.
- Describe the differences between single trait and multiple trait theories of intelligence.
- Explain the differences between the heredity and environment positions on intelligence.
- Describe the different forms of student grouping and explain how they influence learning in the classroom.
- Define socioeconomic status and explain how it may influence school performance.
- Explain the role that culture plays in school success.
- Describe the interaction of gender on various facets of school success.
- Explain how knowledge of learning styles can be used by classroom teachers.
- Describe ways that schools and classrooms can be adapted to meet the needs of at-risk students.

## CHAPTER OVERVIEW

The students we teach differ on a number of significant dimensions which affect not only their ability to learn but also their ability to grow up happy and healthy. These individual differences also influence our effectiveness as teachers and impact the teaching strategies that we employ.

One of the most powerful of these differences lies in the area of general ability or intelligence. There are many definitions of intelligence, but most recent ones center around the ability to problem solve, reason abstractly and acquire knowledge.

Ideas about intelligence have changed over the years. Current ideas about intelligence view it as a multi-dimensional concept that is alterable by the environment. This view suggests that schools should be created that nurture and develop students' intellectual potential and that students should be helped to develop intellectually in diverse ways.

Classrooms accommodate individual differences in intellectual ability in a number of ways ranging from increased time and instructional support to ability grouping. Ability grouping attempts to place students of different abilities in different instructional environments. The potentially negative effects of ability grouping suggest cautions in its use.

A second powerful factor influencing learning is socioeconomic status (SES), which is a measure of a family's relative position in the community, determined by a combination of a family's income, occupation and education level. SES influences physical and experiential growth in young children and continues to influence children in the school years through differential attitudes and values about schooling and language use in the home.

Culture, or the combination of attitudes, values and beliefs, and ways of acting of different groups influences learning in a similar way. An important part of culture is ethnicity which refers to a student's ancestry or national reference group. Culture interacts with schooling through attitudes and values, patterns of adult-child interactions, and the compatibility of classroom organization and communication patterns with students' culture. Culturally responsive teaching acknowledges cultural diversity and attempts to match instruction to the unique backgrounds of students.

Gender differences also impact the effectiveness of our instruction. Though research suggests that boys and girls are quite similar in aptitude, it also reveals differences in how they are treated in school as well as the type of careers they pursue. Teachers can do much to encourage females to explore careers in math and science.

The final area of individual differences is learning styles, which are the preferred ways that students process information and solve problems. Learning styles remind us of the unique individuality of all our students and the need to offer a variety of teaching strategies.

At-risk students are in danger of failing to complete their education with the skills necessary to survive in a technological society. Three approaches to helping at-risk students focus on: 1) personalized teaching that emphasizes caring; 2) creating stable and supportive learning environments, and 3) challenging programs with high expectations and emphasis on thinking skills.

# CHAPTER FOUR
# INDIVIDUAL DIFFERENCES

## CHAPTER-AT-A-GLANCE

| MAIN TOPICS | KEY POINTS | KEY TERMS |
|---|---|---|
| Intelligence | • Key components of intelligence include abstract thinking and reasoning, problem solving ability, and the capacity to acquire knowledge.<br>• Experience is an important factor in intelligence test performance.<br>• Guilford, Gardner and Sternberg all developed models based on the premise that intelligence is a combination of traits, not just one.<br>• Heredity or nature advocates argue that intelligence is transmitted primarily through genes; environment or nurture advocates argue that it is primarily influenced by the cumulative experiences a child gathers.<br>• Interactionists claim that genes provide raw material for intelligence which is then shaped by the environment.<br>• Homogeneous grouping places students of similar ability in the same class; heterogeneous grouping mixes students of different abilities.<br>• Teachers need to be aware that research has pointed out a number of problems with grouping and tracking, and guard against these problems in their classrooms. | • Intelligence, 148<br>• Multiple intelligence models, 149<br>• Nature/nurture, 154<br>• Ability grouping, 156<br>• Heterogeneous grouping, 156<br>• Homogeneous grouping, 156<br>• Between-class ability grouping, 157<br>• Joplin Plan, 158<br>• Within-class ability grouping, 157<br>• Tracking, 158 |
| Socioeconomic Status (SES) | • SES, encompassing parent income, occupation and level of education, has a powerful influence on intelligence test performance as well as school success. | • Socioeconomic status, 160-161 |
| Culture | • The match between a child's culture and the school is a powerful influence on school success.<br>• Attitudes and values of parents and how they are translated into specific childrearing practices can have a tremendous impact on school success.<br>• Effective teachers of culturally diverse learners are sensitive to cultural differences, create environments that meet diverse emotional needs, are committed to using cultural differences in a positive way, and consciously develop creative instructional strategies that build on and complement the strengths of different cultural groups. | • Culture, 165<br>• Ethnicity, 165-166<br>• Cultural inversion, 167<br>• Cultural deficit models, 171<br>• Cultural difference models, 171<br>• Culturally responsive teaching, 172 |

| | | |
|---|---|---|
| Gender Differences | • Gender differences in terms of aptitude or intelligence are minor and primarily due to differential treatment of boys and girls in society as well as schools.<br>• Teachers can minimize the negative effects of gender differences by treating boys and girls equally in the classroom and by actively combating negative sexual stereotypes in their teaching. | |
| Learning Styles | • Learning styles are the preferred ways in which learners process and organize information and respond to the environment.<br>• Research on the effectiveness of matching classroom environments to students' learning styles has been inconclusive.<br>• The concept of learning style suggests the need to vary instruction and to be sensitive to differences in students' behavior. | • Learning styles, 180<br>• Cognitive styles, 181<br>• Field dependence/independence, 181<br>• Impulsive students, 181<br>• Reflective students, 181 |
| At-risk Students | • At-risk students have learning problems and adjustment difficulties; they often exit school with subminimal skills even though they have the capacity to achieve.<br>• Effective instruction for at-risk students provides greater structure and support, more active teaching, greater student engagement, more feedback with higher success rates, and greater challenge. | • At-risk students, 184 |

# CHAPTER FOUR
# INDIVIDUAL DIFFERENCES

## GUIDED REVIEW _____

The chapter discusses the different sources of learner individuality, including intelligence, culture, SES, gender and learning styles.  As teachers we must continually remember that our students bring a wide variety of abilities and other differences with them to the classroom .

(4-1)  List the major sources of learner individuality discussed in this chapter.  (p. 147)

- _____

- _____

- _____

- _____


## INTELLIGENCE _____


Intelligence is a commonly used term in everyday language.  Because of its impact on school learning, it is an important concept to know and understand.

(4-2)  Although most people have a general idea of what is meant by intelligence, experts have identified three key components:  (p. 148)

_____

_____

_____

The relative impact of experience on intelligence, versus the influence of genetics, is at the core of a continual debate often termed nature versus nurture.

(4-3)  Defend the statement:  Experience is a major factor in intelligence test performance.  Use Piaget's theory of development to help support your answer.  (p. 148-149)

_____

_____

_____

_____

## THEORIES OF MULTIPLE INTELLIGENCE

Three contemporary thinkers in the field of intelligence have each developed theories based on the idea that intelligence is not a single trait but rather a combination of many traits.

(4-4) For each phrase below, identify to which theory it belongs: write SOI for Guilford's Structure of Intellect, GMI for Gardner's theory of multiple intelligences, or TTI for Sternberg's triarchic theory of intelligence. (pp. 149-154)

_____describes seven major dimensions of intelligence

_____describes the intellect as the intersection of a cognitive operation, a content area and a product

_____explains intelligence in terms of processing components of problem solving, plus two "hows": how intelligence relates to our environment and how intelligence is modified by experience

_____metacomponent, performance component and knowledge-acquisition component

_____five operations: evaluation, convergent production, divergent production, memory and cognition

_____musical intelligence

_____difficult to apply formally in the classroom because of its complexity

_____interpersonal and intrapersonal intelligence

_____implies that extensive experience with novel problems is preferred over drill and practice of basic skills

_____suggests expansion of school curriculum to develop skills in imaginative writing, visual arts, and music

_____six products: units, classes, relations, systems, transformations, and implications

## INTELLIGENCE: NATURE VS. NURTURE

Experts disagree about the relative contributions of heredity and environment. Current views emphasize the interaction of these two components.

(4-5) A child with high intellectual potential is raised in a non-stimulating environment. Another child with average intellectual potential is raised in a very stimulating environment. Explain how these examples depict current thinking about the influence of nature and nurture. (p. 154)

_____

_____

_____

_____

## INSTRUCTIONAL ADAPTATIONS FOR DIFFERENCES IN ABILITY

Teachers attempt to adapt their instruction to accommodate student differences in ability. These modifications provide greater flexibility and increased instructional support.

(4-6)  Match the instructional adaptation on the left with its characteristics on the right.  (pp. 154-156)

_____  Flexible time requirements

_____  Increased instructional support

_____  Strategy instruction

_____  Peer tutoring and cooperative learning

_____  Ability grouping

A.  Attempts to teach students more effective ways to learn.

B.  Attempts to make instruction more effective by minimizing student heterogeneity.

C.  Helps students by providing additional teaching help.

D.  Gives students extra time to complete work.

E.  Uses students as instructors.


## GROUPING

Grouping attempts to improve instruction by placing students with similar abilities into instructional groups. Research on the negative effects of grouping suggests caution with the practice.

(4-7)  Match the terms on the left with their definitions on the right.  (p. 156-160)

_____  The placement of students of different abilities in the same class.

_____  The mixing of different grade level students of similar ability in content classes.

_____  The practice of grouping students on the basis of some chosen educational need.

_____  Lowered teacher expectations and student self-esteem.

_____  The placement of students of similar abilities in the same class.

_____  The practice of breaking a class into subgroups based on a particular ability.

_____  The practice of dividing students at a certain grade into levels and classes.

A. ability grouping

B. heterogeneous grouping

C. homogeneous grouping

D. between-class ability grouping

E. a potentially negative effect of grouping

F. with-in class ability grouping

G. Joplin Plan

58

(4-8)  What are the main criticisms of ability grouping?  (p. 158-160)

_____

_____

_____

(4-9)  Choose one of above criticisms and describe in your own words the potential problems involved.  Suggest possible solutions for teachers.  (p. 160)

_____

_____

_____

_____

_____

SOCIOECONOMIC STATUS (SES)_____

Socioeconomic status is one of the most powerful individual differences influencing school performance.  SES affects learning through its influence on students' physical needs and experience, through differential interaction patterns in the home, and through attitudes and values.

(4-10)  Complete the following outline.  (p. 160-165)

I.  Socioeconomic status

A.  Factors determining SES

    1._____

    2._____

    3._____

B.  Consistent school problems of low SES students

    1._____

    2._____

    3._____

    4._____

C. Factors related to SES that influence learning

   1. Physical needs

      a._____

      b._____

      c._____

      d._____

   2. Experiential needs

      a._____

      b._____

   3. Family interaction patterns

      a._____

      b._____

      c._____

   4. Attitudes and values

      a._____

      b._____

## CULTURE

Culture, another major factor influencing school learning, is the combination of attitudes, values, beliefs, and ways of acting and interacting of a social group. Teachers who build upon students' culture form links between home and school and make schools more productive learning environments.

(4-11) List four components of ethnicity: (p. 165-166)

_____

_____

_____

_____

(4-12)  List and describe four ways that culture affects learning.  (pp. 166-170)

_____

_____

_____

_____

(4-13)  What are three problems with cultural deficit models of learning?  (p. 171)

_____

_____

_____

(4-14)  List the three characteristics of culturally responsive teaching and provide an example of each.  (pp. 172-174)

_____

_____

_____

_____

_____

_____

## GENDER DIFFERENCES

Gender differences are so enmeshed in our society as well as our schools that a teacher must be careful not to overlook them as a factor influencing learning.

(4-15)  List some behaviors or characteristics that are often considered gender specific that are not necessarily so. (p. 175-177)

_____

_____

_____

_____

(4-16) Use pages 177-180 to complete the following sentences regarding gender differences.

- Society projects different _____ for boys and girls.

- Girls are less likely to take nonrequired _____ and _____ courses.

- _____ receive more approval and disapproval according to a recent classroom study.

- _____ develop at an earlier age, especially in verbal    and motor skills.

- In junior high and high school, _____ do better on    visual and spatial tasks.

- _____ are punished more promptly and explicitly for   aggressive behaviors.

- Differences in achievement in math in Sweden tend to be small because
  _____.

- Achievement differences in math between boys and girls decrease when
  _____.

- When asked in a study to analyze videotapes of classroom interaction containing differential treatment of boys and girls,  teachers <u>failed</u> to see that _____ actually received more teacher attention than _____.

- _____ are more likely to experience reading problems.

## LEARNING STYLES

Learning styles refer to the preferred ways that students like to learn and process information.  The interest in learning styles has risen partially as an explanation for the influence of personality on intelligence and learning.

(4-17)  Classify the following as to whether they are characteristic of field dependence (D) or field independence (I).  (p. 181)

_____ A.  More social, liking to work with others

_____ B.  More organized in terms of note taking

_____ C.  Benefit from teacher efforts to structure content

_____ D.  Better at breaking problems into parts

_____ E.  May have an advantage in math and science

(4-18) Reflect on your own experiences in school. Classify yourself as field dependent or field independent, and impulsive or reflective. Give a example of why you think so. (p. 181-182)

_____

_____

_____

_____

## AT-RISK STUDENTS

At-risk students are those who are in danger of not profiting from our schools. It can be inferred from the profile of the class of 2001 by Kellogg (1988) (see text p. 184) that the number of possible at-risk candidates in our schools is growing every year. Developing ways of teaching these students has become a priority in many cities in the U.S.

(4-19) Would you be considered an at-risk student according to the characteristics in Table 4.4? Explain your answer. (p. 185)

_____

_____

_____

(4-20) Classify each of the following as a characteristic of an effective school (S) or an effective program (P) for at-risk students. (p. 185-186)

_____ additional resources are targeted for students with at-risk characteristics

_____ strong leadership, especially by the principal

_____ students are taken out of the regular classroom for extra hours of reading or math instruction

_____ school climate is safe and orderly

_____ regular classroom teachers involved in planning with resource teachers to achieve common goals

_____ parents are involved

(4-21) Describe in your own words three different approaches to teaching at-risk students. (pp. 187-189)

- _____

- _____

- _____

# CHAPTER FOUR
## INDIVIDUAL DIFFERENCES

## APPLICATION EXERCISES _____

Exercise 4.1 measures your understanding of topics covered on pages 147-160 of your text.

Exercise 4.1

Examine the episode involving Tony moving to a new math group (pages 156 & 157 of your text). Using information in this section, identify four positive characteristics or practices illustrated there.

_____

_____

_____

Exercise 4.2 measures your understanding of topics covered on pages 160-174 of your text.

Exercise 4.2

You are a teacher with a class of 24 students, 17 of whom fit Ogbu's description of involuntary minorities. Describe specifically what you might do in your teaching to help overcome the concept of cultural inversion in your class.

_____

_____

_____

_____

Exercise 4.3 measures your understanding of topics covered on pages 174-180 of your text.

Exercise 4.3

Consider the situation in which Marti Banes found herself on the first day of her advanced-placement chemistry class.

1. What is the best explanation for the low number of girls in her class?

_____

_____

2. What short- and long-term strategies might she pursue to correct this problem?

Exercise 4.4 measures your understanding of topics covered on pages 181-183 of your text.

_____

_____

```
┌─────────────────────────────────────────────────────────────────────┐
│┌───────────────────────────────────────────────────────────────────┐│
│└───────────────────────────────────────────────────────────────────┘│
└─────────────────────────────────────────────────────────────────────┘
```

Exercise 4.4

Using the concept of field dependence/independence, explain the students' behavior in Nate Crowder's class when he switched to small-group work.

_____

_____

```
┌─────────────────────────────────────────────────────────────────────┐
│┌───────────────────────────────────────────────────────────────────┐│
│└───────────────────────────────────────────────────────────────────┘│
└─────────────────────────────────────────────────────────────────────┘
```

Exercise 4.5 measures your understanding of topics covered on pages 183-191 of your text.

Exercise 4.5

Look again at the example of Mrs. Higby's lesson (on page 188 of your text) with her students. Identify in it each of the six characteristics of effective instruction for at-risk students. Cite specific information from the case study to illustrate the characteristics.

_____

_____

_____

_____

_____

_____

_____

_____

# CHAPTER FOUR
# INDIVIDUAL DIFFERENCES

## SELF-HELP QUIZ _____

TRUE/FALSE QUESTIONS:  Write T in the blank if the statement is true, and write F if the statement is false.

_____ 1.  Lack of experience is a major factor contributing to poor performance on intelligence tests.

_____ 2.  Experts agree that the best way to teach at-risk students is through diagnosis and remediation.

_____ 3.  Gardner's theory of multiple intelligences adds dimensions to intelligence that help explain how a person selects effective problem solving strategies.

_____ 4.  The success of attempts to improve intelligence by directly teaching cognitive skills measured on intelligence tests adds support to the environment's case in the nature/nurture argument.

_____ 5.  Homogeneous ability grouping has had little effect on the expectations of teachers and the motivation of low ability students.

_____ 6.  Lower SES parents place greater emphasis on conformity and obedience than do their middle and upper SES counterparts.

_____ 7.  Teachers should help culturally diverse learners by creating a structured classroom environment where cultural differences are ignored.

_____ 8.  Title I programs in the elementary schools have been found to be generally well taught, congruent with regular school instructional goals, and efficient in use of time.

_____ 9.  Although teachers can model and actively teach to dispel commonly accepted gender biases, there is little they can do to combat values already ingrained in students.

_____10.  Field-dependent students take more time to analyze and deliberate before they answer, and are good at identifying inconsistencies in text.

MULTIPLE CHOICE QUESTIONS:  Circle the best answer for each question.

11. Intelligence is best defined as:
   a.  the ability to do well in school.
   b.  the ability to learn, deal with abstractions, and solve problems.
   c.  the ability to adapt to unique environments.
   d.  the ability to think clearly and make decisions after adequate deliberation.

12. Sternberg's view of intelligence suggests that:
   a.  intelligence is made up of fluid and crystallized abilities uninfluenced by school and culture.
   b.  schools should use more time and resources to address divergent thinking, the search for relationships and memorization of important content.
   c.  schools should treat intelligence not as a single trait, but a complex series of interacting components.
   d.  nature is more important than nurture in shaping intelligence.

13. According to Gardner's theory of multiple intelligences:
   a.  the curriculum should be broadened to include emphases on alternate subjects and topics.
   b.  schools should renew their focus on basic skills
   c.  teachers should use teaching strategies linked to students' learning styles.
   d.  female students should be taught to think like male students and vice versa.

14. Individual teachers can allow for differing reading abilities in a classroom by dividing students into subgroups for teaching reading. This is known as:
  a. between-class ability grouping.
  b. within-class ability grouping.
  c. the Joplin Plan.
  d. heterogeneous grouping.

15. Which of the following is **NOT** a problem associated with ability grouping?
  a. Low groups are stigmatized by peers as well as teachers.
  b. There is potential for placement in the wrong group.
  c. Placement in a group tends to be inflexible.
  d. Low groups are often given work that is too difficult.

16. Low SES parents are more likely to interact with their children in the following manner:
  a. explain ideas to their children rather than simply tell them.
  b. use elaborate language and clear directions.
  c. encourage independent problem solving.
  d. none of the above

17. Cultural conflict most often occurs when:
  a. schools embrace a philosophy of acceptance towards cultural diversity.
  b. there is a disparity between school and home language or language patterns.
  c. competition is used as a motivational tool.
  d. children from different cultures mix in one school.

18. One outcome that schools with at-risk programs must especially guard against is:
  a. excessively high expectations for students.
  b. a lack of emphasis on higher level thinking.
  c. excessive teacher warmth and enthusiasm.
  d. all of the above.
  e. none of the above.

19. Which of the following statements best explains the difference in achievement scores in math between boys and girls after elementary school?
  a. girls start to feel the influence of the difference in roles for boys and girls projected by society.
  b. junior high and high school teachers are not able to make up for the influences of society by the time girls reach them.
  c. boys are more naturally talented in math because of their better visual and spatial abilities.
  d. the physical differences between boys and girls at the junior high and high school level are more apparent.

20. A realistic approach to allow for learning style differences would be:
  a. pair students on the basis of their learning styles into learning teams.
  b. administer a learning style inventory and use the results to adapt instruction to each individual's learning style.
  c. develop strategies that teach impulsive students to be more reflective and reflective students to be a little more impulsive.
  d. develop a variety of teaching methods and styles, including opportunities for students to work individually and in groups.

# CHAPTER FIVE
# TEACHING STUDENTS WITH EXCEPTIONALITIES

## CHAPTER OUTLINE _____

I. Students with Exceptionalities: Who Are They?
    A.      Roles of the Regular Classroom Teacher
         1.     Teaching
         2.     Identification
         3.     Acceptance

II. Public Law 94-142
    A.      Due Process through Parental Involvement
    B.      Protection against Discrimination in Testing
    C.      Least Restrictive Environment
    D.      Individualized Education Program
         1.     Functions of the IEP
         2.     Making IEP's work

III. Students with Learning Problems: The Mildly Handicapped
    A.      Referral Procedures
    B.      Mental Retardation
         1.     Levels of mental retardation
         2.     Causes of mental retardation
         3.     Programs for the mentally retarded
    C.      Specific Learning Disabilities
         1.     Characteristics of students with learning disabilities
         2.     Causes of learning disabilities
         3.     Learning disabilities and attention deficit disorder
         4.     Working with LD students who have learning disabilities
              a.     Complications in identification
              b.     Testing and diagnosis
              c.     Prescription
         5.     Research: Promising directions
              a.     Adapting instruction
              b.     A successful homework program
              c.     Caution: The dangers of labeling
    C.      Behavior Disorders: Emotionally Disturbed Students
         1.     Prevalence of behavior disorders
         2.     Kinds of behavior disorders
         3.     Teaching students with behavior disorders
              a.     Behavioral management strategies
              b.     Self-management skills
              c.     Teacher flexibility and sensitivity
    D.      Cross Categorical Special Education Programs

# CHAPTER OBJECTIVES

- Explain the role of the classroom teacher in working with exceptional students.
- Describe the major provisions of Public Law 94-142 and explain how they impact the classroom teacher.
- Describe the three major kinds of students having mild learning handicaps and explain how these are similar and different.
- Explain how physical impairments influence student success in the classroom.
- Describe different approaches to the identification and teaching of gifted and talented students.
- Explain how instructional strategies can be adapted to meet the needs of mainstreamed students.

# CHAPTER OVERVIEW

Students with exceptionalities are those who require special help to reach their full potential. Students with exceptionalities fall at both ends of the ability continuum, including mildly retarded and gifted and talented. The category also includes learning and behaviorally disordered students as well as students with physical impairments like visual handicaps, hearing impairments, and communication disorders.

Mainstreaming, the practice of placing students with exceptionalities in as normal a learning environment as possible, has increased the classroom teacher's role in working with these students. The classroom teacher is in the best position to identify students needing special help and can do much to help them gain acceptance and develop friendships with other students. In addition, the classroom teacher will team with specially trained special education teachers to adapt instruction to meet these students' unique academic needs.

The way that students with exceptionalities are helped in our schools has changed dramatically with the passage of Public Law 94-142, which was designed to provide a quality education for all exceptional students. A major provision of this law, the least restrictive learning environment, requires that students be placed in a learning setting that is as normal as possible while still meeting a student's needs. Other provisions of this law include 1) due process through parental involvement, 2) protection against discrimination in testing, and 3) an individualized education program. This individualized education program is a specifically tailored plan designed to match the educational capabilities and meet the educational needs of a specific student.

Most of the exceptional students in regular classrooms are mildly handicapped. Mentally retarded, or intellectually handicapped, have significantly limited intellectual ability resulting in problems in adapting to classroom tasks. Students with learning disabilities, by contrast, have normal general intellectual capabilities but have problems with specific classroom tasks such as listening, reading, writing, spelling or math operations. Behaviorally disordered students display serious and persistent behaviors that interfere with their classroom capabilities and interpersonal functioning. Cross-categorical programs look for similarities across these specific areas and help students succeed through a structured program.

Classroom teachers will also encounter students with physical handicaps. Students with visual impairment have problems using regular text materials and regular classroom visual displays. Hearing impairments hamper students' ability to benefit from oral lessons. Communication disorders involve problems in students' ability to use language to learn and talk with other people.

Students who are gifted and talented are exceptional because they also need special help to reach their full potential. Once narrowly defined by intelligence test performance, this category has been broadened to include creative talents in such diverse areas as math, music and art. Present programs for the gifted and talented either provide acceleration, or learning at a faster pace, or enrichment, which broadens the learning options for these students.

Effective teaching practices for mainstreamed students provide extra support so that students can experience high rates of success. This support often occurs in the regular classroom through the use of collaboration consultation, the regular Education initiative and Mainstream Assistance Teams which bring special educators into the classroom to help the regular teacher adapt instruction. Other strategies for working with mainstreamed students include cognitive strategy instruction, the use of computers to teach and to track educational progress, and strategies to accomplish social integration and growth.

# CHAPTER FIVE
# TEACHING EXCEPTIONAL STUDENTS

CHAPTER-AT-A-GLANCE _____

| MAIN TOPICS | KEY POINTS | KEY TERMS |
|---|---|---|
| Students with Exceptionalities: Who Are They? | • Teachers assist students with exceptionalities by helping to identify those needing special help, by modifying instruction to meet their unique needs, and by fostering their acceptance in the classroom. | • Students with exceptionalities, 199<br>• Least restrictive environment, 201<br>• Mainstreaming, 201 |
| Public Law 94-142 | • Public Law 94-142 was designed to insure that an appropriate, free educational program would be provided for all children with exceptionalities.<br>• Parents are guaranteed procedural safeguards in the classification and placement of their children.<br>• Any test used for placement must be given by qualified personnel in the student's native language, and will not be used as the sole basis for placement.<br>• Each child has the right to learn in an environment that fosters academic and social growth to the maximum extent possible.<br>• An individually prescribed instructional program must be devised for each student by special education and regular teachers plus parents (parental involvement and approval). | • PL 94-142, 204<br>• Due process, 204<br>• Individualized Education Program (IEP), 206<br>• Curriculum-based measurement, 206 |
| Students with Learning Problems: The Mildly Handicapped | • Students with mild handicaps learn well enough to remain in the regular classroom but need special help to benefit from this placement.<br>• Students who are mentally retarded or intellectually handicapped have below-average intellectual functioning and some impairment in adaptive behavior.<br>• Students can have learning disabilities that hamper learning in a specific area even though they have normal intelligence.<br>• Behavioral disorders involve serious, persistent, age-inappropriate behaviors that interfere with normal social development or functioning in the classroom.<br>• Cross-categorical approaches to teaching children with exceptionalities treat mild learning handicaps as basically similar and approach them using the same instructional strategies. | • Mildly handicapped students, 208<br>• Mental retardation, 209<br>• Specific learning disabilities, 211<br>• Attention Deficit Disorder (ADD), 213<br>• Behaviorally disordered students, 218<br>• Cross-categorical special education programs, 221 |

| MAIN TOPICS | KEY POINTS | KEY TERMS |
|---|---|---|
| Physical Impairments | • Visual handicaps interfere with many crucial processes in the classroom such as reading and writing, but cause little or no impairment in intellectual development.<br>• Learning problems caused by hearing impairments show up in speech and language use that affect reading, writing, and some math.<br>• While speech disorders involve problems in producing understandable speech, language disorders include fundamental problems with the ability to understand or produce language. | • Visual handicaps, 222<br>• Hearing impairments, 225<br>• Speech disorders, 226<br>• Language disorders, 226<br>• Articulation problems, 226<br>• Stuttering, 227<br>• Voice disorders, 227 |
| Students Who Are Gifted and Talented | • Students who are gifted and talented are at the upper end of the ability continuum in intelligence, creativity, or a unique talent.<br>• Definitions of creativity usually include the ability to think divergently, solve problems in an original way, and produce multiple solutions to a problem.<br>• Experts recommend flexible, culturally independent measures for identifying students who are gifted and talented, while questioning the sole use of achievement or intelligence tests for this purpose.<br>• Accelerated programs attempt to meet the needs of students who are gifted and talented by increasing the pace and depth of study; enrichment programs broaden the focus to other areas of study. | • Gifted and talented students, 228<br>• Creativity, 229<br>• Acceleration, 232<br>• Enrichment, 232<br>• Curriculum compacting, 232 |
| Teaching Students with Exceptionalities in the Regular Classroom | • Effective teaching for mainstreaming uses the same principles of efficient use of time, supportive environment, effective management, and high success rates--strategies that work with regular students.<br>• The regular education initiative uses collaboration between special education and classroom teachers to adapt the regular classroom to special needs students.<br>• Students with mild handicaps can be helped through strategy training, attacking learning tasks by matching a strategy to a specific goal.<br>• Computers, used strategically and integrated into the regular program, can be a valuable aid in teaching students with exceptionalities, as well as for tracking student progress.<br>• Regular students accept students with handicaps better when they understand the nature of the handicap and have opportunities to interact with these students. | • Consulting teacher model, 233<br>• Regular Education initiative, 236<br>• Mainstream assistance team, 237<br>• Strategy training, 237 |

# CHAPTER FIVE
# TEACHING STUDENTS
# WITH EXCEPTIONALITIES

## GUIDED REVIEW

### STUDENTS WITH EXCEPTIONALITIES: THE ROLE OF THE CLASSROOM TEACHER

A perceptive teacher knows that every child is special in some way. Many times that special trait or ability fits right into the life of a regular classroom. Sometimes, however, the student <u>and</u> the teacher need help accommodating a special need whether it is a physical handicap or a mental one.

(5-1) Why is the concept of least restrictive environment such an important one in terms of the education of a student with an exceptionality? Include examples to support your answer. (p. 201, 204-205)

_____

_____

_____

_____

Consider this scenario: A fifth grade teacher of middle to low SES students in an urban neighborhood receives a new student mid-year. Throughout Alicia's first week, the teacher notices that she is reluctant to speak in class and has a slight stutter when she becomes nervous.

(5-2) Make specific suggestions how the classroom teacher could help Alicia in the following areas: (p. 202-203)

• Teaching (to accommodate her needs)

_____

_____

• Identification (of her specific problem)

_____

_____

• Acceptance (of Alicia by her peers)

_____

_____

73

PL 94-142 was designed to provide a free and appropriate education for all school age students with exceptionalities.

(5-3)  Summarize the following components of PL 94-142 and the rationale behind each.  (p. 203-207)

- Due process

_____

_____

- Protection again discrimination in testing

_____

_____

- Least restrictive environment

_____

_____

- Individualized education program (IEP)

_____

_____


## STUDENTS WITH LEARNING PROBLEMS:  THE MILDLY HANDICAPPED


Students with mild handicaps learn well enough to benefit from the regular classroom when provided with extra help.

(5-4)  Reread the Gail Toomey/Stacy scenario in the text on pp. 209.  Using the definition of mental retardation on p. 209, what evidence is given that supports the possibility that Stacy may be mildly or educable mentally retarded?  (p. 209-210)

_____

_____

What further information is needed in order to make a complete diagnosis, according to the definition?

_____

_____

Mental retardation has been divided into three levels. Although all individuals do not always fit neatly into these categories, the characteristics are guidelines to assist in identification and education.

(5-5) Classify the following as descriptions of educable (E), trainable (T), or severely (S) mentally retarded. (p. 209-210)

_____are taught independent living skills in special classes

_____have an IQ below 35 (approximately)

_____are taught reading, writing and math plus social skills

_____makes up about 75% of the retarded population

_____are taught vocational skills

_____have an IQ between 70 and 50-55 (approximately)

_____make up about 5% of the retarded population

_____are often mainstreamed into regular classes

_____often have physical handicaps

_____have an IQ between 50-55 and 35-40 (approximately)

_____are taught self-care and social adaptation in separate school facilities

_____make up about 20% of the retarded population

_____are rarely found in the mainstream classroom

(5-6) List the two main program modifications for students who are mildly mentally retarded. Explain the purpose of each modification and give an original example of its application in a classroom. (p. 210)

_____

_____

_____

_____

_____

_____

Learning disabilities are the largest and most recently recognized category of exceptional children. Typically these children are of average or above average intelligence but have problems in specific areas like reading, writing, listening, speaking or math. There is still much disagreement among experts about the definition, diagnosis and remediation of these children, but all agree that the problem does indeed exist.

(5-7)  What are two major differences between a student with mental retardation and a student with a learning disability?  (p. 211-213)

_____

_____

_____

(5-8)  What are three possible causes of learning disabilities?  (p. 213)

_____

_____

_____

(5-9)  What similarities do ADD and ADD-HD have with learning disabilities?  (pp. 213-214)

_____

_____

_____

(5-10)  How would you use IQ and achievement tests results, school achievement, and information about general adaptive behavior to distinguish between a student with a learning disability, a mildly retarded student, and a minority student with a language problem?
(p. 211, 214, 215)

_____

_____

_____

_____

Researchers have found a variety of strategies that help learning students with learning disabilities learn. Since not all students need the same strategies, it is important to be familiar with the many possibilities.

(5-11)  Describe strategies for helping students with learning disabilities in the following categories:  (p. 215-217)

Student management strategies:

_____

_____

Instructional strategies:

_____

_____

Homework strategies:

_____

_____

(5-12)  List the four kinds of behavior disorders and describe their characteristics. (p. 219)

_____

_____

_____

_____

(5-13) Complete the table below comparing mental retardation, learning disabilities, and behavior disorders.  (p. 209-221)

| | Definition/ Characteristics | Causes | Educational Prescription |
|---|---|---|---|
| Mental Retardation | | | |
| Learning Disabilities | | | |
| Behavior Disorders | | | |

(5-14) Summarize in your own words the arguments for and against cross-categorical special education programs. (p. 221-222)

_____

_____

_____

_____

## PHYSICAL IMPAIRMENTS

At first glance, a physical impairment might seem less serious in the classroom than a learning problem, but a physical handicap can interfere with learning and require as much adaptation in the educational setting as other types of learning difficulties.

(5-15) Match the following terms with their descriptions.  (pp. 222-228)

_____learned helplessness

_____negative self-concept

A.  an articulation problem involving the use of one sound in place of another (e.g. "rion" for "lion")

_____ visual handicap

_____ symptom of potential vision problems

_____ partial hearing impairment

_____ symptom of hearing problems

_____ deafness

_____ substituting

_____ distorting

_____ omitting

_____ stuttering

_____ voice disorders

_____ language disorders

B. constantly asking about classroom procedures when information is already on the board

C. an unhealthy dependence upon others to do things that could be done alone

D. problems in ability to understand or express ideas through language

E. the repetition of the first sound of a word

F. asking people to repeat what they had said, or misunderstanding or not following directions

G. hearing impairment severe enough to require other senses to communicate

H. an articulation problem in which a sound is left out (e.g. "ocket" for "pocket")

I. a side effect of a visual handicap affecting self-esteem as a result of overdependence upon others

J. a type of speech impairment involving problems with the larynx or air passageways in the nose or mouth

K. hearing impairment characterized by the use of a hearing aid for receiving auditory messages

L. an articulation problem involving the changing of a sound (e.g. "thorry" for "sorry")

M. a handicap so severe that it cannot be corrected by glasses

(5-16) Suggest ways that the classroom teacher can help in the identification and acceptance of students with communication disorders. (pp. 226-228)

● Identification _____

_____

_____

● Acceptance _____

_____

_____

Students who are gifted and talented are considered exceptional because they, like other students with exceptionalities, need extra resources in order to achieve their full potential.

(5-17) Compare the three definitions of gifted and talented students on p. 228-229 in the text. Which do you think is a more comprehensive and accurate definition? Why? Has anything been left out or has anything been included erroneously, in your opinion? If so, what has and why do you think so? (p. 228-229)

_____

_____

_____

_____

(5-18) What is creativity? How is it measured? (pp. 229-230)

_____

_____

_____

(5-19) What are the four most common methods of identifying students who are gifted and talented? Which criterion should be given the most weight and which the least? Why? (p. 230-231)

_____

_____

_____

_____

(5-20) How are acceleration and enrichment programs similar? How are they different? (pp. 232-233)

_____

_____

_____

The three goals of mainstreaming are to bolster academic achievement, improve self-concept and promote integration and acceptance by other students.

(5-19) Classify the descriptions of effective teaching practices for mainstreaming (found in Table 5.8 on p. 236 in the text) under one of the headings below. Some may fit under more than one, since the goals of mainstreaming are interrelated. The first one has been done for you as an example. (p. 238-239)

| Improve academic achievement | Improve student self-concept and attitude toward school | Improve quality of social interactions with peers |
| --- | --- | --- |
| high rates of on-task behavior | | |

(5-20) Explain in your own words how each of the following can be used to help exceptional students achieve their educational goals. (p. 233-240)

• Consulting Teacher Model

_____

_____

• Mainstream Assistance Team

_____

_____

• Strategy training

_____

_____

• Computers

_____

_____

81

• Peer tutoring

_____

_____


• Cooperative learning

_____

_____

_____


(5-21)  List and describe three approaches to foster social integration and growth.  (p. 240-242)

_____

_____

_____

_____

_____

# CHAPTER FIVE
## TEACHING STUDENTS WITH EXCEPTIONALITIES

## APPLICATION EXERCISES _____

Exercise 5.1

Exercise 5.1 measures your understanding of topics covered on pages 201-203 of your text.

Read the following classroom episode, and identify in it the different functions that the classroom teacher performs in working with exceptional students.

Toni Morrison had been working with her class of second graders for a week trying to get them into reading and math groups that matched their abilities. Marisse, a transfer student, was hard to place. She seemed to understand the material but lost attention during different parts of lessons. When Toni worked with her one-on-one, she did fine, but Toni often noticed her staring out the window.

One day as Toni watched the class work in small groups, she noticed that Marisse held her head to one side when she talked to the other side. Toni wondered . . . She spoke to the principal, who recommended that Marisse be referred to the school psychologist for possible testing.

Two weeks later, the school psychologist came by to discuss her findings. Marisse had a hearing problem in one ear that would require a hearing aid as well as special help from Toni.

In a few days, Marisse came to school with her hearing aid. She obviously felt funny about it and wasn't sure if this was a good idea. Toni moved her to the front of the room so she could hear better, made sure to give directions while standing in front of Marisse's desk, and double-checked after an assignment was given to ensure that the directions were clear to her.

After a couple of days, Toni took Marisse aside to talk about her new hearing aid. Marisse could hear better, but she still felt a little strange with it. Some of the kids looked at her curiously, and that made her uneasy. Toni had an inspiration: Why not discuss the hearing aid in class and let the others try it? This was a risky strategy, but Marisse reluctantly agreed to it.

It worked. During show-and-tell, Marisse explained about her new hearing aid and gave the class a chance to try it out themselves. The strange and different became understandable, and Marisse's hearing aid became a normal part of the classroom.

Explain how Toni Morrison performed each of the functions--teaching, identification, and acceptance--required of teachers in working with exceptional students. Supply examples taken directly from the case study.

1. Teaching

_____

_____

2. Identification

_____

_____

3. Acceptance

_____

_____

Exercise 5.2

Exercise 5.2 measures your understanding of topics covered on pages 203-207 of your text.

Read the following description of a team developing an IEP.

Pablo Martinez had been falling further and further behind in math and reading. Mrs. Henderson, his second-grade teacher, felt it was time to act. She talked with the special education teacher, who called a meeting with Pablo's parents. At the meeting, the special education teacher explained why they were there and what they hoped to accomplish. English as a second language was explored as one possible source of Pablo's problem. Mrs. Henderson shared Pablo's reading and math scores with them as well as his standardized achievement scores from the previous year. Everyone concurred that Pablo was having troubles, and the parents agreed to have the school psychologist test him for possible placement in a special program. Fortunately, the school psychologist was bilingual and was able to administer his tests in Spanish.

At the next meeting, the results of the tests were shared with the parents. They showed that Pablo had normal intelligence but that he performed poorly on the verbal parts of the scale. Everyone agreed that Pablo should remain in the regular classroom but that he would benefit from a resource program that was taught in his native language.

Using information from the episode, describe how each of the following provisions of PL 94-142 was met:

1. Due process

_____

_____

2. Protection against discrimination in testing

_____

_____

3. Least restrictive environment

_____

_____

Exercise 5.3

Exercise 5.3 measures your understanding of topics covered on pages 207-242 of your text.

Examine the following list of descriptors and decide whether they apply to all three types of mild learning handicaps (G = General) or whether they are more characteristic of a specific learning problem (MR = Mental Retardation; LD = Learning Disability; BD = Behavior Disorder).

_____ 1. Problems functioning in regular classrooms.
_____ 2. Below-average performance on intelligence tests.
_____ 3. Problems often involving language.
_____ 4. Management problems often interfering with learning.
_____ 5. Discrepancies between two measures of achievement.
_____ 6. Students sometimes withdrawn and extremely shy.
_____ 7. Failure and frustration often interfering with learning.

# CHAPTER FIVE
# TEACHING STUDENTS WITH EXCEPTIONALITIES

## SELF-HELP QUIZ

TRUE/FALSE QUESTIONS: Write T in the blank if the statement is true, and write F if the statement is false.

_____ 1. One of the classroom teacher's main responsibilities is to help students with exceptionalities overcome negative attitudes of others towards them.

_____ 2. To maintain consistency in identification of children with exceptionalities, results of IQ and achievement tests should be given more weight than less objective information like classroom performance and adaptive behavior.

_____ 3. Students with mild handicaps can usually learn well enough to remain in the regular classroom with little special help if they are accepted by their peers.

_____ 4. A student with a learning disability is often hyperactive, lacks organization, exhibits uneven performance in academics, and is below normal intelligence.

_____ 5. Experts place the actual incidence of behavior disorders at around 2% even though up to 60% of students may be classified as having a behavior problem at least once in their school life.

_____ 6. A common problem of the visually impaired is poor language development, a result of limited opportunities to experience variations in concepts.

_____ 7. People who score high on IQ tests typically also score high on measures of creativity.

_____ 8. Research on mainstreaming reveals that knowledge and strategies that teachers use effectively with regular students need to be fundamentally changed in order to reach special education students.

_____ 9. Computers can be used to teach students with handicaps problem-solving and thinking skills but should be avoided for the memorization of basic facts because of an overdependence on technology and lack of transfer.

_____10. For peer tutoring to be most effective, students with handicaps should have an opportunity to be tutored and to tutor another student, either regular or handicapped.

MULTIPLE CHOICE QUESTIONS: Circle the best answer for each question.

11. The component of PL 94-142 that guarantees parent involvement in the classification and placement of their children, as well as access to their children's school records is called:
    a. due process.
    b. protection against discrimination in testing.
    c. provision for the least restrictive environment.
    d. mainstreaming.

12. The purpose of curriculum-based measurement is to:
    a. measure intelligence of the special education student in comparison to the rest of the regular class.
    b. assess achievement of the special education student in comparison to the rest of the regular class.
    c. identify specific areas that are encountered in the regular classroom in which the special education student needs help.
    d. identify long-term curriculum goals for the special education student.

13. Which of the following is true about students with mild handicaps?
    a. These students can be mentally retarded, learning disabled, or behaviorally disordered.
    b. These students make up about 20% of the total population.
    c. These students usually have other physical handicaps such as sight or hearing impairments.
    d. All of the above are true.

14. Children with learning disabilities are difficult to identify because:
   a. they have many of the same characteristics of the educable mentally retarded.
   b. they are easily confused with developmentally slow children or students with behavior problems.
   c. discrepancies between IQ and achievement tests do not show up when testing the learning disabled.
   d. high levels of creativity often compensate for problems in other areas.

15. The more difficult kind of behavioral disorder to identify is:
   a. the student displaying hyperactivity.
   b. the child who is defiant and hostile.
   c. the child who does not respond to regular rules and consequences.
   d. the shy, timid, depressed child.

16. When teachers and other students overreact to a physical handicap by doing everything for the student, an unhealthy dependence upon others can result. This is called:
   a. negative self-concept.
   b. learned helplessness.
   c. a behavioral disorder.
   d. a communication disorder.

17. Which of the following is a symptom of a language disorder?
   a. tuning out when information is presented on the chalkboard
   b. poorly articulating words, especially consonants
   c. using few words or very short sentences
   d. stuttering

18. Which of the following is **NOT** considered a trait of a student who is gifted and talented?
   a. highly organized and logical
   b. unconventional and nonconforming
   c. likes to work alone
   d. talented in one specific area

19. Which of the following is **NOT** true of accelerated programs for the gifted and talented?
   a. They challenge students by increasing the pace.
   b. They broaden student interests by introducing them to other topics.
   c. They result in improved achievement in accelerated areas.
   d. They sometimes work by allowing students to skip grades or test out of classes.

20. The development of "meta" skills like meta-attention and metacommunication are a part of:
   a. strategy training.
   b. effective feedback.
   c. cooperative learning.
   d. an accelerated curriculum.

# CHAPTER SIX
## BEHAVIORAL VIEWS OF LEARNING

### CHAPTER OUTLINE _____

# CHAPTER OBJECTIVES _____

. Identify examples of learning in everyday experiences.
. Identify examples of contiguity in classroom situations.
. Identify examples of classical conditioning in classroom situations.
. Explain cases of student behavior using concepts such as reinforcement, punishment, generalization, discrimination, satiation, and extinction.
. Explain the impact of different reinforcement schedules on student behavior.
. Identify examples of modeling and vicarious conditioning in classroom situations.

# CHAPTER OVERVIEW _____

The first section of your text focused on the learner and learner characteristics. General patterns of learner development-- intellectual, social and emotional, moral, and physical--were presented in chapters 2 and 3. In chapter 4, you saw how differences in ability, socioeconomic status, culture, gender, and even preferred ways of learning cause individuals to vary from these general patterns. Your survey of learners culminated in a further examination of individual differences in chapter 5 when you studied the effects of various exceptionalities on a student's ability to succeed in school.

We now turn to the first of three chapters devoted to the learning process itself. In this chapter we examine Behaviorism, and in chapters 7 and 8 we discuss Information Processing views of learning. As you study your text and work your way through this study guide, keep the following question in mind: "How does the information I'm studying here explain the way people learn and how they behave?" This question can serve as a reference point or "hook" to which the ideas you study can be attached.

Behaviorism is a well-developed view of learning that focuses exclusively on the relationship between observable behavior and experience. It doesn't consider internal processes, such as insight or perception, nor does it consider needs such as belonging to social groups or self-esteem. Four different types of learning--contiguity, classical conditioning, operant conditioning, and observational learning all fit under the general heading of behaviorism.

Contiguity describes learning as the simple association of two sensations--a stimulus and a response. It explains learning by saying that the more often the two are paired the more likely one will result in the other, as in the question, "What is nine times six?" (a stimulus), which results in "Fifty four" (a response).

Classical conditioning expands on the ideas of a simple S-R pairing to suggest that formerly neutral stimuli become associated with the original stimulus and result in responses identical or similar to the original responses. The formerly neutral stimulus is then called a conditioned stimulus and the response it elicits is called a conditioned response. Classical conditioning can be used to explain involuntary, emotional, and physiological responses to stimuli, such as test anxiety (a conditioned response resulting from the conditioned stimuli--tests). Ivan Pavlov, a Russian physiologist, is the founder of the original ideas about classical conditioning.

In contrast with classical conditioning, which views learning as an involuntary response to stimuli, operant conditioning describes learners as voluntarily acting, or "operating" on their environments. It explains behavior in terms of the consequences that follow the behavior--positive and negative reinforcement, which increase behavior, and presentation and removal punishment, which decrease behavior.

The way positive reinforcers are administered influence the rate and durability of learning. Continuous reinforcement increases behavior more rapidly than do intermittent schedules, but the behavior is less durable. Fixed interval schedules result in rapid increase in a behavior immediately before the reinforcer is given and decreases rapidly right after, such as giving a test each Friday; students study on Thursday and don't study again until the next Thursday.

Behaviors left unreinforced gradually disappear, or become extinct, such as students who are never praised for their efforts, On the other hand the overreinforcement of behaviors can lead to satiation, thereby reducing the potency of the reinforcer, such as students who are praised and complimented for nearly every behavior. Satiation is more likely with older than with younger children.

Observational learning describes the effects of watching others on our behavior. The tendency to imitate behaviors we see in others is called modeling. Modeling can be direct--simple imitation of another's behavior, symbolic--imitating behavior displayed in books, plays, movies, or television, synthesized--developing complex behaviors by combining portions of observed acts, or abstract--inferring systems of rules by observing examples of the rules being applied. Modeling can result in learning new behaviors, facilitating existing behaviors, focusing attention, changing inhibitions, or arousing emotions. Models who are perceived as competent and similar to the observer are more effective than their opposite counterparts.

Vicarious conditioning is the process of observing the consequences of another person's behavior and adjusting our behavior accordingly. For instance, when a student is openly praised for diligent work, other students' diligence is likely to increase; the first student is positively reinforced, the student serves as a model for the others, and the others are vicariously reinforced.

# CHAPTER SIX
# BEHAVIORAL VIEWS OF LEARNING

## CHAPTER-AT-A-GLANCE

| MAIN TOPICS | KEY POINTS | KEY TERMS |
|---|---|---|
| Learning from a Behaviorist Perspective | • Behaviorists focus on observable behaviors that are acquired as a result of experience.<br>• Behaviors occurring as a result of maturation, reflex, or instinct, and temporary behavior that results from illness or drugs are not considered learning. | • Learning, 255 |
| Contiguity | • Contiguity, sometimes called associative learning, describes the relationship between simple stimuli and responses. It can be used to explain fact learning and some stereotyping. | • Contiguity, 256<br>• Stimuli, 256<br>• Response, 256 |
| Classical Conditioning | • Classical conditioning, sometimes respondent learning, explains involuntary, emotional and physiological responses to stimuli.<br>• Unconditioned stimuli elicit reflexive or instinctive responses called unconditioned responses.<br>• Initially neutral stimuli, which aren't necessarily related to the unconditioned stimuli in any way, become associated with the unconditioned stimuli and become capable of elicited conditioned responses similar to the unconditioned responses.<br>• Learners generalize when stimuli similar to the conditioned stimuli elicit conditioned responses. They discriminate when they respond differently to related but not identical stimuli.<br>• Learners eventually stop responding to conditioned stimuli if the conditioned stimuli are continually presented in the absence of the unconditioned stimuli. | • Unconditioned stimulus, 258<br>• Unconditioned response, 258<br>• Neutral stimulus, 258<br>• Conditioned stimulus, 258<br>• Conditioned response, 258<br>• Generalization, 260<br>• Discrimination, 261<br>• Extinction, 261 |

| Operant conditioning | • Operant conditioning explains voluntary actions that are affected by the consequence of behavior.<br>• Positive and negative reinforcers increase behavior, and presentation and removal punishers decrease behavior.<br>• Secondary reinforcers increase behavior when they are paired with primary reinforcers-- reinforcers that meet basic needs.<br>• When a preferred activity is used as a reinforcer for a less preferred activity, the Premack Principle is in effect.<br>• Generalization occurs when learners are reinforced for giving the same response to similar but not identical stimuli. Learners discriminate when feedback indicates that the same response to related stimuli is not appropriate.<br>• Praise, an important form of feedback, is effective when it is immediate, specific, genuine, and encourages effort.<br>• Learner responses are shaped when the learners are given reinforcers for partially correct responses.<br>• The way reinforcers are administered affects how quickly behaviors are learned and how durable they remain. Continuously reinforced behaviors are learned rapidly, but intermittently reinforced behaviors are more durable.<br>• Too much reinforcement can lead to a learner becoming satiated, because the reinforcer has lost its potency, and too little reinforcement can lead to extinction. | • Consequence, 262<br>• Positive reinforcement, 263<br>• Negative reinforcement, 264<br>• Primary reinforcer, 265<br>• Secondary reinforcer, 265<br>• Premack Principle, 265<br>• Presentation punishment, 266<br>• Removal punishment, 266<br>• Generalization, 271<br>• Discrimination, 271<br>• Praise, 271<br>• Shaping, 273<br>• Continuous reinforcement, 274<br>• Intermittent reinforcement, 274<br>• Fixed-interval schedule, 274<br>• Variable-interval schedule, 274<br>• Fixed-ratio schedule, 274<br>• Variable-ratio schedule, 274<br>• Potency, 276<br>• Satiation, 277<br>• Cues, 279 |
|---|---|---|
| Observational | • Modeling refers to changes in individuals that result from observing the actions of others.<br>• Modeling can be direct, symbolic, synthesized, or abstract.<br>• Vicarious conditioning occurs when observers adjust their behavior based on the consequence a model receives.<br>• Modeling can result in learning new behaviors, facilitating existing behaviors, focusing attention, inhibiting or arousing emotions.<br>• Models are most effective if they are perceived as competent and similar to the observer. When observers are fearful or uncomfortable, coping models are more effective than mastery models.<br>• When they observe the consequence of others' behaviors and adapt their behaviors accordingly, vicarious conditioning is taking place. | • Attentional component, 290<br>• Attentional component, 290<br>• Retention component, 290<br>• Reproduction component, 291<br>• Motivational component, 292 |

*CHAPTER SIX*
*BEHAVIORAL VIEWS OF LEARNING*

GUIDED REVIEW _____

## LEARNING FROM A BEHAVIORIST PERSPECTIVE

Learning is an enduring change in behavior that occurs as a result of experience.

(6-1) Would a behaviorist describe blinking when a object flies near our eyes as learning? Explain. Identify two changes in behavior that would not be described by behaviorists as learning. (p. 255)

_____

_____

_____

## CONTIGUITY

Contiguity is the process of pairing simple stimuli and responses.

(6-2) Explain why contiguity could be called "associative learning." (p. 256)

_____

_____

(6-3) Explain how learning a fact like "The capital of California is Sacramento," and forming stereotypes is similar. (p. 256)

_____

_____

_____

## CLASSICAL CONDITIONING

Classical conditioning helps us explain the occurrence of involuntary, emotional and physiological responses. It describes learning in terms of unconditioned and conditioned stimuli, and unconditioned and conditioned responses.

(6-4) Look again at the case study on page 254 of your text. Identify the unconditioned and conditioned stimuli and the unconditioned and conditioned responses in it. (pp. 257-258)

_____

_____

_____

(6-5) You were assigned to make a persuasive argument in your English class, and you lost your train of thought a stumbled through it, feeling very embarrassed. Now you're nervous whenever you have to make or defend an argument in English, and the same is true in history. You're fine in physics, though, where the focus is on solving problems rather than making arguments. Explain your behavior in history and physics. (p. 260)

_____

_____

_____

(6-6) Look again at 6-5. What might your teacher do to help you get over your nervousness in English. (p. 261)

_____

_____

_____

## OPERANT CONDITIONING

Operant conditioning explains changes in behavior as the relationship between voluntary behaviors and consequences that follow the behaviors.

(6-7) Identify three differences between classical and operant conditioning. (p. 263)

_____

_____

_____

(6-8) Identify at least five examples of positive reinforcers commonly found in classrooms. (pp. 263-264)

_____

_____

_____

(6-9) You nag your spouse or roommate to do a better job of picking up after himself or herself. Surprisingly, you find that it works.  Explain why your nagging was effective. (pp. 264-265)

_____

_____

_____

(6-10) Your students want to watch a short video in class, after which they promise faithfully that they will do their homework. How should you respond? Explain. (pp. 265)

_____

_____

_____

(6-11) Give three original examples of presentation punishment. (pp. 266)

_____

_____

(6-12) Identify two ways in which negative reinforcement and removal punishment are different. (p. 267)

_____

_____


(6-13) Mr. Wilson has put John, a disruptive third grader, in time-out. Mr. Wilson says, "John, when you are ready to behave you can come and join the rest of the class. Until then you stay where you are. Is Mr. Wilson technique positive reinforcement, negative reinforcement, presentation punishment, or removal punishment? Explain. (p. 269)

_____

_____

_____


(6-14) Describe an original classroom example of generalization and discrimination. (pp. 270-271)

_____

_____

_____


(6-15) Compare the characteristics of effective feedback and effective praise. How are they similar and different? (pp. 271-273)

_____

_____

_____


(6-16) You're observing a teacher interacting with her students. In response to one student's answer, she says, "Very good, Sue," but after another's she replies, "Good answer, Kathy. You correctly noted that all regular polygons have sides that are equal." What can we infer about the two students' answers based on the teacher's feedback? (p. 273)

_____

_____

(6-17) Describe an original classroom example of shaping. (pp. 273-274)

_____

_____

_____

(6-18) Explain why giving students, such as yourselves, frequent announced tests is more effective than giving them only a midterm and a final. Frequent announced tests illustrate what kind of reinforcement schedule? (p. 274-276)

_____

_____

_____

(6-19) Nicole, first clarinet in the band, beams when Mr. Stoun, the band instructor comments on how nice she looks, but she reacts impassively when Mr. Rowe the football coach does the same thing. Explain the difference. (p. 276)

_____

_____

(6-20) Why must teachers carefully monitor their students' efforts in question and answer sessions? (pp. 278)

_____

_____

(6-21) Teachers are encouraged to prompt students who are unable to answer rather than turn to other students for the answer. Explain why prompting is effective teaching behavior. (pp. 278-279)

_____

_____

## OBSERVATIONAL LEARNING

Modeling is the imitation of behaviors observed in others and vicarious conditioning occurs when we adjust our own behavior based on our observations of others' behaviors and the consequences of those behaviors.

(6-22) Give an original example of direct, symbolic, synthesized, and abstract modeling. (p. 283)

_____

_____

_____

_____

(6-23) Give an original example of the following modeling outcomes: learning new behaviors, facilitating existing behaviors, focusing attention, changing inhibitions, and arousing emotions. (pp. 284-285).

_____

_____

_____

_____

(6-24) Look again at the case study on page 254 of your text. Explain why Tim would be more apt to imitate Susan's than Karen's behavior. Suppose Susan began to do poorly on the tests in algebra II. What might Tim do then? (pp. 285-286)

_____

_____

_____

_____

(6-25) Suppose you're teaching students to identify adjective and adverbial phrases in paragraphs and you want to capitalize on observational learning in the process. Describe and illustrate each of the observational learning steps that you would follow in the process. (pp. 286-289)

_____

_____

_____

_____

(6-26) You have a new student with an ethnic background different than your own. Describe how you might use classical conditioning with the student to help him or her feel comfortable in your class. In doing so identify the unconditioned and conditioned stimuli and the unconditioned and conditioned responses. (pp. 292-293)

_____

_____

_____

_____

# CHAPTER SIX
## BEHAVIORAL VIEWS OF LEARNING

<u>APPLICATION EXERCISES</u>

EXERCISE 6.1

Exercise 6.1 measures your understanding of topics covered on pages 255-262 of your text.

Look at exercises 1 through 3. If the behavior described in the underlined portion of the example is primarily the result of learning, put an <u>L</u> in the space in front of the example. Otherwise leave the space blank.

_____ 1. Mrs. Smith is doing a demonstration with air pressure and blows up a balloon. The balloon bursts, and Cathy, sitting in the front row, <u>jerks her head back.</u>

_____ 2. Ronnie, age 8, is going in for some booster shots. He <u>cries</u> when he sees the nurse with the needle.

_____ 3. Donnell, a senior, wants to be a good football player. He was a bit slow last year, running a 5.4-sec 40-yd dash. He lifted weights all summer, and to his pleasure, he <u>now runs a 4.9-sec 40-yd dash.</u>

4. Read the following case study.

> Duranna is a conscientious and good student, although she is a bit unsure of herself. She's typically very attentive in class, and her classmates regard her as someone who will usually be able to answer questions.
> One day, Mr. Harkness, her American history teacher, was conducting a question-and-answer session, and Duranna jerked when she heard her name called, suddenly realizing that she hadn't heard the question. A couple of the boys giggled as Mr. Harkness stared at her. Her stomach clenched, and she felt her face turn red. She started to stammer, then fell silent.
> Now Duranna is uneasy whenever Mr. Harkness starts calling on students in class, and she doesn't like geometry as well as she did either, because she never knows when Mrs. Drake might call on her. She's relieved when she's in the safe confines of Spanish class, where Mrs. Lopez always calls on students in order up and down each row.

Consider this scenario as an example of classical conditioning, and identify each of the following from it.

a. Unconditioned stimulus

_____

_____

b. Unconditioned response

_____

_____

c. Conditioned stimulus

_____

_____

d. Conditioned response

_____

_____

e. Generalization

_____

_____

f. Discrimination

_____

_____

5. Think about the concept of <u>extinction</u>. Describe how Mr. Harkness could help Duranna eliminate her conditioned response, that is, help it become extinct.

_____

_____

_____

_____

EXERCISE 6.2

Exercise 6.2 measures your understanding of topics covered on pages 262-270 of your text.

Read the following scenario and answer the questions that follow it.

Miguel is an inquiring student who asks good, probing questions in class, and the other students seem to appreciate him because his questions often help clear up some of their uncertainties. However, Miguel's questioning periodically makes Mr. Orr uneasy because he doesn't always have the answers.

One day when Miguel started to ask his fourth question in a row, Mr. Orr responded derisively: "Well, look at the brain. He's at it again."

Miguel stopped in mid-sentence.

During class a couple days later, Miguel asked one question and raised his hand to ask another. Mr. Orr looked at him and sneered, "Let's hear from the brain again."

The following day, Miguel quietly took notes the entire period.

1. Explain Miguel's behavior (his question asking)? Use information from the case study to defend your answer.

_____

_____

_____

_____

_____

2. Explain Mr. Orr's behavior (his sarcasm)? How do we know? Use information from the case study to defend your answer.

_____

_____

_____

_____

_____

3. In the text we cited the statement, "All right, as soon as you've finished identifying the longitude and latitude of the five cities I've given you, you can begin your map projects," as an example of a teacher using the Premack Principle. For the Premack Principle to be in effect, what must be true about the students attitudes toward longitude and latitude problems compared to map work?

_____

_____

_____

_____

## EXERCISE 6.3

Exercise 6.3 measures your understanding of topics covered on pages 270-279 of your text.

Read each of the following short case studies. For each, select from the following concepts--generalization, discrimination, the specific reinforcement schedules, potency, satiation, extinction, and shaping--the one that is most clearly illustrated in the example. In each case, explain the illustration.

1. Mrs. Thornton arrives at the door of her classroom at 7:35 a.m. She takes out her key, puts it in the lock, and attempts to open the door. The door won't budge. "Hmm," she says to herself. "That's never happened before." She jiggles the key a couple more times, and then heads for the workroom to try and find a janitor.

_____

_____

_____

2. Mrs. Green's fifth-grade class is studying insects. They've examined grasshoppers, beetles, a roach, and a water strider. "Hey!" Mary exclaimed while looking at a spider. "This isn't an insect."

_____

_____

_____

3. Ken, a senior, wants to be as well prepared as possible for college. He's taking analytic geometry, even though math is not his strong suit, and he plans to major in a foreign language in college. He studied very hard for his first analytic geometry test and got a low C. He tried hard on the second test too, but it came back a D. He's having a difficult time trying now and is spending less time on the homework. He studied only haphazardly for his last test.

_____

_____

_____

"I always give partial credit at the beginning of the year," Jane Howe, a geometry teacher, commented. "The kids have so much trouble with proofs. As time goes on, I make them do more to earn points on the problems, and by the end of the year, they have to get the whole thing right for any credit."

_____

_____

_____

5. "I'm quitting sending notes home to parents," Mrs. Starke, a fourth-grade teacher, commented to a colleague in the teachers' lounge one day. "We had a workshop in which we were encouraged to write positive notes to send home when the kids are good. I tried it, and the children responded for a while. Now they hardly react, and the notes don't seem to affect their behavior. I even saw one child throw the note away rather than take it home."

_____

_____

_____

6. Steve Weiss, a chemistry teacher, gives his students one problem each day when they come to class that counts five points on their overall quiz grade for the 9 weeks. "Generally, they're doing well," he noted. "I always give back their papers the next day, and they're about to the point where they like it. They ask me stuff like, 'Is this going to be another easy one today?'"

_____

_____

_____

EXERCISE 6.4

Exercise 6.4 measures your understanding of topics covered on pages 282-294 of your text.

1. Think about the children's story about the three little pigs. What form of modeling described in Table 6.4 is demonstrated in the story? When the two lazy little pigs get eaten by the wolf, what effect does this have on the reader? Explain. When the conscientious little pig outwits the wolf, what effect does this have on the reader? Explain.

_____

_____

_____

2. Think about the book A Tale of Two Cities. We described it in chapter 2 as a piece of literature that has a moral dilemma embedded in it. Explain the dilemma in its effect on readers using the concepts of vicarious reinforcement and vicarious punishment when the character Sidney Carton chooses to die in his friend's place. What form of modeling is demonstrated by Sidney Carton?

_____

_____

_____

3. Read the following case study and answer the questions that follow.

   Mrs. Holmes was working with her seventh-grade geography students on specifying geographical locations. They knew the concepts of longitude and latitude and could read the numbers on a map.
   She stood next to a large world map.
   1. "Look at the map, everyone," she began. "Today we're learning an important skill that we'll use throughout the course. To start, let's find ourselves. Where do we look first? Jody?"
   2. "We're in the United States," Jody responded. "It's right there," she continued, pointing.
   3. "Good," Mrs. Holmes smiled. "Now let's be more precise."  She had the students locate their state and city and went on.
   4. "Next we're going to locate another city. Name a famous city."      Several examples were suggested, and she decided on Mexico City.
   5. "Now watch," she commanded. "I'm looking at these numbers up here. They're what? Karen?"
   6. ". . . Longitude."
   7. "Excellent, Karen. Now look, everyone. I'm going to find one that runs as close to Mexico City as possible. Here we go," and she traced a line from the top of the map through Mexico City with her finger. "It's very close to 100°," she noted, pointing to the number at the top. "We see we're west of England, where we said the zero line of longitude is, so Mexico City is 100° west longitude."
   8. She repeated the process to find Mexico City's latitude.

9. "Give me another city," she continued. Settling on Chicago, she said, "Okay. Put your own maps on your desk." After waiting a few seconds, she asked, "What is its longitude? Joanie?"
10. ". . . It looks like it's about 88°."
11. She smiled at Joan. "Okay. West or east? Jack?"
12. ". . . West."

Mrs. Holmes continued the process, helping the students locate Chicago's latitude and then the location of Paris. Finally, she had them work independently to locate three more cities, saying that they would get five points on their homework grade for correctly identifying all three.

Analyze Mrs. Holmes's lesson as an example of applying observational learning in the classroom by identifying each of the four processes of observational learning in the lesson. Using the numbers at the beginning of each paragraph of the case study, make specific reference to the case study in your analysis.

a. Attention

_____

_____

b. Retention

_____

_____

c. Reproduction

_____

_____

d. Motivation

_____

_____

4. Read the following case study and answer the questions that follow.

Joe, a junior high teacher, has a faculty meeting every Wednesday at 2:00 p.m. One week, Karen, the assistant principal, arrived for the meeting at 1:55 p.m. with overheads and handouts, ready to go. Joe got up from his classroom desk at 1:55 prepared for the meeting. As he stepped out into the hall, he glanced through the lounge doorway and saw four other faculty members sitting working. "I'll wait for them to walk by," he said to himself, and he sat back down and scored some more tests. The others walked by about 2:10, so he went to the meeting then. Everyone was there and settled by 2:15, and the meeting began.

The next week, the meeting again got started at about 2:15, and the following week at about 2:20. The fourth week, Joe was in his office at 2:15 on Wednesday when his friend Sue walked by. "Aren't you coming to the meeting?" she asked.

"I'll be there in a minute," Joe responded with a smile, as he always did in response to a question. He came to the meeting at 2:25.

a. Identify an example of modeling in the scenario.

_____

_____

b. Identify an example of contiguity in the scenario.

_____

_____

c. We see that Joe started going to the meetings later and later.
Which concept from operant conditioning, <u>positive reinforcement</u>, <u>negative reinforcement</u>, <u>presentation punishment</u> or <u>removal punishment</u> best explains why he is going later? How do you know it is that concept?

_____

_____

_____

# CHAPTER SIX
# BEHAVIORAL VIEWS OF LEARNING

SELF-HELP QUIZ _____

TRUE/FALSE QUESTIONS. Write T in the blank if the statement is true, and write F if the statement is false.

_F_ 1. For operantly conditioned behaviors the influence of the environment (stimulus) precedes the behavior, but for classically conditioned behaviors it follows the behavior.

_F_ 2. Operantly conditioned behaviors must be reinforced to prevent extinction, but classically conditioned behaviors do not become extinct.

_F_ 3. Generalization occurs with operantly conditioned behaviors but not with classically conditioned behaviors.

_T_ 4. A flushed face in an embarrassing situation is better explained by classical than by operant conditioning.

_F_ 5. While positive reinforcement is an increase in behavior, negative reinforcement is a decrease in behavior.

_T_ 6. In a classical conditioning situation, the conditioned stimulus initially has no effect on behavior one way or the other.

_F_ 7. When classically conditioned learning takes place, the unconditioned and the conditioned stimuli will be similar to each other.

_T_ 8. In a classical conditioning situation, the unconditioned and the conditioned responses will be similar to each other.

_F_ 9. Learners can be vicariously reinforced, but they can't be vicariously punished.

_T_ 10. Learner behaviors that are intermittently reinforced are likely to be more enduring than are continuously reinforced behaviors, once the reinforcers are removed.

MULTIPLE-CHOICE ITEMS. Circle the best response in each case.

11. Mrs. Lincoln wants her second graders to know their addition and subtraction facts, so she does five minutes of drill and practice at the beginning of every school day. The type of learning that results is best described as:
   a. contiguity.
   b. classical conditioning.
   c. generalization.
   d. discrimination.
   e. vicarious conditioning.

12. You're anticipating taking a test from an instructor with a reputation for being "tough." As you wait for the test, you feel jittery and your mouth is dry. Your jitters and dry mouth are best described as:
   a. unconditioned stimuli.
   b. conditioned stimuli.
   c. unconditioned responses.
   d. conditioned responses.

13. Mr. Powell's students are getting a bit rowdy as the end of the day nears. He comments, "If the trash around your desks isn't picked up, and if you're not quiet in one minute, we'll be spending 10 minutes after school." The students immediately pick up the papers around their desk and are sitting quietly as the bell rings. Mr. Powell's technique would be best described as:
   a. negative reinforcement
   b. presentation punishment
   c. removal punishment
   d. discrimination
   e. satiation

14. Mr. Allen tries to be judicious in praising his students. He wants to praise them enough but not too much. To implement this he praises his students when he feels like they give an insightful response or a response reflecting considerable effort. His schedule would be best described as:
   a. continuous.
   b. fixed ratio.
   c. variable ratio.
   d. fixed interval.
   e. variable interval.

15. Mr. Allen's desire to give "enough praise" but not "too much" indicates that he's aware of two concepts. The two concepts are best described as:
   a. potency and satiation
   b. potency and extinction
   c. generalization and discrimination
   d. extinction and satiation
   e. generalization and extinction

16. In a lesson on place value, Kim sees the numbers 42 and 24 and says, "In the first number the four is in the tens column, and in the second it's in the ones column." Kim's comment best illustrates which of the following?
   a. Classical conditioning
   b. Discrimination
   c. Generalization
   d. Vicarious conditioning

17. In item 16, Kim's learning would be best classified in which of the following categories?
   a. Contiguity
   b. Classical conditioning
   c. Operant conditioning
   d. Observational learning

18. Joanne is being disruptive in Mrs. Henderson's class. Exasperated, Mrs. Henderson tells Joanne to pull her desk out into the hall and sit there until she is told otherwise. Mrs. Henderson's technique is best describe as an attempt to administer:
   a. negative reinforcement
   b. presentation punishment
   c. removal punishment
   d. vicarious punishment

19. Two of your students are whispering instead of doing their assigned seatwork. You go to them and tell them to stop whispering. They comply. This incident best illustrates:
   a.   negative reinforcement
   b.   presentation punishment
   c.   removal punishment
   d.   satiation

20. Mr. Parker comments to his second graders as they are beginning a seat work assignment, "I'm very pleased to see that Debbie has already working and has finished the first two problems." Mr. Parker's comment is best described as an attempt to which of the following with his class?
   a.   Positive reinforcement
   b.   Negative reinforcement
   c.   Vicarious reinforcement
   d.   The Premack Principle

# CHAPTER SEVEN
# COGNITIVE VIEWS OF LEARNING

## CHAPTER OUTLINE

I. Cognitive Learning Theory
II. An Information Processing model
    A. Models: Aids to understanding
    B. The environment
    C. The sensory registers
    D. Short-term/Working memory
        1. Chunking
        2. Working memory as a screening device
        3. Consciousness
        4. The limitations of working memory
            a. Automaticity
            b. Working memory and teacher behavior
    E. Long-term memory
    F. The structure of long term memory
        1. Episodic and semantic memory
        2. Declarative and procedural knowledge
        3. Declarative knowledge: Propositional networks
        4. Schemata: Combining declarative and procedural knowledge
            a. The role of background knowledge
            b. Expert and novice thinking
        5. Networks and schemas: Implications for teachers
III. Cognitive processes
    A. Attention: Information processing from a student perspective
        1. Attracting student attention
        2. Lesson beginnings
    B. Perception: Finding meaning in stimuli
        1. Experience and perception
        2. Expectations and perception
    C. Rehearsal: Retaining information through practice
        1. Short-term retention through rehearsal
        2. Transfer to long-term memory through rehearsal
        3. The nature of rehearsal
    D. Encoding: Making connections in long term memory
        1. Accuracy of encoding
        2. Activity
        3. Organization
            a. Teacher organization versus learner organization
            b. Charts and matrices as organizers
            c. Hierarchies as organizers
            d. Other types of organization
            e. The development of organizational strategies
        3. Elaboration

        a.  The power of elaboration
        b.  Analogies
        c.  Elaboration in learning activities
        d.  Elaboration: research results
     4.  Combining activity, organization, and elaboration
     5.  Mnemonic devices
        a.  Method of loci
        b.  The pegword method
        c.  The key word method
        d.  Embedded letter strategies
  E.  Forgetting
     1.  Interference
     2.  Forgetting as retrieval failure
     3.  Retrieval and encoding
        a.  The role of context
        b.  Problems as contexts
IV.  The Impact of Diversity on Information Processing
  A.  Diversity and perception
  B.  Diversity and encoding
     1.  Instructional adaptations for background diversity
  C.  Diversity and forgetting
V.  Metacognition: Knowledge About Cognitive Processes
  A.  Meta-Attention
     1.  The development of meta-attention
  B.  Metacommunication
     1.  The development of metacommunication
     2.  Communication
  C.  Metamemory
     1.  The development of metamemory
  D.  Metacognition and self-regulation
IV.  The Development of Memory Strategies
  A.  Metamemory

# CHAPTER OBJECTIVES _____

- Identify the characteristics of the sensory registers, working memory, and long-term memory.
- Explain how attention affects further processing.
- Explain how orienting stimuli influence attention.
- Describe the role of perception in moving information from one information store to another.
- Describe the role of rehearsal in retaining information in working memory.
- Explain how to increase the effectiveness of rehearsal.
- Explain how activity, organization, elaboration, and mnemonic devices improve encoding.
- Explain how interference can be reduced.
- Explain how context is a factor in retrieval.
- Identify examples of meta-attention, metacommunication, and metamemory.
- Explain how teachers can help students develop metacognitive abilities.

# CHAPTER OVERVIEW _____

In chapter 6 we saw that behaviorists focus exclusively on observable behaviors as they are influenced by experience. In this chapter we turn to information processing, a view that describes learning using information stores and internal mental processes.

We cannot directly observe these information stores and internal processes so we create a model to help us visualize our information processing system, much in the same way as we create models to help us visualize the structure of atoms and molecules. As you read the following paragraphs, open your text to page 307, and relate the information you read to the respective parts of the model.

The Information Processing Model is composed of three parts. The first is composed of three places that store information--the sensory registers, working memory, and long-term memory. The second is composed of cognitive processes--attention, perception, rehearsal, encoding, and retrieval--that govern the transfer of information from one store to another, and the final component is metacognition, which is knowledge--stored in long-term memory--about cognitive processes.

The sensory registers--probably a separate one for each sense--have virtually unlimited capacity, and they essentially photograph information. Information enters the sensory registers without our being conscious of it, but it is quickly lost from them if we don't begin to process it by attending to the stimuli.
Processing begins with attention. Attractive or unique objects, events that behave in unpredictable ways, the sound of our own name, and commands are called orienting stimuli because they attract our attention, or in other words, we orient to them. The fact that we see fewer lines to right than to the left of attention in the model on page 307 is intended to remind us that stimuli unattended to are lost.

We attach meaning to, or interpret, the stimuli we attend to through the process of perception. Perception is critical. For example, if learners see a whale and perceive it as a fish, whales enter working memory as fish for them, and the rest of their processing will be invalid as a result. Our perceptions are influenced by our past experience and expectations. The wavy lines to the right of perception in the model are intended to remind us that the meaning we attach to stimuli isn't always valid.

Working memory is the conscious part of our information processing system. It is here that new information from the sensory registers together with already-learned information retrieved from long-term memory are combined for additional learning. Working memory is capable of holding only a few items of information for a matter of seconds, but the capacity can be effectively increased by combining separate items into "chunks," or making knowledge and skills automatic through overlearning, and retention can be maintained through rehearsal. The rehearsal "loop" above working memory in the model is intended to remind you that information can be retained in working memory through rehearsal. To avoid overloading learners' working memories, which results in information being lost, teachers should proceed in short steps and provide students with ample opportunities to practice working with new knowledge and skills. The fact that working memory is smaller than the other two stores in the model on page 307 is intended remind you of working memory's limited capacity.

Rehearsal, such as repeating addition facts over and over, can also be used to move information to long-term memory by "brute force," but encoding information by forming associations between new and prior learning is much more effective. The more associations formed, the more meaningful the information is. Meaningfulness can be increased, and encoding made more efficient, if information is carefully organized, if new learning is consciously attached to old through elaboration in the form of reviews and comparisons, and if learners are put in active roles during learning activities. Fact learning can be enhanced through mnemonics, such as "Thirty days has September, April, June, and November, . . ." The more meaningful the information is when encoded, the easier it is to retrieve, and the less likely it is to be forgotten.

Research indicates that the context information is in is encoded with the information itself. For example, if parts of speech are presented in the context of paragraphs, they are more likely to be meaningful than if they are learned in sentences out of context.

Long-term memory is our permanent information store. Declarative knowledge--knowledge of facts, definitions, generalizations, and rules--and procedural knowledge--knowledge of how to perform activities--exists in long-term memory. Declarative knowledge exists in propositional networks, which are sets of interconnected items of information, and procedural knowledge exist in the form of schemata, which combine items of information with procedures for taking action. Experts in an area have more "links" among the items of information in their memories and they have more procedural knowledge of the field.

The process of receiving, processing, storing and retrieving information is more complex than the previous paragraphs imply. Our awareness of our cognitive processes and our ability to control them, called metacognition, further impact how effectively we process information. Meta-attention, metacommunication, and metamemory are all forms of metacognition.

Metacognition is developmental; for example, older learners are better than younger ones at purposefully directing their attention toward important information (a form of meta-attention), recognizing when they aren't communicating and then making adjustments (a form of metacommunication), and using strategies to encode information into long-term memory (a form of metamemory). When learners develop their metacognitive abilities they can become self-regulated, meaning they are equipped to learn effectively on their own.

# CHAPTER SEVEN
# COGNITIVE VIEWS OF LEARNING

## CHAPTER-AT-A-GLANCE

| MAIN TOPICS | KEY POINTS | KEY TERMS |
|---|---|---|
| Cognitive Learning Theory | • Learning is a change in individuals' mental structures giving them the capacity to change their behavior.<br>• Cognitive theory studies internal mental processes, such as attention, perception, imagery, and insight. | • Cognitive learning theory, 305<br>• Learning, 305<br>• Information processing, 306 |
| An Information Processing Model | • Models help us visualize what we cannot directly observe.<br>• The Information Processing Model is composed of information stores and cognitive processes.<br>• The sensory registers essentially photograph information. They hold exact copies of stimuli from the environment for a very brief period.<br>• Working memory is our conscious processing component. It can hold about seven "bits" of information for about 20 seconds.<br>• The capacity of working memory is effectively increased if information are "chunked" into larger meaningful units.<br>• If operations are made automatic--overlearned to the point where they require little mental effort--working memory space is made available for higher order operations.<br>• Episodic memory holds personal experiences in the form of images, and semantic memory, that holds the information we know and skills we have.<br>• Long-term memory contains declarative knowledge--knowledge of facts, rules, definitions and generalizations--and procedural knowledge--knowledge of how to perform activities.<br>• Declarative knowledge exists in propositional networks, and procedural knowledge exists in the form of schemata.<br>• Experts' schemata are more inter-related than are those of novices in a field, and experts possess more procedural knowledge of the field. | • Model, 306<br>• Information stores, 307<br>• Cognitive processes, 307<br>• Sensory registers, 308<br>• Chunking, 310<br>• Automaticity, 312<br>• Long-term memory, 312<br>• Episodic memory, 313<br>• Semantic memory, 314<br>• Declarative knowledge, 314<br>• Procedural knowledge, 314<br>• Propositional network, 314<br>• Schemata, 316 |

| | | |
|---|---|---|
| Cognitive Processes | • If we quickly attend to information in our sensory registers, it can be processed further; if not, it is lost.<br>• We attach meaning to the information we attend to through the processes of perception.<br>• Rehearsal can be used to retain information in working memory. With extended rehearsal, some information will be transferred to long-term memory.<br>• Information in working memory is encoded by connecting it to information that already exists in long-term memory.<br>• The more connections made between new information and existing information, the more meaningful the new information is.<br>• Elaboration, organization, activity, and mnemonics aid encoding by making new information meaningful.<br>• The ability to retrieve existing information is critical to further processing.<br>• Information encoded in context enhances retrieval. | • Attention, 322<br>• Orienting stimuli, 322<br>• Perception, 323<br>• Rehearsal, 326<br>• Encoding, 327<br>• Meaningfulness, 327<br>• Organization, 331<br>• Elaboration, 334<br>• Analogy, 335<br>• Mnemonic device, 336<br>• Retroactive interference, 339<br>• Proactive interference, 339<br>• Retroactive facilitation, 339<br>• Proactive facilitation, 339<br>• Retrieval, 340<br>• Context, 341 |
| The Impact Of Diversity On Information Processing | • Teachers can accommodate diversity in their students' by assessing their backgrounds, providing experiences when they are lacking, and using students' experiences to augment the backgrounds of their classmates. | |
| Metacognition: Knowledge About Cognitive Processes | • Knowledge and control of our attention, communication, and memory are forms of metacognition called meta-attention, metacommunications, and metamemory, respectively.<br>• Metacognition is developmental; young children are less aware of their powers of attention, communication and memory, and they are less able to control them than are older students.<br>• As students' metacognition develops they become self-regulated; equipped to learn effectively on their own. | • Meta-attention, 347<br>• Metacommunication, 349<br>• Metamemory, 350<br>• Self-regulation, 351 |

# CHAPTER SEVEN
# COGNITIVE VIEWS OF LEARNING

## GUIDED REVIEW

## COGNITIVE LEARNING THEORY

Cognitive learning theories explain learning using stimuli, responses, and the internal mechanisms that exist between the two.

(7-1) Identify at least three concepts ignored by behaviorists that are important to cognitive learning theorists. (p. 305)

_____

_____

_____

## AN INFORMATION PROCESSING MODEL

Models help us visualize what we cannot directly observe.

(7-2) How is a model of the atom similar to the information processing model, and how are they different from the globe as a model? (pp. 305-306)

_____

_____

_____

The sensory registers hold exact copies of information for a very short period of time.

(7-3) Why are the sensory registers critical in the information processing system? (pp. 308-309)

_____

_____

_____

(7-4) Explaining something or giving directions to students while they are taking notes is unwise teaching practice.  Explain why. (p. 309)

_____

_____

Working memory is the conscious part of our information processing system.

(7-5) In calling directory assistance for a phone number, the recorded message responds, for example, "six four one, five three hundred" rather than "six four one, five three zero zero." Explain why phone companies would prepare messages in this way? (p. 310)

_____

_____

_____

(7-6) Teachers often use drill and practice activities, such as flash cards, to help students learn their basic addition, subtraction, and multiplication facts. Why is this necessary? (p. 312)

_____

_____

(7-7) Identify three things we might do as teachers to help accommodate the limitations of learners' working memories. (p. 312)

_____

_____

_____

Long-term memory is our permanent information repository.

(7-8) In chapter 6 you learned information about positive and negative reinforcement and presentation and removal punishment. This information is what kind of knowledge? Create a propositional network that illustrates the relationships among the types of reinforcement and the types of punishment. Suppose you identify an example of negative reinforcement in your everyday experience. What kind of knowledge do you use to identify the example? Explain. (pp. 314-315)

_____

_____

_____

_____

(7-9) What is the primary difference between propositional networks and schemata? (p. 316)

_____

_____

(7-10) Identify two differences between the thinking of experts in a field and the thinking of novices in that field. (pp. 317-318)

_____

_____

_____

(7-11) You have taught your students about amphibians, and are now teaching them about reptiles. To be consistent with information processing theory, identify at least two specific things you should be doing in the process? (p. 319)

_____

_____        _____

_____

Cognitive processes determine how much and how efficiently information is moved from one information store to another.

Processing begins with attention.

(7-12) Provide an original example of each of the types of orienting stimuli in Table 7.2 on page 324 of your text. (p. 324)

_____

_____

_____

_____

Perception is the meaning we attach to stimuli.

(7-13) Two students look at the model at the top of page 307 of your text. One says, "Oh, those look like 'p' electron orbitals," and the other says, "Those thinks look like balloons tied in the middle." How can we explain the difference in the two students' responses? (p. 324)

_____

_____

(7-14) You have taught your students about adjective clauses in sentences, and you want to check your students' perceptions of what they have learned about them. What might you do to check their perceptions? (p. 324)

_____

_____

Rehearsal is the process of repeating information over and over without altering its form.

(7-15) Identify two functions of rehearsal. Give an example of each. (pp. 326)

_____

_____

(7-16) You have found that your students don't know their multiplication facts, so you are planning to conduct some drill and practice activities with them using flashcards. How should you conduct the drill in order for it to be the most effective? (p. 327)

_____

_____

_____

When mental representations of information are created by connecting new information to information that already exists in long-term memory, we say the information has been encoded.

(7-17) Someone comments about an experience, "That simply wasn't meaningful to me." Based on information processing theory, what does that comment mean? (p. 327-328)

_____

_____

(7-18) Does information have to be accurately encoded in order for it to be meaningful? Explain why or why not. (p. 328)

_____

_____

_____

(7-19) Identify four tools that help enhance encoding by making information more meaningful. Give an example of each with a classroom topic. Your textbook authors have attempted to capitalize on each of these in writing the book. Identify an example of each from the text. (pp. 328-338)

_____

_____

_____

_____

_____

_____

(7-20) In chapter 6 you learned that punishment was a decrease in behavior as a result of something undesirable being given or something desirable being taken away. You were comfortable with the concepts until you learned that extinction was the disappearance of a behavior due to nonreinforcement. Now you're slightly confused about punishment. What concept does this best illustrate? Explain. (p. 339)

_____

_____

_____

(7-21) You're a math teacher, and you want to introduce the topic of equivalent fractions to your students. Suggest a way of introducing the topic that would allow you to capitalize on context. (pp. 341-344) (The teacher in the case study introducing chapter 12 does a nice job of this. You may want to refer to this case study. [pp. 584-587])

_____

_____

_____

(7-22) Your class is composed of students having several different ethnic backgrounds in it, and you have just done a science demonstration with them where you soak a piece of cloth in a water-alcohol mixture and then light the cloth. (The alcohol burns off but the cloth doesn't ignite, because the water keeps it below its kindling temperature.) What would be a good question to ask to begin your lesson? Explain. (p. 346)

_____

_____

_____

(7-23) Identify an original example of meta-attention, metacommunication, and metamemory. (pp. 347-351)

_____

_____

_____

_____


(7-24) A first grader takes a phone call while his mother is in the shower. His mother asks him to write down the number, so she can return the call. He hunts for a pencil and a piece of paper to write the number on. The same thing happens to a fifth grader. How are the behaviors of the first grader and the fifth grader likely to differ while they search for the paper and pencil? Why are the behaviors likely to differ? (p. 351)

_____

_____

_____

_____

# CHAPTER SEVEN
# COGNITIVE VIEWS OF LEARNING

## APPLICATION EXERCISES

### EXERCISE 7.1

Exercise 7.1 measures your understanding of topics covered on pages 301-320 of your text.

1. A prealgebra teacher has written the following on the chalkboard:

4 + 5(7-3) - 9/3

She then asks, "What are we going to do first to simplify this expression? What is important to remember whenever we simplify something like this?" Criticize her questioning based on your understanding of the sensory registers.

_____

_____

_____

2. Describe a simple alternative to improve the teacher's questioning.

_____

_____

_____

3. You are introducing a unit on the Far East in your world history class. You present information outlining the impact of religion on life in Japan in the early 20th century, exploitation by the British and other Western nations, the indignation Japan felt after World War I, Japan's overpopulation and scarce natural resources in the 1920s and 1930s, and how all these factors led to Japan's decision that it had no choice but to attack the United States. The students seem interested, watching you attentively as you present the information.

However, the next day when you begin your review of the previous day's information, it's as if they hadn't listened after all. Using your understanding of working memory as a basis, explain why this might have happened.

_____

_____

_____

_____

4. Based on what we know about working memory, why is a textbook an important supplement to teacher lectures?

_____

_____

5. Two high school teachers were discussing their classes. The physics teacher commented,

> "I'm having a terrible time. The kids seem to understand the problems when I explain them, but they get lost in their algebra when they try to do them on their own, so they wind up confused."

Relate the physics teacher's description to our discussion of working memory, and explain why her students are having difficulty. Include the concept of automaticity in your explanation.

_____

_____

_____

6. When students perform each of the following, which type of knowledge--declarative or procedural--primarily being demonstrated? Explain.
a. Identify Abraham Lincoln as the president of the United States during the Civil War.

_____

_____

b. Ride a bicycle.

_____

_____

c. State that isosceles triangles have two equal sides.

_____

_____

d. Identify isosceles triangles in a group of plane figures.

_____

_____

7. Consider these definitions:
a. Common nouns are parts of speech that name persons, places, and things.
b. Proper nouns name specific persons, places, and things.

Create a propositional network that would incorporate the two definitions.

---

EXERCISE 7.2

Exercise 7.2 measures your understanding of topics covered on pages 320-326 of your text.

For items 1 through 3, look at the topics and describe lesson beginnings that could be used to attract the students' attention and pull them into the lesson. (A variety of lesson beginnings are possible. Suggest at least two different ways of beginning each.)

1. You are beginning a unit on longitude and latitude in your geography class.

_____

_____

_____

_____

2. You want your students to understand the rule for punctuating possessive nouns--a singular possessive uses an apostrophe s, and a plural possessive uses only an apostrophe if the plural noun ends in s and an apostrophe s if the plural noun does not end in s.

_____

_____

_____

_____

3. You are beginning a lesson on the skeletal system with your science students.

_____

_____

_____

4. You have taught your students about direct and indirect objects and you begin a review by writing the following sentence on the chalkboard:

Kathy handed Tim the papers.

What question could you now ask that would be an excellent way of diagnosing the students' perceptions. (Be specific. Either write down or say to yourself the exact question you would ask.)

_____

_____

5. Read the following case study and explain the difference in the two teachers' reactions based on the information you've studied in this section.

> Two young teachers were interviewed by a principal for jobs at the same school. (There were two openings, so they each hoped to get a job.) They were very excited about the prospect of working together, so they went to lunch and discussed their respective interviews.
> "How was it?" Marianne asked.
> "Awful," Katarina responded. "He grilled me and made me feel like I was the dumbest thing in the world. How about you?"
> "I thought mine went really well," Marianne said tentatively, with a puzzled look on her face. "He asked me a lot of questions, but it seemed to me that he was just trying to see if I knew what I wanted from teaching."
> "I should never have applied for this job," Katarina continued disconsolately. "Donna (a friend of hers who teaches at the school) warned me about this guy. After today, I don't think I could ever work for him."
> "Gosh, I'm really looking forward to it," Marianne responded. "I went to a workshop last week on what to do in an interview. They said we'd be asked a lot of questions, and it's the interviewer's way of finding out how we think, so I guess I was sort of ready for it."

_____

_____

_____

_____

EXERCISE 7.3

Exercise 7.3 measures your understanding of topics covered on pages 326-338 of your text.

In items 1 through 4, the examples involve a learner using (a) organization, (b) elaboration, (d) rehearsal, or (e) a mnemonic, to transfer the information into long-term memory. Classify each and explain your answers.

1. Nikki was confused about the solution to a force and acceleration problem involving friction. She went back to a problem she had worked in which no friction was involved, and then went through a sample problem in the book involving friction. She then used the information from the first two to help her understand the new problem.

_____

_____

2. Tanya knew there would be an essay question on the strengths and weaknesses of the Colonial and British armies during the Revolutionary War. To prepare for the test, she drew a matrix with England and the Colonies on one side and advantages and disadvantages on the top.

_____

_____

3. Meg knew there would be names and dates on the test on Wednesday, so she got some 3 x 5 index cards, wrote the important facts on the cards, and used them as flash cards to study on the bus ride to and from school.

_____

_____

4. To remember the correct order of the different phases of mitosis (prophase, metaphase, anaphase, telophase), Juan formed the word <u>Pmat</u> and used it as a retrieval guide.

_____

_____

5. Students--particularly young children--often believe that mammals are warm-blooded animals that live on land and have four legs, and they further believe that anything that lives in the water is a fish. Are these conceptions meaningful to them? Explain. Explain how they might come to these conclusions based on the information in this section.

_____

_____

_____

6. You're teaching your students about the North and South prior to the Civil War. Describe how you might organize the information in your unit to help make it meaningful for the students.

_____

_____

7. You have been doing a unit on the areas of plane figures with your math students. They understand how to find the areas of squares, rectangles, and triangles. How might you use this information to capitalize on the process of elaboration as you move to a discussion of the areas of parallelograms and trapezoids?

_____

_____

_____

EXERCISE 7.4

Exercise 7.4 measures your understanding of topics covered on pages 338-344 of your text.

1. For each of the following items, classify the example as illustrating proactive interference, retroactive interference, proactive facilitation, or retroactive facilitation.

a. In her home economics class, Joan first learned about natural fibers. The concepts she learned there helped make sense of the teacher's presentation on synthetic fibers.

_____

_____

b. Diane understood how to convert numbers to base 2, but when the class went on to base 3, she became confused. In several cases, she converted numbers to base 2 instead of base 3.

_____

_____

c. Jill had been reading Romeo and Juliet for a week and couldn't quite understand what the story was about. One day her teacher made a presentation on tragedies, and the play all came together for Jill.

_____

_____

d. Steve understood what antonyms were and could give an opposite term when the teacher asked for one in class. When the class turned to synonyms, he had trouble differentiating the two. When asked to give an antonym, he often gave a synonym instead.

_____

_____

128

2. Think again about the rule, "A singular possessive uses an apostrophe s, and a plural possessive uses only an apostrophe if the plural noun ends in s and an apostrophe s if the plural noun does not end in s." Describe a context in which the rule could be taught that would aid meaningfulness and retrieval.

_____

_____

_____

3. We would predict that Juan would be able to retrieve information about the solar system more readily than would Randy. Explain why we would make this prediction based on the information in this section.

_____

_____

_____

┌─────────────────────────────────────────────────────────────────────────────┐
│ ┌───────────────────────────────────────────────────────────────────────┐ │
│ └───────────────────────────────────────────────────────────────────────┘ │
└─────────────────────────────────────────────────────────────────────────────┘

## EXERCISE 7.5

Exercise 7.5 measures your understanding of topics covered on pages 344-352 of your text.

Classify each of the following examples as best illustrating meta-attention, metacommunication, or metamemory. Explain in each case.

1. Mrs. Jensen was giving directions for the social studies test on Friday. Marissa raised her hand and asked, "I'm sorry, but I'm not sure what you said about the second part of the test. Will it be multiple choice or essay?

_____

_____

_____

2. Steve was doing his homework while listening to the radio. He noticed that he was periodically listening to the radio instead of focusing on his work, so he got up and turned off the radio.

_____

_____

_____

3. Billy was reporting on the major exports of the southern colonies. As he looked up from his paper, he saw some confused looks on his classmates' faces. He paused and asked, "Are there any questions?"

_____

_____

_____

4. Claudia was studying her notes for her science test. "Why can't I remember the difference between spring tide and neap tide?" she mumbles to herself. "I'll read it once more." She then went back to her text and highlighted the description of each.

_____

_____

_____

5. A high school sophomore was up late baby-sitting on a school night and knew that she was going to have a rough time staying awake at school the next day. As she walked into her English class, she said to herself, "I'll sit in the most uncomfortable position I can, and that will keep me awake."

_____

_____

_____

# CHAPTER SEVEN
# COGNITIVE VIEWS OF LEARNING

## SELF-HELP QUIZ

TRUE/FALSE QUESTIONS. Mark T in the blank if the statement is true, and mark F if the statement is false.

F 1. While information in working memory is in the form of perceived reality, information in long-term memory is in the form of objective, or true, reality.

F 2. Since working memory is what we call consciousness, its capacity is larger than that of long-term memory, which is unconscious.

F 3. Information that is not accurately perceived is lost from working memory.

F 4. Information is normally quickly lost from the sensory registers, but it can be retained there with rehearsal.

F 5. Much of the information from the sensory registers enters working memory even though we're not consciously aware of it.

F 6. The concept of meaningfulness cannot be applied to fact learning.

T 7. Information that is "automatic" effectively occupies no working memory space.

F 8. To enhance learner encoding, lecture is probably more effective than teacher questioning because more content can be covered.

F 9. Metamemory refers to the process of accurately perceiving stimuli.

T 10. According to research results, the context information exists in when it is learned is encoded with the information itself.

MULTIPLE-CHOICE ITEMS. Circle the best response in each case.

11. A teacher is giving a lecture on the differences in the way the Spanish interacted with the natives in the Americas compared to the way the English and French interacted with them, and she included some graphic pictures depicting various forms of mistreatment from all parties. In an effort to cover all the factors in a class period, she lectures quite rapidly. Based on the case study, of the following, which is the most likely result?
    a. The information she is presenting won't enter the sensory registers.
    b. The students' attention won't be attracted.
    c. The information is likely to be misperceived.
    d. Some of the information will be lost from working memory.

12. As an eighth grade science teacher, you're beginning the study of inertia (Motionless objects remain at rest, and moving objects continue moving in a straight line unless a force acts on them.) At this point they have no experience with the concept. Based on the information process model, which of the following would be the best way to begin the lesson?
    a. Ask the students what inertia means to them.
    b. Tell the students what inertia is and why it is important.
    c. Tie a string around a pair of socks, swing it around your head, and let it go.
    d. Ask a student to give an example of inertia.

13. You are showing a film about bats to your third graders. Afterward one of the students comments, "I didn't know that birds have teeth." Of the following, the process most closely related to the comment is:
    a. attention.
    b. perception.
    c. rehearsal.

d.  encoding.

14. A teacher wants his students to know the most common prepositions, so he gives them a list and tells them that they have to know all the prepositions by the following week. The process the students will most likely use to learn the prepositions is:
    a.  perception.
    b.  rehearsal.
    c.  elaboration.
    d.  organization.

15. A third grade teacher in continuing her work with place value is introducing the concept of the 100's column. She begins the lesson by having them make several numbers, such as 24, with interlocking cubes. She then uses the cubes to demonstrate 124 for them and asks them to compare it to the other numbers they made. Of the following, the process she is most trying to capitalize on to enhance encoding is:
    a.  attention.
    b.  perception.
    c.  organization.
    d.  elaboration.

16. In conducting the lesson the way she did, she is also attempting to capitalize on another process used to enhance encoding.  Of the following, her efforts best illustrate attempts to capitalize on:
    a.  attention
    b.  perception
    c.  rehearsal
    d.  activity

17. You find that your algebra students are having problems solving equations, because they get mixed up on simplifying simple arithmetic expressions.  You decide to give them some additional practice.  Of the following, which is the most desirable schedule?
    a.  25 minutes every Monday to kick off the week.
    b.  10 minutes on Tuesday and 15 minutes on Thursday.
    c.  15 minutes on Monday and 10 minutes on Friday.
    d.  5 minutes every day.

18. Consider the concept of interference. For which of the following pairs of ideas is interference most likely?
    a.  Nouns and verbs
    b.  Nouns and adverbs
    c.  Verbs and direct objects
    d.  Direct objects and indirect objects

Use the following information for items 19 and 20.

A busy mother is working at her desk at home and asks Billy, her son, to run the nearby store to pick up several items.  She tells him what she wants and continues with her work. He leaves the house and heads for the store. A second mother does the same thing with her son, Ken. Ken says, "Wait a second, Mom, what were the last two things you wanted?" as he writes the items down. She tells him, Ken writes them down, and he heads out the door.

19. Based on the information in the case study, the best estimate of Billy's age is:
    a.  7
    b.  10
    c.  14
    d.  17

20. Based on the case study, of the following, the youngest we would expect Ken to be is:
    a. 8
    b. 10
    c. 14
    d. 17

# CHAPTER EIGHT
# COGNITIVE VIEWS OF LEARNING: APPLICATIONS

## CHAPTER OUTLINE _____

I. Different Instruction For Different Learning

II. Types Of Cognitive Learning
- A. Concepts
  - 1. Discriminations: Prerequisites to concept learning
  - 2. Characteristics
  - 3. Concept prototypes
  - 4. Concepts: Ease of learning
  - 5. Examples: The key to concept learning
  - 6. Concept analysis: A planning tool
  - 7. Rule - Eg: A concept teaching strategy
  - 8. Concept Mapping: Connecting concepts in long-term memory
- B. Relating concepts: Principles, generalizations, and academic rules
  - 1. Principles
  - 2. Generalizations
  - 3. Academic rules
  - 4. Examples and applications
- C. Declarative knowledge
  - 1. Concept learning and declarative knowledge: Implications for teaching
- D. Dealing with diversity in students' background knowledge
  - 1. Instructional strategies for dealing with diversity in background knowledge
    - a. Assessment
    - b. Adaptive instruction

III. Cognitive strategies
- A. Effective strategy users: Developing self-regulation
  - 1. Strategy use and goal setting
- B. Study skills
  - 1. Study skills: Research results
  - 2. Basic study strategies
    - a. Underlining
    - b. Note taking
    - c. Summarizing
    - d. Spacial representations
  - 3. Comprehensive study strategies
    - a. SQ4R
    - b. MURDER
    - c. Reciprocal teaching
- C. Thinking skills
  - 1. Basic processes
  - 2. Domain-specific knowledge
  - 3. Metacognitive knowledge
  - 4. Attitudes and dispositions

D. Problem solving
  1. Problem solving stages
    a. Understanding the problem
    b. Expert vs. novice thinking
    c. Devising a plan
    d. Implementing the plan
    e. Evaluating the results
  2. Open-ended problem solving
    a. Understanding the problem
    b. Devising a plan
    c. Implementing the plan
    d. Evaluating the results
IV. Teaching for transfer
  A. Specific and general transfer
  B. Meaningfulness: The key to transfer
  C. Transfer of concept learning
    1. Transfer of principles, generalizations and
       academic rules
  D. Transfer of problem-solving ability
  E. Transfer of study skills
    1. Transfer of study skills: The role of domain knowledge
  F. Transfer of thinking skills
    1. Global transfer
    2. The role of domain-specific knowledge
    3. General transfer: Dispositions and self-regulation
  G. Transfer of declarative knowledge
    1. Ausubel's theory of meaningful verbal learning
      a. Expository teaching
      b. Advance organizers
      c. Deductive sequencing
      d. Forming associations
  H. The importance of discovery: The work of Jerome Bruner
    1. Unstructured and guided discovery
    2. Research on discovery learning

## CHAPTER OBJECTIVES

- Describe different types of cognitive learning.
- Explain the application of concept learning to classroom activities.
- Explain how principles, generalizations, and academic rules are learned.
- Explain how study skills can be used to increase student learning.
- Explain how thinking skills can be used in classroom learning activities.
- Identify similarities and differences in convergent and open-ended problem solving.
- Describe effective procedures for promoting transfer of learning.
- Describe Ausubel's theory of meaningful verbal learning applied to classroom activities.
- Explain the similarities and differences between discovery learning and expository teaching.

| Cognitive Strategies | • Cognitive strategies are mental operations learners use that go beyond the processes directly required to carry out a task.<br>• Effective strategy users are self-regulated; they understand the strategy, they know when to use it, and they have adequate background knowledge to which it can be applied.<br>• Study skills are cognitive strategies learners use to increase their comprehension of written materials and teacher presentations.<br>• Thinking skills depend on the understanding of specific content, skills with basic processes, attitudes and dispositions, and metacognitive knowledge.<br>• To make problem solving more understandable it can be broken into four steps: understanding the problem, devising a plan, implementing the plan and evaluating the results.<br>• Convergent problem solving strategies lead to a single, correct answer. Divergent problem solving can lead to more than one acceptable solution.<br>• Experts in a field have more links between the individual items of information in a schema, and they see problems in a larger context than do novices in the same field. | • Cognitive strategies, 380<br>• Domain-specific knowledge, 382<br>• Study skills, 389<br>• Thinking Skills, 389<br>• Basic processes, 390<br>• Problem solving, 393<br>• heuristics, 397 |
|---|---|---|
| Teaching for Transfer | • Transfer occurs on a continuum ranging from settings closely related to the learning situation (specific) to those essentially unrelated (general).<br>• The more meaningful the information in long-term memory, the more likely learning is to transfer.<br>• Transfer depends on the *quality*, the *variety*, and the *context* of examples.<br>• Problem solving transfer improves with the variety of applications, comparing similarities and differences between types of problems.<br>• Transfer of study skills is promoted by practice in a variety of settings, metacognitive knowledge about the skill and adequate domain-specific knowledge.<br>• Transfer of thinking skills is domain specific; an expert thinker in one domain may not be an expert thinker in another.<br>• Attitudes and dispositions transfer in a general sense.<br>• Ausubel stresses the importance of meaningful learning through the use of an expository method, advanced organizers, deducting sequences, and forming associations.<br>• Bruner's discovery learning is a strategy that presents students with data and guides them into finding patterns. | • Transfer, 400<br>• Specific transfer, 402<br>• General transfer, 402<br>• Generative knowledge, 407<br>• Inert knowledge, 407<br>• Expository teaching, 408<br>• Advance organizer, 408<br>• Deductive sequence, 409<br>• Discovery learning, 410<br>• Unstructured discovery, 411<br>• Guided discovery, 411 |

# CHAPTER EIGHT
## COGNITIVE VIEWS OF LEARNING: APPLICATIONS

GUIDED REVIEW _____

## DIFFERENT INSTRUCTION FOR DIFFERENT LEARNING _____

Not all learning is the same and should not be taught in the same manner. A good teacher recognizes the different types of learning and uses different instructional methods appropriate for each type.

(8-1) Identify two important themes of the chapter. What implications do these themes have for teaching? (p. 365)

_____

_____

_____

_____

## TYPES OF COGNITIVE LEARNING _____

Declarative knowledge and procedural knowledge in the form of concepts and the relationships among them, study skills, thinking skills, and problem solving are different types of cognitive learning outcomes.

(8-2) Give an original example of each of the five specific cognitive outcomes listed in Figure 8.1. (p. 366)

_____

_____

_____

_____

Concept teaching involves helping students link essential characteristics to positive and negative examples. Concepts lacking well-defined characteristics are best represented with prototypes. Concepts with a small number of tangible characteristics are easier to learn than concepts with several, abstract characteristics.

(8-3) Consider the concept adjective. Identify its characteristics, and concepts superordinate, coordinate, and subordinate to it. Write a definition of it. Is a noun or an adverb a more important nonexample for it? Explain why. How easy is the concept to learn compared to the concept Republican? Explain why. (pp. 366-369).

_____

_____

_____

_____

_____

Concept maps visually represent relationships among concepts.

(8-4) Create a network for the concept information processing. (pp. 372-373)

Principles, generalizations, and academic rules describes relationships among concepts.

(8-5) What is the difference between a principle and a generalization? Give an example of each that illustrates the difference. (pp. 372-374)

_____

_____

_____

_____

(8-6) How are academic rules different from either principles or generalizations? Give an example of an academic rule. (p. 374-375)

_____

_____

_____

Declarative knowledge includes names, dates, facts, definitions, and organized bodies of information.

(8-6) Throughout your study of your text, you learned concepts such as <u>equilibrium</u> in chapter 2, <u>negative</u> <u>reinforcement</u> in chapter 6, and <u>perception</u> in chapter 7. What part of this learning was declarative knowledge? Explain. (pp. 375-376)

_____

_____

_____

_____

(8-7) You have a class in which the backgrounds of the students vary dramatically. You want to teach them about the skeletal system. Describe specifically what you would do to accommodate the differences in the students' backgrounds. (p. 380)

_____

_____

_____

_____

Cognitive strategies are mental operations that go beyond the basic processes needed to perform a task. Self-regulated learners understand the differences among strategies, know when a particular strategy is most appropriate, and have adequate content knowledge.
Study skills are cognitive strategies applied to written materials and teacher presentations.

(8-8) A student uses summarizing as a study skill--a particular type of cognitive strategy--as he reads his social studies text. Using the definition, ". . . operations over and above the processes directly entailed in carrying out a task," what are the "operations," and what are the "processes directly entailed in carrying out the task," in the student's case. What is the student's goal in using the strategy? (pp. 380-382)

_____

_____

_____

_____

142

(8-9) A seventh grader is reading about worms in her life science book. She comments to her mother, "When I study this weird stuff, I draw sort of a picture of each thing and write the big word by it. The picture helps me remember it." Does the girl demonstrate the characteristics of a self-regulation? Explain why or why not. (p. 382)

_____

_____

_____

_____

(8-10) What is the most important aspect of using underlining or note taking as a study strategy? (pp. 385-386)

_____

_____

(8-11) Study the four comprehension monitoring steps in reciprocal teaching outlined in Table 8.7 and then apply them in your study of "Thinking Skills" (which is covered on pages 389 through 392), the next section of the chapter. (pp. 388-389)

_____

_____

_____

_____

Thinking skills allow learners to efficiently process information. Effective thinking requires use of basic processes, awareness of the processes being used, adequate background knowledge, and dispositions such as open-mindedness and a desire to be informed.

(8-12) A teacher stands still holding a can of paint. She asks the students how much "work" she is doing, and Kevin says, "None." She responds, "How do you know?" to which Kevin answers, "Because the can isn't moving, and movement is required for work to be done." What basic process and subprocess is Kevin demonstrating with his responses? Briefly describe Kevin's domain-specific knowledge. (pp. 389-392)

_____

_____

_____

_____

The purpose of engaging students in problem solving activities is not only to help them gain specific knowledge but also to develop problem solving skills that can be applied to new situations. The more experiences a thinker has in solving problems, the more expertise is gained.

(8-13) You are trying out a used car for several days, and you want to see if it is as economical as you hope it will be, so you want to check its gas mileage. Describe each of the problem solving steps in this example. (pp. 393-397)

Understanding the problem

_____

_____

Devising a plan

_____

_____

Implementing the plan

_____

_____

Evaluating the results

_____

_____

(8-10) Describe at least two differences in the way an expert would approach the gas mileage problem compared to the way a novice would approach the problem. Be specific in your explanation. (p. 395)

_____

_____

_____

_____

# TEACHING FOR TRANSFER

Students' ability to transfer learning to new situations depends on the variety, the quality, and the context of examples used in teaching.

(8-11) Refer to the teaching example on pp. 371-372 of your text. Assess the lesson based on the quality of the teacher's examples, the variety of examples, and the context in which the examples were presented (pp. 402-403)

_____

_____

_____

_____

(8-12) You have taught your students the rule for setting off nonessential clauses with commas. What would be the best way of having them apply the rule to most capitalize on *context*? (p. 403).

_____

_____

_____

(8-13) Research indicates that convergent problem solving is content specific, and the skills used often do not transfer to other areas. Give and example that illustrates this research result. What can you do as a teacher to increase the likelihood that problem solving ability will transfer? Give an example that illustrates your idea. (pp. 403-404).

_____

_____

_____

_____

(8-14) You want your students to learn <u>summarizing</u> as a study skill. What can you do to increase the chance that this skill will transfer? (pp. 404-406)

_____

_____

_____

_____

(8-15) Research indicates that general transfer for the most part does not exist. What aspect of transfer is an exception to the previous statement? Support your statement with an illustration. (pp. 406-407)

_____

_____

_____

(8-17) Earlier in the chapter we discussed generalizations, principles, and academic rules. Describe how you would teach someone to understand generalizations, principles and rules using Ausubel's work as a basis for designing your instruction. (pp. 407-409)

_____

_____

_____

(8-18) Consider generalizations, principles, and academic rules again. Describe how you would teach them using a guided discovery approach. (pp. 409-413).

_____

_____

_____

_____

# CHAPTER EIGHT
# COGNITIVE VIEWS OF LEARNING: APPLICATIONS

## APPLICATION EXERCISES _____

### EXERCISE 8.1

Exercise 8.1 measures your understanding of topics covered on pages 359-378 of your text.

For items 1 through 5, read the episode and decide whether the lesson was aimed primarily at a *concept*, a *principle*, a *generalization*, a *rule*, or *declarative knowledge*. Explain how you know in each case.

1. Mary Jo Fernandez wanted her students to understand the theory of continental drift. She began by giving an overview of the theory, complete with an outline and slides. Then the students broke into study groups to investigate geological formations, fossil forms, magnetic clues, and data from the seafloor. As each group gathered information, they put it in a chart that the class discussed at the end of the unit.

_____

_____

_____

2. Bill Stanton wanted his art students to know how color influences depth perspective in paintings. To reach his goal he displayed and asked students to compare a series of color prints, ultimately guiding them to the conclusion that "dark colors appear to recede" and "light and bright colors look closer."

_____

_____

_____

3. Dan Shafer wanted his language arts students to be able to identify inferences in written essays. He began by defining inferences and explaining why they're important. He then displayed a paragraph on the overhead and went through it line by line, underlining each inference and explaining his thinking. Finally, he displayed a second paragraph and had the students identify inferences and explain their thinking.

_____

_____

_____

4. Juanita Kennedy was teaching a unit on farm animals to her kindergarten class, most of whom had never been to a farm. Juanita wanted her students to know the names of both the animals and their babies, what they eat, and the products they give us. In teaching the unit, she used pictures, stories, such as The Little Red Hen and The Ugly Duckling, and songs. She completed the unit with a trip to the zoo and petting farm.

_____

_____

_____

5. Kathy Connor's prealgebra students were having trouble simplifying simple arithmetic expressions such as 8/4 + 6(8 - 2)/9. She presented several examples, explained and demonstrated each step in the process, and then gave the students several problems on which to practice. Each was discussed and explained.

_____

_____

_____

6. Read the following case study and answer the questions that follow it.

> Jan Schwartz's fifth-grade music class was learning a ballad about cowboys. As they turned to the page in the music book, a hand went up.
> "What's a dogie?"
> "Actually, Kim, it's pronounced dō-gē--long *o* and long *e*. It does kind of look like the word doggy, doesn't it? Who knows what a dogie is? . . . Anyone? . . . Well, let's look at the sentence and see if we can find out. It says, 'Get along, little dogie.' What are the cowboys doing? Jed?"
> ". . . They're herding cattle."
> "Good, and so a little cow would be a? . . . Tanya?"
> ". . . Calf."
> "Very good! A dogie is a calf, but a special kind of calf--one that's lost its mother. Why would that be important to a cowboy? Shannon?"
> ". . . Because they wouldn't know who to follow or where to go."
> "Excellent, Shannon! Class, look at the picture of the cattle drive on the front of the album. Can you see any potential dogies?" she asked, holding the picture up for them.

Identify each of the following:

a. The concept being taught_____

b. A superordinate concept_____

c. A coordinate concept_____

d. A characteristic_____

e. An example_____

How "easy" was this concept to learn? Explain why._____

_____

_____

_____

EXERCISE 8.2

Exercise 8.2 measures your understanding of topics covered on pages 378-399 of your text.

Read the following descriptions of a class involved in problem solving and identify each of the problem solving steps in it.

Bill Watson's algebra class was working on applications of problem solving. To begin the class, Bill put the following problem on an overhead:

A goat is tied to the corner of a 40-ft-square barn with a 30-ft rope. If it can graze everywhere outside of the barn that its rope allows it to reach, what is the size of its grazing area?

"What do we need to do first?" he began. "Taffy?"
" . . . Figure out what we know and need to find out."
"Good, Taffy. Let's start with givens. What do we know? Betty?"
"Well, we know how big the sides of the barn are--40 ft--and we know that the rope is 30 ft long."
"Okay. Now would anyone like to come up and draw us a picture to help us see what we are trying to figure out? Shanda?"
"Well, I think the problem looks like this. We have a circle with a radius of 30 ft. But the barn is here. It cuts out part of that circle. We have to find the area of the circle that's not in the barn because no grass grows in the barn, and he couldn't get in to eat it anyway."
"Excellent drawing, Shanda. So how do we translate this into a formula? Kerry?"
"The formula for the area of a circle is A equals pi times the radius squared. So we need to find that and subtract 1/4 from it--to allow for the barn."
"Who can do that on their calculator and then share with us on the board? Brad?"
"Hmmm . . . Okay. I think the answer is 2,826."
"It's 2,826 what, Brad?"
"Oh, right! Square feet. Does that sound about right?"
"Is that what everyone else got? Kim?"
"No, he forgot to subtract the quarter of a circle in the barn. So it should be 2,119.5 square ft."
"Good, Kim. Is that what everyone else got? Class, two things we can learn from this problem. First, always go back to the notes you took when you set up the problem. If Brad had checked with the diagram we drew, he would have caught his mistake. Second, make sure you have the right units. If it's area, it needs to be square something."

Understanding the problem

_____

_____

_____

Devising a plan

_____

_____

_____

149

Implementing the plan

_____

_____

_____

_____

Evaluating the results

_____

_____

_____

[ _____ ]

EXERCISE 8.3

Exercise 8.3 measures your understanding of topics covered on pages 399-413 of your text.

1. The following descriptions show how three teachers taught their students about reptiles. Analyze the three episodes in terms of the discussion of transfer in the chapter and decide which teacher's students would have the highest likelihood of transfer and which would be least likely to transfer. Explain your reasoning in the analysis.

Mrs. Jung carefully explained what reptiles are, where they live, and what they eat. She then told her students that animals such as alligators, crocodiles, turtles, and snakes are reptiles.

Mrs. McManus brought her son's pet snake to class. She also showed the students colored pictures of an alligator, a turtle, and a horned toad. She had the students observe the snake and the pictures and discuss the characteristics they all had in common.

Mr. Hume explained what reptiles are and told the students that snakes, lizards, alligators, and turtles are reptiles. He also showed the students a picture of a sea turtle, so they knew that some reptiles live in water.

Most likely to transfer

_____

_____

_____

Least likely to transfer

_____

_____

_____

_____

2. Identify one important aspect of concept teaching that each of the teachers neglected to do in the lesson.

_____

_____

_____

3. Read the following episode, which describes a teacher using Ausubel's ideas to structure a lesson. Then respond to questions a, b, and c.

Ann Kenderson began her biology class by displaying the following outline on the board:

The parts of the blood are like a baseball team. Each has a job to do. Their job is to carry different materials in the blood.

She then began, "We looked at this outline yesterday. Let's briefly review. What are the components of the blood shown here? Katrina?"
"Plasma, white blood cells, and red blood cells."
"Okay. How is plasma different from the other two? Jake?"
"It doesn't have any cells--it's mostly water and protein."
"And how is plasma similar to the other two? Tamara?"
"I . . . I'm sorry," Tamara said hesitantly.
"Look at the statement at the top."
" . . . Oh, yes. It carries stuff too."
"Good, Tamara. Each of the components of the blood carries different materials.
"Now today, we're going to focus on the red blood cells." Ann wrote the following statement on the board:
Red blood cells are our body's oxygen railroad.
"Class, I'd like everyone to look at the board. What do you think that statement means, Sasha?"
"Well, the red blood cells must carry something."
"And what do you think they carry, Sasha? Read it carefully."
"Oh, yeah. They carry oxygen."
"How does this relate to our first statement of yesterday? Kim?"
"It says that each component of the blood carries some materials. The material for the red blood cells is oxygen."
"Good, Kim. Now, class, how does a railroad carry materials? Rodney?"
"There are railroad cars that they fill up."
"Good. Class, red blood cells are like railroad cars. They fill up with oxygen at the lungs and take it to the rest of the body. The rest of the body uses the oxygen and releases carbon dioxide."

a. Identify two advance organizers in this case study.

_____

_____

_____

_____

b. How does the episode illustrate a deductive teaching sequence?

_____

_____

_____

c. Identify specific points in the case study that illustrate forming associations.

_____

_____

_____

4. Read the following teaching episode and respond to the questions that follow.

   Jill Sharman, a preschool teacher, wanted her students to learn about triangles. She gathered her class in the front of the room and made two yarn circles on her felt board. In one circle, she put triangles of different sizes and colors; in the other, she put squares, circles, and other shapes. She asked the children what the triangle shapes had in common and led them to conclude that each had three sides and was made out of straight lines. She also led them to conclude that the size and color didn't really matter since they were all grouped together.

a. Identify the abstraction being taught.

_____

b. Identify the data provided to students to help them "discover" the abstraction.

_____

_____

c. What did Jill do that is inconsistent with one of the themes of this chapter.

d. Describe how the same content might be taught using a deductive sequence (as Ausubel would suggest).

# CHAPTER EIGHT
# COGNITIVE VIEWS OF LEARNING: APPLICATIONS

## SELF-HELP QUIZ _____

TRUE/FALSE QUESTIONS. Write T in the blank if the statement is true and write F if the statement is false.

**F** 1. Although there are different types of learning, the way content is learned is the same and therefore it can be taught basically in the same manner.

**F** 2. The rule-eg teaching strategy is one example of discovery learning.

**T** 3. Generalizations describe relationships between concepts, but are less certain than principles.

**F** 4. "Raise your hand when you wish to speak" is an example of an academic rule.

**F** 5. Research reveals that most study skills are learned independently without instruction from a teacher.

**T** 6. Although the basic processes of thinking skills should be taught individually and specifically, they are used to process information in a general sense.

**F** 7. Open-ended problem solving involves understanding a well-defined problem, devising a plan, implementing the plan and arriving at a specific solution.

**F** 8. Transfer of learning for concepts is more dependent upon students' ability to access information in working memory than on the context of examples used to teach the concept.

**T** 9. Dispositions are one element of the thinking process that transfer well in a general sense, as opposed to domain-specific knowledge which transfers poorly to non-related situations.

**T** 10. Expository teaching is an efficient teaching strategy because it consists of the use of advance organizers and carefully organized teacher lectures.

MULTIPLE CHOICE QUESTIONS: Circle the best response in each case.

11. You want your students to learn about fractions. You introduce the topic by saying, "Fractions are <u>numbers</u> that you use to describe what you have when you break a whole number or thing into smaller parts. If I break a cookie into two pieces that are the same size, I have two halves of a cookie." The first sentence of the statement to the students can also be called a:
   a. discrimination.
   b. definition.
   c. characteristic.
   d. rule.
   e. principle.

12. In item 11, "numbers" is the
   a. concept.
   b. subordinate concept.
   c. coordinate concept.
   d. superordinate concept.
   e. definition.

13. In item 11, the second sentence of the statement to the students can also be called a(n):
   a. example.
   b. definition.
   c. academic rule.
   d. generalization.
   e. principle.

14. The statement, "In writing possessives, the apostrophe is written before the 's' if the noun is singular but is written after the 's' if the noun is plural," best describes which of the following?
    a. Concept
    b. Principle
    c. Definition
    d. Rule
    e. Discrimination

15. Which of the following best illustrates a cognitive strategy?
    a. Reading an assigned passage in history
    b. Finding the lowest common denominator when adding fractions
    c. Identifying an example of an inference in a written paragraph
    d. Writing notes in the margins of your textbook

16. You want to teach your students about prepositions. Of the following, which is most effective for promoting transfer?
    a. Present a list of prepositions and explain how they're used.
    b. Present a list of sentences that have prepositions in them.
    c. Present a paragraph that includes several prepositions.
    d. Explain to the students that prepositions are always in phrases, and all they have to do is identify the phrase.

17. The aspect of transfer that is the focus of item 16 is:
    a. variety of examples.
    b. quality of examples.
    c. context for examples.
    d. both variety and quality of examples.

18. The statement "Students learn best when they are presented with information in an organized, logical manner and are involved actively in questions and answers with the teacher" is most consistent with the philosophy of:
    a. Piaget
    b. Skinner
    c. Ausubel
    d. Bruner
    e. Montessori

19. Maurice has learned to add fractions in math. When he encounters a word problem in science he is able to use fractions to solve it. This situation most closely relates to:
    a. hierarchical learning.
    b. a study skill.
    c. discovery learning.
    d. specific transfer.

20. You have taught your students the concept rhombus (figures with four equal sides and opposite angles equal). Of the following, which is the best way to determine if transfer has occurred?
    a. Show them a parallelogram and ask them if it is a rhombus.
    b. Show them a square and ask if it is a rhombus.
    c. Show them a trapezoid and ask if it is a rhombus.
    d. Show them a regular hexagon (six equal sides and six equal angles) and ask if it is a rhombus.

# CHAPTER NINE
## INCREASING STUDENT MOTIVATION

CHAPTER OUTLINE _____

# CHAPTER OBJECTIVES

- Identify the differences between general and specific motivation to learn
- Explain motivation on the basis of behavioral, humanistic, cognitive, and social learning theories.
- Plan a learning activity that capitalizes on the effects of arousal in motivation.
- Identify from a classroom case study a teacher's attempt to meet students' needs for control and self-determination.
- Identify desirable and undesirable teacher behaviors according to attribution theory.
- Identify applications of Maslow's Hierarchy of needs in the classroom.
- Explain the importance of goal-setting in promoting motivation and self-efficacy.
- Identify applications of teacher personal characteristics that promote student motivation.
- Identify applications of classroom climate variables that promote student motivation.
- Identify applications of instructional variables that promote student motivation.
- Explain how cooperative learning can enhance achievement and capitalize on diversity.

The key concept on which the study of your text has focused is learning and what we as teachers can do to increase it. In order to effectively promote learning we must understand the characteristics of the people we're trying to teach--the content of chapters 2-5 of your text. In chapters 6-8 we examined the nature of the learning process itself, first from a behaviorist point of view and then from a cognitive orientation. Now we turn to motivation, an extremely important factor that influences student learning. In this chapter we're trying to answer the question, "What is the nature of learner motivation and what can we as teachers do to increase it?"

Theories of motivation explain both general motivation to learn--learner tendencies that extend beyond specific teachers and classes--as well as specific motivation to learn, which depend more on the behavior of teachers.

Behavioral theories describe motivation in terms of effective use of reinforcers; it is extrinsic motivation. The use of reinforcers is criticized on the grounds that they decrease the desire to learn for its own sake, they cause learners to focus only on learning that is being reinforced, reinforcers are difficult to systematically administer, and the application of reinforcers doesn't take learners' perceptions and beliefs into account.

According to humanistic views of motivation human beings have an innate need for personal growth and development. The humanistic view focuses on the whole person, and self-concept is fundamental. The student-teacher relationship and classroom climate are critical for student motivation according to this view.

Cognitive theories suggest that people are instinctively motivated by a need to understand the way the world works, and these theories emphasize the importance of learner perceptions in explaining motivation.

Social learning theorists believe learners are motivated to the extent that they expect to succeed on tasks and value achievement on the tasks. If learners believe that they are making genuine progress toward valued goals, they can develop a sense of self-efficacy. Learners with high self-efficacy approach rather than avoid challenging tasks, persist on the tasks, focus on thoughts of success, and perform better than counterparts of equal ability who are low in self-efficacy.

Personal factors--arousal, needs, beliefs, and goals--can also affect an individual's motivation.

An optimum level of arousal--a physical and psychological response to the environment--is needed for high performance, but arousal to the point of anxiety can detract from performance and motivation. Teachers can capitalize on the effects of arousal by appealing to learners' curiosity with thought-provoking questions, demonstrations that behave counter-intuitively, and dressing or behaving in incongruous ways.

Personal needs are described differently by different theorists. Abraham Maslow, a humanistic thinker, asserts that people have an instinctive drive for self-fulfillment, which he called self-actualization. To reach self-actualization, deficiency needs--survival, safety, belonging, and self-esteem must be first met. Upon fulfillment of deficiency needs, individuals move to growth needs--intellectual achievement, aesthetic appreciation, and self-actualization. The growth needs are never "met," however, and in fact expand as individuals acquire experience in those areas.

Other thinkers describe needs as a drive for competence--the need to master skills and tasks in order to cope with the environment, the need for control over their own destiny and a sense of autonomy, and the need to achieve and experience pride in accomplishment.

Attribution theory, a well-developed cognitive description of motivation, examines students' explanations for their successes and failures, describing them most commonly in terms of ability, effort, task difficulty, and luck. The different explanations (attributions) impact their continuing effort, the difficulty of the tasks they select, and their perceptions of themselves.

Researchers examining learners' beliefs assert that individuals will go to great lengths, such as making a point of not trying, or procrastinating, to preserve their self-worth when it is threatened. This tendency is more pronounced in older than in younger learners.

Learners' motivation can be enhanced if they set short-term, quantitative, and specific goals that focus on challenge and mastery of tasks. A task orientation helps learners eliminate worries about failure and comparisons with others.

Teachers can do much to promote motivation in their classrooms. Personal characteristics like modeling, enthusiasm, warmth, and high expectations, together with promoting an orderly and safe environment, where students are involved, challenged, and successful significantly increases motivation even in reluctant learners.

Cooperative learning, a set of instructional procedures that promotes collaboration in mixed-ability groups, can be used to increase motivation by capitalizing on features of both extrinsic and intrinsic views of motivation. When students are held individually accountable, have an equal opportunity for success, and contribute to the success of the group, motivation for all ability levels is increased. Research documents the effectiveness of cooperative learning for increased achievement and motivation as well as a means for capitalizing on the background diversity of learners, promoting acceptance of students with exceptionalities, and enhancing self-esteem.

## CHAPTER NINE
## INCREASING STUDENT MOTIVATION

### CHAPTER-AT-A-GLANCE

| MAIN TOPIC | KEY POINTS | KEY TERMS |
|---|---|---|
| General and Specific Motivation to Learn | • Students with general motivation to tend to study and work conscientiously regardless of the class, topic, or teacher<br>• Students with specific motivation to learn tend to work conscientiously in some classes but not others.<br>• Specific motivation to learn depends more on the topic and teacher than does general motivation to learn. | • General motivation to learn, 427<br>• Specific motivation to learn, 427 |
| Theories of Motivation | • Behaviorists describe motivation as occurring as the result of reinforcement; it comes from outside the learner.<br>• Humanistic views describe motivation as an instinctive need for growth and development.<br>• Motivation is a response to a need to understand how the world works according to cognitive theories.<br>• According to social learning theorists, learners are motivated if they expect to succeed on tasks they perceive as worthwhile. | • Reinforcement, 428<br>• Humanistic psychology, 432<br>• Cognitive theories, 433<br>• Social learning theories, 434<br>• Expectancy X value theories, 434<br>• Self-efficacy, 434 |

| Personal Factors in Motivation | • Optimum arousal--a state of alertness-- is needed for high performance; arousal to the point of anxiety detracts from performance.<br>• Surprising or discrepant events can capitalize on arousal through the effects of curiosity motivation.<br>• Maslow described humans' need for growth and self-fulfillment in a hierarchy. In this hierarchy, deficiency needs, such as survival and safety, disappear when they are met, but growth needs, such as learning and achievement, increase as learners have experience with them.<br>• Competence motivation describes people's needs to master skills, which in turn helps them better cope with the environment.<br>• Students' need for control over their own fate can be met by allowing them to have input into decisions that affect them.<br>• People with high need for achievement are motivated by challenging tasks and opportunities to repeat difficult assignments. People with high need to avoid failure withdraw from challenge.<br>• According to Attribution Theory, students typically explain their successes and failures in learning activities as being due to ability, effort, good or bad luck, and the ease or difficulty of the task. The explanations, called attributions, are related to their belief about ability, their motivation to achieve, and their sense of self worth.<br>• Individuals will instinctively try to protect their self-worth when it is threatened.<br>• Short-term, quantitative, and specific goals can result in students focusing on learning rather than mere performance. | • Arousal, 438<br>• Anxiety, 438<br>• Curiosity motivation, 439<br>• Need, 439<br>• Deficiency need, 440<br>• Growth need, 441<br>• Competence motivation, 441<br>• Achievement motivation, 442<br>• Attributions, 444<br>• Attribution theory, 444<br>• Learned helplessness, 445<br>• Incremental view of ability, 446<br>• Entity view of ability, 446<br>• Performance goals, 448<br>• Learning goals, 449 |

| | | |
|---|---|---|
| The Class-room: A Model for Promoting Motivation | • The implications of theories of motivation, together with personal factors and a "learning-focused" classroom can be combined into a classroom model for promoting student motivation.<br>• A learning focused classroom defines success and satisfaction in terms of progress, learning new information as a reason for effort, and ability as incremental.<br>• Modeling, enthusiasm, warmth and empathy, and high expectations are important teacher characteristics for promoting learner motivation.<br>• Students are motivated when they are in a safe and orderly environment, experience success, are challenged, and understand what they are learning, why they are learning it, and how well they are performing.<br>• Teachers can increase student motivation by involving learners in learning activities, personalizing content, beginning lessons with attention-getters, and providing students with feedback. | • Warmth, 455<br>• Empathy, 455<br>• Classroom climate, 457<br>• Comprehension, 459<br>• Introductory focus, 462<br>• Personalization, 463<br>• Involvement, 464<br>• Open-ended questions, 465 |
| Cooperative Learning: A Tool for Promoting Motivation | Cooperative learning involves students of mixed ability, sex, and race in groupwork that can increase achievement, self-esteem, and acceptance of students with exceptionalities, and can help teachers capitalize on the diversity in their students. | • Cooperative learning, 470 |

# CHAPTER NINE
## INCREASING STUDENT MOTIVATION

## GUIDED REVIEW _____

### GENERAL AND SPECIFIC MOTIVATION TO LEARN _____

General motivation to learn describes a broad and enduring disposition toward learning. Specific motivation to learn describes an orientation toward learning that is influenced by individual teachers and classes.

(9-1) Identify two differences between general and specific motivation to learn. Which of the two can we as teachers more influence? (pp. 427-428)

_____

_____

### THEORIES OF MOTIVATION _____

Extrinsic motivation comes from outside learners. Behaviorism describes motivation as effective use of reinforcers.

(9-2) Imagine that you're a teacher of eighth graders and your friend teaches third graders. Describe how your use of reinforcers might be different than that of your friend. (pp. 429-430)

_____

_____

_____

(9-3) Describe a classroom example that would illustrate each of the criticisms of behavioral approaches to motivation that appear on pages 430-431 of your text. (pp. 430-431)

_____

_____

_____

_____

Humanistic views of motivation focus on the development of the whole person. These views suggest that we are motivated by the need for overall well-being and personal growth.

163

(9-4) Explain why humanistic psychology is sometimes called a "third force." (p. 432)

_____

_____

_____

(9-5) Identify an example from the case study at the beginning of the chapter that illustrates the student-teacher relationship and another example that illustrates classroom climate as they are described in this section. (pp. 432-433).

_____

_____

_____

Cognitive theorists suggest that we are all motivated to understand the world and have control over our lives. Learners' perceptions are important in explaining motivation according to cognitive views.

(9-6) A teacher puts a cup of water into a gallon can, heats the can over a hot plate until the water boils rapidly, removes the can from the hot plate and tightly screws the lid on the can. As the students watch, the can "magically" collapses in front of their eyes. Explain why this demonstration would be motivating based on cognitive theories of motivation. (pp. 433-434)

_____

_____

_____

According to social learning theories learners are motivated if they expect to succeed on tasks that they believe are challenging and important. Progress toward valued goals, can lead to feelings of self-efficacy.

(9-8) Success and self-efficacy are closely related but not identical. How do they differ? (pp. 434-435)

_____

_____

(9-9) Two learners of equal ability--one with high self-efficacy and the other with low self-efficacy--are faced with a challenging task. Describe likely differences in the two learners approach to the tasks, thoughts, effort, and performance on the tasks. (p. 435)

_____

_____

Arousal is a response to the environment leaving a learner alert, wide awake, and attentive.

(9-10) Blood pressure and health are in a curvilinear relationship. An optimum level of blood pressure is critical to life, but too much is harmful to health. Explain how this is an analogy for arousal and motivation and performance. (p. 438)

_____

_____

_____

(9-11) How did Kathy Brewster in the opening case study of this chapter capitalize on the motivating effects of arousal in her lesson? (p. 439)

_____

_____

_____

Maslow suggests that we all have a drive for self-fulfillment. In order to be fulfilled, lower needs must be satisfied so that we can reach for higher ones.

(9-12) Describe the difference between deficiency and growth needs. Give a classroom example of teachers' attempts to meets students' needs for safety, belonging, and self-esteem. (pp. 450-453)

_____

_____

_____

_____

The need for competence, the need for control and the need for achievement are all needs strongly relating to cognitive theorists descriptions of individuals' needs to "understand the way the world works."

(9-13) A child is learning how to ride a bicycle. She falls, comes into the house bruised and crying, but five minutes later is back out on the bicycle only to repeat this process over and over. Explain the child's persistence based on the concept of competence motivation. (pp. 441-442)

_____

_____

_____

(9-14) Provide a classroom example of something teachers can do to help students feel like Origins rather than Pawns. (p. 442)

_____

_____

_____

(9-15) Sally usually does the "B" problems (those designed to challenge the students) in algebra, even though they are often difficult for her. Karen rarely does them, in spite of usually being able to solve them. Explain the difference in the two girls' behaviors based on the concept of achievement motivation. (pp. 442-443)

_____

_____

_____

Attribution theory focuses on learners' explanations for their success or failure.

(9-16) Glen and Roni both do poorly on an English test. Glen comments that he didn't study enough, and Roni says she just gets confused with English and everything gets all jumbled up. What are the likely outcomes of these attributions if the students' behavior is consistent with patterns identified by research? (pp. 443-445)

_____

_____

_____

When their self-worth is threatened, people instinctively strive to protect it. Perceptions of ability increase in importance as students progress through school.

(9-17) Fred studies little the night before a test, gets a D and comments to Kevin who got a B+, "Ahh, I would have done just as well if I had studied half as hard as you did." Explain Fred's behavior (his not studying and his comment). (pp. 446-).

_____

_____

_____

(9-18) It is generally believed that underachievers need to experience a great deal of success in order to improve their achievement. Identify a potential danger in "doing whatever it takes" to assure student success. (p. 447).

_____

_____

_____

When learners set goals that are short-term, quantitative, and specific, they begin to focus on mastery of tasks, and stop worrying about failure or comparisons to other students. This orientation can lead to sustained effort and achievement.

(9-19) You know that you will have a test on this chapter at some point during the course you're taking, and you decide to set a goal for yourself. Which one of the following three goals is the most desirable? a) to get at least a B on the test, b) to score in the top third of the class on the test, or c) to answer in writing each of the application exercises in this study guide. Explain why the one you chose is the most desirable. (pp. 448-449)

_____

_____

_____

_____

## THE CLASSROOM: A MODEL FOR PROMOTING MOTIVATION

Behavioral, cognitive, humanistic and social learning theories together with personal factors in motivation and a "learning-focused" classroom all imply specific teacher behaviors that can increase students' drive to learn. These behaviors can be consolidated into a cohesive model that gives teachers guidance in their efforts to increase their students' motivation.

(9-20) Think about two classes that you're now taking. Are they primarily "learning-focused" or "performance-focused?" Describe specifically what makes them that way. (pp. 449-452)

_____

_____

_____

(9-21) You're in a school observing a particular teacher. Identify at least one specific behavior that would indicate each of the following: modeling, enthusiasm, warmth and empathy, and high expectations. (pp. 453-457)

_____

_____

_____

_____

_____

(9-22) Again you're in a classroom observing a teacher. Identify at least one example of a teacher behavior that promotes each of the following: order and safety, success, comprehension, and challenge. (pp. 457-460)

_____

_____

_____

_____

(9-23) Think about the way your textbook authors organized your book. How did they provide introductory focus for the text? (Hint: look back on pages 1 and 2 of the text.) (pp. 461-462)

_____

_____

_____

(9-24) You're teaching your students about direct and indirect objects. Give a specific classroom illustration that will show how you could personalize your examples. (pp. 463-464)

_____

_____

_____

(9-25) You're teaching your class of 28 seventh graders about crustaceans (crabs, lobsters, shrimp, etc.). Describe two specific ways of promoting student involvement in this lesson. (pp. 464-467)

_____

_____

_____

(9-26) Give a specific example of feedback in a "learning-focused" situation and another example of feedback in a "performance-focused" situation. (pp. 467-468)

_____

_____

_____

## COOPERATIVE LEARNING: A TOOL FOR PROMOTING MOTIVATION

Cooperative learning promotes motivation by decreasing competition among individual students and increasing collaboration among mixed ability groups.

(9-27) Slavin suggests three features--group goals, individual accountability, and equal opportunity for success--must all exist for cooperative learning to be successful. Explain how Selina Keyesy accomplished each of these in her work with her students. (pp. 471-472)

_____

_____

_____

(9-28) You are a teacher and have several different ethnic groups in your class. Describe specifically how you will organize your groups to capitalize on the diversity in your classroom. (pp. 476-479)

_____

_____

_____

_____

# CHAPTER NINE
# INCREASING STUDENT MOTIVATION

## APPLICATION EXERCISES _____

EXERCISE 9.1

Exercise 9.1 measures your understanding of topics covered on pages 423-438 of your text.

For each of the following items, be sure to carefully <u>defend your answer</u> based on the information you've studied in this section of the chapter.

1. In the chapter's opening case study, Jim's comment, "It's sort of interesting the way Brewster's always telling us about the way we are 'cause of something that happened a zillion years ago," indicates that his motivation has increased as a result of Kathy's teaching. Which approach to motivation--behavioral, humanistic, cognitive, or social learning--best explains Jim's motivation?

_____

_____

_____

2. Jim also commented, "Besides, you miss a homework assignment in this class, and you're dead. . . .Nobody messes with Brewster." This comment gives us an indication of Kathy's expectations. Which theoretical view of motivation best explains the impact of teacher expectations on student motivation?

_____

_____

_____

_____

3. Later in the case study, we saw the following encounter:
 "Wait a minute!" Joe interrupted. "How about the new fighting techniques they learned? . . ."
 "Joe," Kathy began firmly, "what is one of the principles we operate on in here?"
 "We don't have to agree with someone else's point, but we do have to listen. Sorry, Nikki. It just slipped out."
 Which approach to motivation best explains the importance of the principle, "We don't have to agree, but we have to listen"?

_____

_____

_____

_____

4. Toward the end of the case study Kathy commented, "Now isn't that interesting! . . . Here we see ourselves in the 20th century finding a relationship to people who lived a thousand years ago. That's what history is all about."
a. Explain the motivating effects of this comment from a cognitive point of view.

_____

_____

_____

b. Explain the motivating effects from a humanistic point of view.

_____

_____

_____

5. In the case study, David indicated to Kelly that he perceived that "Brewster loves this stuff." Which approach to motivation best explains the motivating effects of Kathy's behavior that led to David's comment?

_____

_____

_____

EXERCISE 9.2

Exercise 9.2 measures your understanding of topics covered on pages 438-449 of your text.

1. You are a language arts teacher and you're planning a lesson on direct and indirect objects. Offer a specific suggestion for what you might do to capitalize on the effect of arousal in motivation.

_____

_____

_____

2. Think about Maslow's hierarchy of needs and identify two examples in the chapter's opening case study where Kathy Brewster attempted to meet a deficiency need in one of her students. Defend your answer with information taken from the case study.

_____

_____

_____

_____

3. Identify an example in the chapter's opening case study where Kathy Brewster attempted to meet students' needs for control and self-determination.

_____

_____

_____    _____

_____

4. Kathy Brewster attempted to conduct her class so she emphasized the need for achievement and reduced the need to avoid failure. Citing specific evidence from the case study, explain how she attempted to accomplish this.

_____

_____

_____

_____

For items 5 through 8, decide if attribution theorists would recommend (R) or would not recommend (NR) the teacher statement. Explain why in each case.

5. In handing out a test to her class, a teacher says, "Work hard on this test now. It's kind of a tough one."

_____

_____

_____

6. In handing back a test, the teacher notices that Tommy has gotten an A on it. With a smile, he says, "Well done, Tommy. That was easy, wasn't it?"

_____

_____

_____

7. Sympathetically, a teacher says to a student who has just received a D on a math quiz, "Try not to feel too bad about this, Billy. I know math is hard for you."

_____

_____

_____

8. To a girl of average ability who has just received a B on a test, a teacher says, "Very well done, Susan. Your hard work is starting to pay off, isn't it?"

_____

_____

_____

For items 9, 10, and 11, decide on the basis of attribution theory whether or not the students would be likely to make the statements that appear in each case. Explain your reasoning.

9. "I'm generally pretty good in science, but I don't think I'll do well on this next test. I have a funny feeling about it."

_____

_____

_____

10. "I'll never be able to get it. I have a mental block against Spanish. I've never been able to get it straight."

_____

_____

_____

11. "I'm scared of this test. I guessed on four questions last time and got three right. I don't know if I can pull that off again."

_____

_____

_____

_____

```
┌─────────────────────────────────────────────────────────────┐
│                                                               │
└─────────────────────────────────────────────────────────────┘
```

EXERCISE 9.3

Exercise 9.3 measures your understanding of topics covered on pages 449-460 of your text.

1. Identify a student behavior at the beginning of the opening case study that was the direct result of Kathy Brewster's modeling.

_____

_____

_____

2. Identify the one student statement in the case study that best indicates a combination of Kathy Brewster's modeling and her enthusiasm.

_____

_____

_____

3. What concept from the section on teacher characteristics do the statements, "You miss a homework assignment in this class, and you're dead" and "Nobody messes with Brewster," best indicate?

_____

_____

4. Consider the climate variable <u>order and safety.</u> Using the characteristics of the variable described in this section, identify a specific example in the case study that illustrates this variable.

_____

_____

174

5. Look at the ways teachers can promote student success (on page 459 of your text). Other than reteaching, Kathy Brewster applied each of the strategies with her class. Identify an instance in the case study that illustrates each of the strategies.

_____

_____

_____

_____

## EXERCISE 9.4

Exercise 9.4 measures your understanding of topics covered on pages 459-479 of your text.

1. Describe how Kathy Brewster capitalized on the concept of introductory focus when she began her unit on the Crusades.

_____

_____

_____

2. How did Kathy attempt to personalize the content of her lesson?

_____

_____

_____

3. Describe Kathy's techniques for promoting student involvement.

_____

_____

_____

4. Pam Bean decides to implement a cooperative learning program at the beginning of the second grading period in her seventh-grade math class. One of her groups is composed of Steve, Karen, Joe, and Georgette, who respectively got B, B+, C-, and D the first nine weeks. On the first quiz the students' grades were respectively 78, 90, 75, and 65. Using the guide in Table 9.11, find the number of improvement points for each student and the number of improvement points for the team.

_____

_____

_____

_____

# CHAPTER NINE
## INCREASING STUDENT MOTIVATION

SELF-HELP QUIZ _____

TRUE/FALSE QUESTIONS. Write T in the blank if the statement is true and write F if the statement is false.

_____ 1. Teachers typically have a greater impact on general motivation to learn than they do on specific motivation to learn.

_____ 2. The "scarcity principle" usually applies more to elementary students than it does to middle or secondary students.

_____ 3. Your students are finding out what kinds of materials are attracted to magnets and are very involved in the activity. According to research, rewarding them for their participation would be unwise practice.

_____ 4. According to Maslow, people can become self-actualized after they've met their needs for intellectual achievement and aesthetic appreciation.

_____ 5. According to Maslow, belonging to a family or social group will not be a need for people until their need for safety is met.

_____ 6. According to research, people with a high need for achievement avoid challenging tasks in order to assure themselves of success.

_____ 7. According to Bandura, people achieve a sense of self-efficacy primarily according to the extent to which they're successful.

_____ 8. The attribution that is most likely to lead to learned helplessness is lack of effort.

_____ 9. When using a cooperative learning in your classroom, the instruction is not changed.

_____ 10. In cooperative learning activities, students work collaboratively on seatwork, but they take quizzes independently.

MULTIPLE-CHOICE ITEMS. Circle the best response in each case.

11. You have a students who seems to have "given up" and she won't try no matter how much effort you make. According to attribution theory, she most likely has been attributing her lack of success to:
   a. lack of ability.
   b. lack of effort.
   c. bad luck.
   d. tests and assignments that are too hard.

12. You have a student who has an incremental view of ability. He scores poorly on one of your tests. Based on this information, which of the following is most likely?
   a. He will avoid challenging tasks in the future to protect his self-esteem.
   b. He will develop a sense of learned helplessness.
   c. He will consciously avoid trying, so he can attribute lack of success to lack of effort rather than lack of ability.
   d. He will view his lack of success as lack of effort and will try harder in the future.

13. Of the following, the concept most closely related to cognitive views of motivation is:
   a. reinforcement.
   b. competence.
   c. safety.
   d. self-esteem.

14. Susan is getting better in algebra, and she now is able to solve simultaneous equations with considerable skill. According to cognitive theories of motivation, what is the most likely outcome of this experience?
   a. Susan feels reinforced each time she correctly solves a problem.
   b. Susan will develop a sense of self-efficacy.
   c. Susan's self-esteem will improve.
   d. Susan's need for intellectual achievement will be met.

15. Leah seems to have a strong aesthetic need. She very much enjoys the symphony, ballet, and art openings. According to Maslow, which of the following is the best conclusion?
   a. Leah's self-esteem need has been met.
   b. Both Leah's self-esteem and intellectual achievement needs have been met.
   c. Leah's intellectual achievement need has been met, but we don't know about her self-esteem need.
   d. Leah's intellectual achievement need and all of her deficiency needs have been met.

16. Mrs. Richards conducts help sessions for her students two nights a week after school. She also works with them before school and even during their lunch hour if they ask for help. The element of the Model for Promoting Motivation that these behaviors most closely relate to is:
   a. modeling.
   b. warmth and empathy.
   c. personalization.
   d. reinforcement.

17. Mr. Moran always returns his quizzes the day after they're given and he goes over frequently missed items carefully. The characteristic of the Model for Promoting Motivation that this behavior most closely relates to is:
   a. modeling.
   b. expectations.
   c. comprehension.
   d. reinforcement.

18. Whenever students fail to respond to her questions, or they give an incorrect answer, Mrs. McDonald asks another, simpler question that the students are able to answer. The characteristic of the Model for Promoting Motivation that this behavior most closely relates to is:
   a. enthusiasm.
   b. modeling.
   c. expectations.
   d. warmth and empathy.

19. A direct instruction lesson consists of a review and orientation, teacher presentation, guided practice, and independent practice. Which of these does cooperative learning most affect?
   a. Review and orientation
   b. Teacher presentation
   c. Guided practice
   d. Independent practice
   e. Both guided and independent practice

20. Heather has an 84 average to this point in the grading period. She earns a 91 on her latest quiz. The number of improvement points she will earn is:
   a. 30
   b. 20
   c. 10
   d. 0

# CHAPTER TEN
## MANAGING STUDENT BEHAVIOR

## CHAPTER OUTLINE

I. Classroom Management and Discipline
   A. Classroom Management
   B. The Persistence of Management Problems
      1. Sociological factors
      2. Energy and effort
      3. Lack of information
   C. Goals of Classroom Management
   D. Outcomes of Effective Management
      1. Increased achievement
      2. Increased motivation

II. Planning: The Key to Preventing Management Problems
   A. Student Characteristics
   B. The Physical Environment
      1. Visibility
      2. Accessibility
      3. Distractibility
   C. Establishing Procedures
   D. Setting Rules
      1. Class-school consistency
      2. Clarity
      3. Rationales
      4. Positive Statements
      5. A short list
      6. Student input
   E. Basic Rules

III. Making Rules and Procedures Work
   A. Teaching rules and procedures
   B. Monitoring rules and procedures

IV. Preventing Problems: Putting Plans into Action
   A. Teacher Characteristics
      1. Caring: The foundation of positive classroom climate
      2. Firmness: Helping students develop responsibility
      3. The democratic teacher: Combining caring and firmness
   B. The Beginning of the School Year
   C. Essential Management Skills
      1. Organization
      2. Lesson movement
         a. Withitness
         b. Overlapping
         c. Momentum
         d. Smoothness
      3. Communication with learners
         a. Nonverbal behavior
         b. "I-Messages"
         c. Ownership: Whose problem is it?
         d. Assertiveness: Communicating your right to teach
         e. Active listening

# CHAPTER OBJECTIVES

- Identify the elements of effective planning that prevent management problems.
- Differentiate between rules and procedures, and explain how each contributes to effective classroom management.
- Explain how developmental differences in students influence classroom management.
- Identify teacher characteristics associated with effective management.
- Identify examples of essential management skills in cases of classroom practice.
- Identify examples of effective intervention techniques that eliminate management problems when they occur.

# CHAPTER OVERVIEW _____

In chapters 2-5 your study centered on students, how they develop, ways they differ, and the exceptionalities that are sometimes found in them. Your efforts shifted in chapters 6-8 to the nature of the learning process itself. With an understanding of the learner and the learning process as context, this section of the text has focused on motivation and what teachers can do to increase it and now on the management of student behavior. At first glance, it may seem that little relationship exists between motivation and management, but this isn't the case. The two are strongly related, and rarely do we see highly motivated students in classrooms that are not orderly.

Classroom management, which is the combination of classroom organization and teacher behaviors that lead to orderly learning environments, is often confused with discipline, the focus on teacher actions in response to student misbehavior. A major goal of classroom management is to develop student responsibility and self-management. Management and discipline continue to be some of teachers' most chronic classroom problems, particularly for those beginning their careers. Proficient management, on the other hand, leads to both increased student achievement and improved motivation.

Skilled managers begin with careful planning. When they plan, teachers consider the physical environment of their classrooms and the characteristics of their students. For instance, they insure that their displays are visible to all students, traffic areas are clear, and distractions are reduced or eliminated. Student development also affects planning; if they are teachers of kindergartners, for example, they make different plans than they do if they teach fifth, eighth or eleventh graders.

The cornerstone of efficient management is a well-designed system of procedures--the routines that students follow in their daily activities--and rules, which provide the standards for student behavior. To be most effective, teachers prepare a small number of clearly stated rules, they allow the students to provide input into their preparation, and they provide reasons for the rules' existence.

Effective managers tend to be democratic--a combination of sincere caring for all the students together with making students responsible for their own behavior, and holding them accountable. They teach their procedures and rules just as they would teach any concept, principle, or skill. They provide examples of rule compliance and they have students practice procedures until they're essentially automatic. They begin the process the very first day of school, and they continue to monitor rules and procedures throughout the year.

Just as reading, writing, and arithmetic are considered basic skills for learners, essential management skills exist for teachers. They must be well organized and able to maintain the momentum of their lessons while at the same time being constantly aware of what all students are doing all of the time. They communicate clearly, and their verbal and nonverbal behaviors are consistent. They are neither passive or hostile in their dealings with students, but rather assertive, an appropriate middle ground.

Communicating with parents is another essential component of classroom management. Through communication teachers can increase student achievement and create more positive attitudes toward school. Obstacles to communication include economic, cultural and language barriers. Early and continued communication efforts help overcome these obstacles.

While careful planning and well designed and conducted lessons eliminates many management problems before they start, students inevitably break rules. When they do, teachers must intervene. Constructive interventions are brief, teachers follow through to be certain students comply with the rules, and rules are enforced consistently. All the while, they are careful to help students' maintain dignity and self-esteem.

Interventions vary depending on the degree to which the infraction disrupts the class. The least disruptive infractions can be ignored, or alternative, desirable behaviors can be reinforced. Slightly more disruptive behaviors, such as whispering during seatwork, can often be eliminated with simple desists--directives to stop the behavior. More serious infractions, such as chronic talking, or continually leaving seats without permission require the consistent application of consequences.

Severe management problems, such as defiance or violence, require both immediate, short-term attention and longer-term solutions that deal with the sources of the problem. Teachers should immediately get help in the case of a violent or defiant student, and not attempt to solve the problem alone.

Classroom climate is a critical factor in the success of any management system. If students feel that teachers genuinely care about them as individuals and about their learning, many of the common classroom problems disappear. Without this climate, truly effective management is very difficult to accomplish.

# CHAPTER TEN
# MANAGING STUDENT BEHAVIOR

## CHAPTER-AT-A-GLANCE

| MAIN TOPICS | KEY POINTS | KEY TERMS |
|---|---|---|
| Classroom Management and Discipline | • Classroom management includes the teacher planning and classroom behaviors that lead to a safe and orderly learning environment.<br>• Discipline refers to teacher behavior in direct response to student misbehavior.<br>• Students achieve higher and are more motivated in well managed classrooms than they are in poorly managed classrooms. | • Classroom management, 489<br>• Discipline, 489 |
| Planning: The Key to Preventing Management Problems | • Effective managers carefully plan for classroom management. They build their management system around a well crafted system of procedures and rules.<br>• In planning procedures and rules teachers should consider both the characteristics of their students and the physical environment of their classrooms.<br>• Procedures guide students in their daily routines, and rules provide the standards for acceptable behavior.<br>• Rules should be stated positively, rationales should be provided, and students should be allowed input into the rules. The list of rules should be kept short.<br>• Consequences for breaking rules and consequences for obeying rules should be clear and predictable for students. | • Procedures, 495<br>• Rules, 495<br>• Basic rules, 499 |
| Making Rules and Procedures Work | • Rules and procedures should be taught with examples and nonexamples just as any concept would be taught. Once taught, rules and procedures must be continually monitored to be effective. | |

| Preventing Problems: Putting Plans Into Practice | • Teachers who are effective managers are typically democratic--a combination of genuine caring for students together with making students responsible for their own behavior and holding them accountable for their actions.<br>• Skilled managers realize that the beginning of the school year is critical. They begin to establish their management patterns for the year the first day of school, and they immediately open lines of communication with parents.<br>• Effective managers are effective teachers. They are well organized, they maintain the force and flow of lessons, and they are able to simultaneously deal with minor management problems without disrupting the continuity of their learning activities.<br>• Effective managers communicate clearly. Their verbal and nonverbal behaviors are consistent, and they actively listen to their students. They are neither hostile nor passive; rather they are assertive and evenhanded. | • Caring, 503<br>• Firmness, 503<br>• Organization, 505<br>• Lesson movement, 506<br>• Withitness, 506<br>• Overlapping, 507<br>• Momentum, 508<br>• Smoothness, 509<br>• Nonverbal behavior, 509<br>• "I-message," 511<br>• Active listening, 513 |
|---|---|---|
| Accommodating Diversity: Communication With Parents | • Communication between home and school enables a partnership to occur that increases achievement and encourages better attitudes and behaviors.<br>• Obstacles to parental involvement include economic, cultural, and language barriers.<br>• Strategies for involving parents include early communication through letters, orientation meetings, and continued communication through notes, telephone and other proactive efforts. | |
| Interventions: Dealing with Misbehavior | • In spite of careful planning and effective instruction, disruptions will inevitably occur. When they happen, effective managers keep the encounters short, they follow through to be certain that the disruptive behavior has been completely stopped, they are consistent, and they don't get trapped into arguments with students.<br>• The type of intervention a teacher chooses depends on the severity of the disruption; minor incidents can often be ignored or alternate desirable behaviors can be reinforced. Simple desists will stop other behaviors, and consequences can be applied when the behavior is more disruptive.<br>• Absolute consistency is critical in dealing with chronic misbehavior.<br>• Teachers should not attempt to handle serious disruptions or violent students alone.<br>• Short term strategies for dealing with serious management problems stop the behavior and protect the victim; long term solutions deal with the problem comprehensively and instructionally. | • Consequences, 521<br>• Assertive Discipline, 523<br>• Desist, 528 |

*CHAPTER TEN*
*MANAGING STUDENT BEHAVIOR*

<u>GUIDED REVIEW</u>

CLASSROOM MANAGEMENT AND DISCIPLINE

Classroom management includes all the things teachers do to establish and maintain an orderly learning environment. Discipline is a subset of management; it refers to teachers' behaviors that directly respond to student misbehavior.

(10-1) Identify teachers' four most commonly cited management concerns. (p. 489)

_____

_____

(10-2) Describe three reasons that management problems continue to exist. (pp. 490-491)

_____

_____

(10-3) What are the two major goals of classroom management? Which of these is more long term? (pp. 490-491)

_____

_____

(10-4) Identify two important outcomes of effective management. (pp. 491-492)

_____

_____

PLANNING: THE KEY TO PREVENTING MANAGEMENT PROBLEMS:

Careful planning can eliminate many management problems before they occur. Well crafted plans take the physical environment and the characteristics of the students into account, and they are built around an efficient system of procedures and rules.

(10-5) Imagine that you are a 1st grade teacher, and that you have friends who teach 5th, 8th, and 11th grades, respectively. Describe the general characteristics of each of your classes, and specifically describe how each of you will plan to accommodate those characteristics. (pp. 493-494)

_____

_____

(10-6) Identify three factors in the physical environment that you should consider when you plan, and give an example that illustrates each. (pp. 493-495)

_____

_____

(10-7) Explain how procedures and rules differ. Give at least three examples of classroom procedures. (p. 495)

_____

_____

_____

(10-8) Consider the rule, "Don't talk out." Rewrite this rule to state it more clearly. (p. 498)

_____

_____

(10-9) Consider the rule, "Don't speak without permission." Rewrite the rule so it is stated in positive terms. (pp. 498-499)

_____

(10-10) Explain why the list of rules should be kept short, particularly for young children. (p. 498)

_____

_____

(10-11) Look at the case studies on pages 500 and 501 in your text. How is the way Martha Oakes taught her procedure and the way Jordi Arrese taught his rule similar to the way concepts are effectively taught? (pp. 500-501) (Hint: Think about your study of chapter 8. What is critical in order to teach concepts effectively?)

_____

_____

(10-12) Mr. McCoy comments to his 5th graders, "We've been doing mostly a good job of following our procedures, but I see some of you are getting up and putting papers in your folders before you've completely finished your assignments. Now, let's review the process again." What does Mr. McCoy's behavior illustrate? Explain. (p. 501)

_____

_____

## PREVENTING PROBLEMS: PUTTING PLANS INTO PRACTICE

You have designed a well crafted set of procedures and rules and have carefully taught them using examples and nonexamples, in the same way you would teach any concept. You now want to put the plans into practice to eliminate management problems before they get started. Your personal characteristics, the beginning of the school year, communication with parents, and essential management skills are important in this process.

(10-13) You are sitting in a classroom watching a teacher. Identify at least three specific behaviors that the teacher might display that would allow you to infer that he or she is a democratic teacher. (pp. 503-504)

_____

_____

(10-14) You are a new teacher in a new school, anticipating your first day with the students. Describe specifically what you will do on the first day and what you will do during the first week to establish the patterns you want for the remainder of the year. (pp. 504-505)

_____

_____

_____

Essential management skills are the specific behaviors that effective managers demonstrate regardless of the grade level, type of students, or topic being taught. They include lesson organization, lesson movement, and communication.

(10-15) You are sitting in a classroom at 10:13 in the morning. Students are filing into the room, anticipating the start of class, scheduled for 10:15. You sit through the entire class. Identify four specific behaviors you would expect from the teacher indicating that she is well organized. Give an example of each. (p. 505-506)

_____

_____

(10-16) Describe a classroom example of a teacher displaying each of the three features of withitness. (pp. 506-507)

_____

_____

(10-17) Describe lesson momentum. Give an example of each of the four factors that detract from lesson momentum. (pp. 508)

_____

_____

_____

_____

(10-18) Describe lesson smoothness. Give an example of each of the three factors that detract from lesson smoothness. (pp. 509)

_____

_____

(10-19) Write a brief original case study--examples appear on page 510 of your text--that illustrates congruent verbal and nonverbal communication. Write another brief case study that illustrates verbal and nonverbal behavior that are incongruent. (pp. 509-510)

_____

_____

_____

(10-20) A student turns around in the middle of your presentations and starts laughing. Give an example of an "I-Message." Include each of the features of "I-Messages" in the example. (pp. 510-511)

_____

_____

_____

(10-21) In the middle of a lesson, Sharon blurts out, "I'm thirsty. Can I get a drink of water?" Provide an example of a passive, hostile, and assertive teacher response. (p. 512)

_____

_____

(10-22) Write a brief case study illustrating active listening. Include each of the elements of active listening in it. (pp. 513)

_____

_____

_____

## ACCOMMODATING DIVERSITY: COMMUNICATION WITH PARENTS

Communication with parents is helpful with all students, but is especially valuable in working with students from different cultural, ethnic and socioeconomic backgrounds. Communication helps build a partnership that benefits both students and their parents.

(10-23) What are some of the benefits of communication with the home? From a management perspective which of these do you think is most important? (p. 515)

_____

_____


(10-24) Name and describe three barriers to greater parental involvement. (pp. 516-517)

_____

_____


## INTERVENTIONS: DEALING WITH MISBEHAVIOR

You have carefully planned and taught your rules and procedures. Your lessons are smooth and they have momentum. You know what's going on in your classroom, and you communicate clearly. In spite of these efforts, some management problems will occur and you will have to intervene.

(10-25) When using behavioral consequences for misbehavior what two decisions need to be made? (pp. 520-522)

_____

_____

_____


(10-26) Identify the five guidelines for successfully intervening in cases of misbehavior. Give a brief example of each. (pp. 524-537)

_____

_____

_____


(10-27) Give examples of student behaviors where you would respond in each of the following ways: Ignoring the behavior, praising an alternate behavior, using a desist, and applying consequences. (pp. 527-528)

_____

_____

(10-28) What is the major advantage of using logical consequences in dealing with misbehavior? (pp. 529-530)

_____

_____

_____

(10-29) You have a student who is a chronic "talker" in class. He is very social and loves whispering and minor horseplay during lessons and seatwork. His behavior hovers on the line of almost-bad-enough to be called seriously disruptive. Identify the one thing that you must do in order to eliminate this chronic misbehavior. (pp. 530-531)

_____

(10-30) You have a student that defies one of your directives by openly refusing to comply. What should you do short and long term? (pp. 533-536)

_____

# CHAPTER TEN
# MANAGING STUDENT BEHAVIOR

## APPLICATION EXERCISES

Exercise 10.1

Exercise 10.1 measures your understanding of topics covered on pages 489-501 of your text.

1. Identify two factors in Judy Holmquist's physical environment in the opening case study that were less than ideal. One was out of her control. What might she have done about the other?

Read the following episode, then answer the questions about it.

    Joe, a fifth-grade teacher, stopped by to pick up Andrea, his fiancee and an eighth-grade science teacher. They fell into a discussion of student discipline and looked at Andrea's rules, which were listed in her classroom:
    1. Do not speak without permission.
    2. Do not laugh, snicker, make jokes, or in any way react to another student's answer.
    3. Do not leave your desk without permission.
    4. Be prepared and ready when class begins.
    "My list is similar," Joe commented, "except I don't have your second one."
    "I knew I would need it," Andrea responded, "so I laid it on them. And we work on it all the time. Every time it happens, I stop the class for a moment and we discuss it, and they have another example to think about. This is a tough one for junior high students.
    "I originally told them," she explained, "that part of the reason we were in school was to learn to respect each other and treat each other decently, and this rule would help us learn to do that."

2. How do Andrea's comment, "I knew I would need it," in reference to her second rule, and Joe's lack of a similar one relate to our discussion of student characteristics?

_____

_____

_____


3. Using one of the guidelines for forming rules as a basis, critique Andrea's first three rules.

_____

_____

_____

4. Using a different guideline than in question 3, critique Andrea's fourth rule.

_____

_____

5. Using a third guideline, criticize Andrea's second rule in the context of her remark, "so I laid it on them."

_____

_____

6. How does Andrea's comment, "And we work on it all the time," illustrate our discussion about making rules and procedures work?

_____

_____

7. How does Andrea's comment in the last paragraph illustrate one of the guidelines suggested for forming rules?

_____

_____

Exercise 10.2

Exercise 10.2 measures your understanding of topics covered on pages 501-513 of your text.

1. Look again at the examples with Vicki Williams and Donnell Alexander on page 504. Identify two important characteristics of effective organization present in Donnell's case that were missing in Vicki's.

_____

_____

2. Identify at least three characteristics of a democratic classroom that Judy Holmquist demonstrated in our opening case study.

_____

_____

3. Identify at least three examples of withitness and an additional example of overlapping in Judy's behavior in our case study at the beginning of the chapter.

_____

_____

_____

4. Identify at least three specific instances where Judy demonstrated effective communication behaviors in her lesson, and identify the type of communication in each instance.

_____

_____

_____

_____

5. Mr. Adams's class is off-task and disruptive when they are supposed to be doing seatwork. He says, "If you don't do your homework, you'll flunk the test; if you flunk the test, you could flunk the course; if you flunk the course, you'll have to go to summer school. Now none of us wants to go to summer school, do we? So let's get started on our homework."

What concept from our discussion of essential teaching skills was Mr. Adams demonstrating, and what would have been a more effective approach to getting his students on-task?

_____

_____

_____

6. Look again at Isabelle Rodriguez's work with her ninth graders on page 510 of your text. Analyze the effectiveness of her behavior, using the concepts of withitness and overlapping as the basis for your assessment.

_____

_____

7. Translate the following into "I-messages" using the guidelines in the last section.

a. "No assignment? We're never going to learn that way!"

_____

b. "Felicia, be quiet! We can't just blurt out the answers."

_____

c. "Sean, turn around. I like the front of your head better."

_____


Exercise 10.3

Exercise 10.3 measures your understanding of topics covered on pages 513-536 of your text.

Alberto Mancini is an eighth-grade math teacher. He has finished an explanation of decimals and percents, and has assigned the students their homework for the next day. He is circulating among the students when Heather gets up, goes to her locker at the back of the room, and noisily shuffles materials in it.

"Heather," Alberto says evenly, "we don't leave our seats without permission."

"I'm just getting some stuff out of my locker," she shoots back.

Alberto walks up to her, looks her in the eye, and says quietly, "I want you to sit down now."

"I need this stuff. You let Karen go to her locker."

"Heather, you know the rules. That's a behavior point lost."

Heather stomps to her desk and loudly slams her books on the floor.

Alberto steps up to her and whispers, "That's a second point, Heather. Please see me after class."

Heather stops after class, and sits down sullenly. Alberto pulls his chair out from behind his desk and sits facing her directly. "Do you have anything you want to say?" he queries.

She sits sullenly, saying nothing.

"If you have anything that you would like to say to me privately, Heather, I'll be happy to listen anytime," he says, leaning toward her. He hesitates a few seconds, then continues, "Now, let me get to the point so we both understand. We must have rules in our classroom, as we discussed at the beginning of the year. I am going to enforce the rules," he continues emphasizing the last sentence and leaning forward again. "It's your choice to break them or not break them, and you know the results.

"I know that you understand what happened today," he continues pleasantly, "but I'll briefly outline it for you to be sure it's clear. . . . Karen asked for permission, and I gave it. She quietly and quickly went to her locker. I believe that you knew you were breaking the rule, and I believe you also know now that you were being disrespectful to your classmates, yourself, and me by slamming your books on the floor. I'll be calling your parents tonight to explain why you'll be serving detention tomorrow. . . . I'll expect to see no more of this in the future," Alberto says pleasantly, getting up. "Here's a tardy slip that will get you into Mrs. Evans's class."

The next morning, Alberto greets the class as he always does and treats Heather as if nothing happened the day before.

1. Using the guidelines and concepts developed in the section on interventions, write an analysis of Alberto's effectiveness in dealing with Heather. Use illustrations taken directly from the example in your description.

_____

_____

_____

_____

_____

_____   _____


2. Identify at least three examples of effective preventive management techniques that Alberto employed in dealing with Heather. Use illustrations taken directly from the example in your description.

_____

_____

_____

_____

# CHAPTER TEN
# MANAGING STUDENT BEHAVIOR

SELF-HELP QUIZ _____

TRUE/FALSE QUESTIONS. Write T in the blank if the statement is true and write F if the statement is false.

_____ 1. The concept classroom management and the concept discipline mean the same thing.

_____ 2. In general, students are more motivated in well managed classrooms.

_____ 3. The process of planning and administering rules and procedures for first graders is essentially the same as it would be for fifth graders.

_____ 4. Rules are a subset of procedures.

_____ 5. Rules are very important for beginning teachers, but veterans rarely use them.

_____ 6. Rules and procedures are essentially concepts and should be taught the same way any concept is taught.

_____ 7. If rules and procedures are taught well enough at the beginning of the year, monitoring them later on should not be necessary.

_____ 8. Being firm is the most important characteristic a teacher can possess if he or she is to be an effective manager.

_____ 9. Withitness means that a teacher has carefully planned and is well organized when he or she enters the classroom.

_____10. Minor disruptions by students can be appropriately ignored by teachers.

MULTIPLE-CHOICE ITEMS. Circle the best response in each case.

Use the following description for items 11-13.

You are a 7th grade science teacher conducting a lesson on plant parts and the function of each of the parts. You begin the lesson by reaching down behind your desk and picking up a large plant that you bought at a flower shop. You show the students the different plant parts, and as you're explaining the functions of each part, Rodney begins poking Jennifer with a ruler. At the same time Jimmy is whispering to Susan across the aisle.

11. If you are "withit" which of the following best describes how you should respond?
    a.   First stop Jimmy's whispering, since it is least serious, and then concentrate on Rodney.
    b.   First stop Rodney and then stop Jimmy.
    c.   Stop Rodney immediately and ignore Jimmy.
    d.   Stop the lesson and discuss the rule about keeping hands and feet to yourself with the whole class.

12.  Which of the following best describes "overlapping?"
    a.   Stop the lesson and discuss the rule about keeping hands and feet to yourself with the whole class while making eye contact with Rodney.
    b.   While you're explaining the functions of the plant parts move over to Rodney, take his ruler, and continue standing by him for a moment.
    c.   Stop the lesson briefly, admonish Rodney, and then continue with the lesson.
    d.   Stop the lesson briefly, tell Rodney to put his ruler away, tell Jimmy to stop whispering, and continue with the lesson.

13. Having the plant behind your desk at the beginning of the lesson best illustrates:
    a.   lesson organization.
    b.   lesson smoothness.
    c.   lesson momentum.
    d.   lesson overlapping.

14. A chemistry teacher is discussing the charge on common ions. After discussing several of the elements, he says, "Oh, by the way, don't forget to turn in your review problems tomorrow." After a few questions about the problems, he again begins discussing ions and their charges. Which of the following is the best assessment of this incident?
   a.   His behavior will detract from lesson momentum.
   b.   His behavior demonstrates his ability with overlapping.
   c.   His behavior will detract from lesson smoothness.
   d.   His behavior demonstrates withitness, since he remembered to remind the students about their assignment.

15. On Tuesday, after teaching his students that his students that adjectives modify nouns and pronouns, Mr. Grimes gives a seatwork assignment in which the students are required to identify adjectives and the nouns or pronouns they modify in sentences. In monitoring the students during their seatwork, he finds that the students seem to understand the topic very well, with only two of the sentences giving the students any trouble. On Wednesday, Mr. Grimes goes over the assignment carefully, discussing each of the sentences and identifying the adjectives and the nouns or pronouns they identify in each case.
   Which of the following concepts most accurately describes Mr. Grimes's teaching on Wednesday?
   a.   Organization, which increased lesson overlapping.
   b.   Overdwelling, which detracted from lesson momentum.
   c.   Intrusions, which detracted from lesson smoothness.
   d.   Pacing, which increased lesson smoothness.

16. Karen Johnson's 10th graders are working on their next day's English homework as she circulates among them. She is bending over helping Leroy when Jeff and Mike begin whispering loudly behind her.
   "Jeff. Mike. Stop talking and get started on your homework," she says glancing over her shoulder. The boys slow their whispering, and Karen turns back to Leroy. Soon they are whispering as loudly as ever.
   "I thought I told you to stop talking," Karen says over her shoulder again, this time with a hint of irritation in her voice.
   The boys glance at her and quickly resume whispering.
   Which of the following best describes the above incident?
   a.   Karen is demonstrating effective overlapping since she attends to a management incident at the same time she conducts instruction.
   b.   Karen is demonstrating ineffective communication, since her verbal and nonverbal behavior are incongruent.
   c.   Karen is demonstrating effective lesson momentum, since most of the students are working diligently.
   d.   Karen is demonstrating ineffective communication, since she didn't actively listen to the students.

17. You have a rule that prohibits talking without permission. As your 5th graders are doing seatwork, Sonja briefly whispers something across the aisle and then resumes working. Based on the discussion of the "intervention continuum" in the chapter, which of the following is the best course of action.
   a.   Ignore the behavior since it was brief.
   b.   "Desist" the behavior immediately, to prevent it from happening again.
   c.   Openly praise one of the students who is working conscientiously and diligently.
   d.   Remind Sonja of the rule, and suggest that she come to you if she has a question.

18.      Mrs. Harkness is teaching the rule, "Bring all needed materials to class each day," to her students. She discusses the rule, provides examples, and then places considerable emphasis on why the rule is important. Of the following, the best prediction of the grade level Mrs. Harkness teaches is:
   a.   first grade.
   b.   fifth grade.
   c.   seventh grade.
   d.   tenth grade.

19. Which of the following rules is best stated?
    a.    Do not speak unless you are called on by the teacher.
    b.    Always come to class prepared.
    c.    Avoid embarrassing your classmates.
    d.    Leave your desk only when given permission.

20. One of your sixth graders has been chronically disruptive. You warn him, he stops briefly, and then becomes disruptive again. You state, "Please go to the timeout area." He looks at you and says, "Do I have to?"
 Of the following, your best course of action is:
    a.    Assertively restate your demand, reminding him of the consequences for defiance.
    b.    Explain to him the reason for the no-talking rule and leave it at that.
    c.    Ask him why he is refusing to comply with your demand.
    d.    Send him a non-verbal signal to be quiet.

# CHAPTER ELEVEN
## PLANNING FOR INSTRUCTION

## CHAPTER OUTLINE _____

## CHAPTER OBJECTIVES

- Explain the different uses for planning.
- Identify the different aspects of the instructional process.
- Describe the role of objectives in planning.
- Identify different kinds of objectives.
- Explain how task analysis can be used in the planning process.
- Identify objectives in the three domains of learning.
- Explain the relationship between long term, unit, weekly, and daily lesson plans.
- Describe the results of planning research.

## CHAPTER OVERVIEW

Teacher planning is a complex process in which teachers select topics, form goals, organize content, select and sequence learning activities, and consider management, motivation and evaluation. Planning performs three major functions: it provides emotional security for the teacher; it helps organize instruction for students; and it provides an opportunity for reflection about goals and purposes. The products of planning, typically teacher notes and plans, provide a false impression of the enormous amounts of work that go into the process.

The Linear Rational Model proposed by Ralph Tyler describes planning as a logical, sequential process in which teachers specify objectives, select and organize learning activities, and design evaluation procedures. Central to this model is the construction of behavioral objectives which describe in observable, performance terms what the learner will be able to do at the end of instruction.

Task analysis is a useful tool of organizing and sequencing learning activities. It breaks complex knowledge and skills into substeps through a sequential process that first specifies the terminal behavior, then identifies requisite skills, sequences these skills, and then diagnoses students' entry skills level.

Planning is a nested process in which individual daily lesson plans are embedded with larger, more global and more comprehensive plans. The process starts with long-term plans that map out the year's or semester's work in terms of topics and dates. Unit plans convert these global plans into specific, integrated plans of action for periods of two or three weeks. Weekly plans adjust unit plans to the realities of school calendars. Finally, lesson plans help teachers deliver daily instruction in concrete ways.

Planning goals can be divided into three areas or domains--cognitive, affective, and psychomotor. Cognitive objectives focus on knowing and understanding facts, concepts, principles, rules and skills as well as problem-solving. Bloom's Taxonomy provides a way to sequence objectives in the cognitive domain. The affective domain deals with attitudes and values, and an affective taxonomy based on internalization can also be used to sequence objectives. A third taxonomy in the psychomotor domain focuses on the development of coordination and strength.

Research reveals that because objectives are often either implied in the learning activity or supplied to the teacher they often aren't a starting point for teacher planning. However, objectives play an important role in the development of professional vocabulary and skills and can be a powerful tool for teacher analysis and reflection.

# CHAPTER ELEVEN
# STUDENT DEVELOPMENT:
# APPLICATIONS

## CHAPTER-AT-A-GLANCE

| MAIN TOPICS | KEY POINTS | KEY TERMS |
|---|---|---|
| Teacher Planning | • Planning is a complex consideration of content, student needs, materials available, and management.<br>• Written plans range from elaborately detailed documents to cryptic notes. | |
| Planning Functions | • Planning offers emotional security to teachers; this insecurity may be due to lack of experience or unfamiliarity with content.<br>• Planning aids the teacher by forming an organizational link between curriculum and instruction.<br>• Planning allows teachers the opportunity to reflect on their own teaching and its effect on student learning. | • Reflection, 547 |
| Planning: The Linear Rational Model | • The steps of the Linear Rational Model are: 1) stating behavioral objectives, 2) preparing and organizing learning activities consistent with the objectives, and 3) designing evaluations that match the objectives and the learning activities.<br>• Mager's objectives have an observable behavior, the conditions under which the behavior is demonstrated, and the criterion for acceptable performance.<br>• Gronlund's objectives have a general goal followed by specific behaviors providing evidence that the goal has been reached.<br>• Task analysis consists of specifying what the students will accomplish, sequencing the subskills required, and diagnosing which of these skills students lack. | • Linear Rational Model, 548<br>• Behavioral objectives, 549<br>• Mager's objectives, 549<br>• Gronlund's objectives, 549<br>• Task analysis, 551 |
| Comprehensive Planning: Long-Term, Unit, Weekly, and Individual Lesson Plans | • Long-term plans are descriptions of broad topics to be covered over a period of time such as a year, a semester or a grading period.<br>• Unit plans take long-term plans and organize them into smaller segments based on central topics or themes.<br>• Weekly plans fit unit plans into a particular week, specifying what is expected to be accomplished within that given time frame.<br>• Daily lesson plans delineate the particulars of what will be taught and how it will be done for a specific lesson. | • Long-term plans, 553<br>• Unit plans, 554<br>• Weekly plans, 554<br>• Lesson planning, 555 |

| | | |
|---|---|---|
| Domains of Instruction | • Teachers' goals may fall in the cognitive domain, which focuses on knowledge, understanding, and intellectual skills; the affective domain, which includes attitudes and values; or the psychomotor domain, which examines physical skills and abilities.<br>• Taxonomies help to classify objectives in each domain into different levels requiring different learner behaviors. | • Cognitive domain, 558<br>• Bloom's Taxonomy, 558<br>• Affective domain, 560<br>• Psychomotor domain, 561 |
| Planning: Research Results | • State and school district curriculum requirements commonly use behavioral objectives as their framework.<br>• Veteran teachers include the elements of the Linear Rational Model in their planning but don't follow the sequence or write out complete plans. | |
| Planning: Implications for Teacher Training and Practice | • The Linear Rational Model and the objectives within it provide an effective model to help teachers think through the planning process even though they may not apply it the way it was originally designed. | |

# CHAPTER ELEVEN
# PLANNING FOR INSTRUCTION

## GUIDED REVIEW

### TEACHER PLANNING

Planning is a complex process that requires both practice and effort. The physical written product of teacher planning depends on the experience and needs of the individual teacher. The planning process is also on-going, taking place before, during, and after the actual act of teaching a lesson.

(11-1) A teacher is planning a lesson on insects. Select a grade level perspective with which you are comfortable, and then suggest questions for each of the planning components below that this teacher might need to ask and answer in the process of making planning decisions. For example, for "organization of content" an elementary teacher might ask, "Should I expose students to examples of insects first and study similarities and differences, or should I define insects, present examples, and then explore their habitats?" (p. 545)

- Grade level:

_____

- Organization of content

_____

_____   _____

- Selection of learning activities

_____

_____

- Sequence of learning activities

_____

_____

- Student grouping

_____

_____

- Assignments

_____

_____

- Grading practices

_____

_____

- Classroom management

_____

_____

- Student motivation

_____

_____

- Student emotional well-being

_____

_____

- Social interaction

_____

_____

## PLANNING FUNCTIONS

Planning fulfills three primary functions: emotional security, organization, and reflection. Again, the written plan may not appear to reflect all of these functions, but the process is more than the written product.

(11-2) Reread the scenario about Vicki Williams and Karen Stevens on p. 508 in the text. Predict how the planning that each teacher did will affect her emotional security. (pp. 545-546)

_____

_____

How did the organization of the two teachers affect each one's classroom? (pp. 546-547)

_____

_____

What might Vicki and Karen each conclude upon reflecting over the day's outcomes? (pp. 547-548)

_____

_____

## PLANNING:  THE LINEAR RATIONAL MODEL

The Linear Rational Model is a logical, sequential method for relating planning and instruction.  Although it has been criticized, it still can be a valuable planning and teaching tool.

(11-3) List the four steps of the Linear Rational Model:  (pp. 549)

_____

_____

_____

_____

(11-4)  Select one content area within each of the domains of instruction (see Tables 11.5, 11.6 and 11.7 for examples).  Write an example of an objective for each using first Mager's approach and then Gronlund's.  (pp. 549-550)

I. Cognitive domain:

_____

A._____

_____(Mager's)

B. _____

_____(Gronlund's)

II. Affective domain:

_____

A._____

_____(Mager's)

B._____

_____(Gronlund's)

III. Psychomotor domain: _____

    A. _____

    _____ (Mager's)


    B. _____

    _____ (Gronlund's)


(11-5) After writing objectives using both formats, which do you prefer? Why? (p. 549-550)

_____

_____

_____


(11-6) Select one of the objectives from exercise 11-4 and suggest five different learning activities that could be used to teach the content or skill in that objective. (pp. 550-551)

_____

_____

_____


(11-7) Perform a task analysis on the content or skill selected in exercise 11-6. The steps are broken down for you below. (pp. 551-553)

● Terminal behavior

_____

● Prerequisite subskills

_____

_____

● Sequence of subskills

_____

_____

•Diagnosis of students (Lacking students, how would you determine which students had the prerequisite subskills required?)

_____

_____

(11-8) Design an evaluation item that could be used to determine whether or not a student had accomplished the objective selected for the task analysis in exercise 11-7.  (p. 553)

_____

_____

## COMPREHENSIVE PLANNING:  LONG-TERM, UNIT, WEEKLY, AND INDIVIDUAL LESSON PLANS

Each step in the planning process builds on the previous one to form a coherent workable whole.  Although planning can be time-consuming, especially at first, the result can directly influence teacher effectiveness on a daily basis.

(11-9)  Classify each of the following as a characteristic of long-term planning (L), unit planning (U), weekly planning (W) or individual lesson planning (I).  (pp. 553-555)

_____  often finalized on Friday afternoon or over the weekend

_____  typically covers a time period of 2 to 3 weeks

_____  specifies an objective, procedures, and evaluation method

_____  must take into consideration holidays, assemblies, etc.

_____  serves as basic framework for all other planning

_____  often based on chapters in students' texts or groups of objectives from curriculum guides

_____  describes broad topics with very general time lines

_____  specifies materials to be used

(11-10)  Construct a plan statement for each of the areas below in one particular subject area as if you were a teacher beginning the year or semester.  (pp. 553-555)

• Long-term plan

_____

_____

- Unit plan

_____

_____

- Week plan

_____

_____

- Lesson plan

_____

_____

## DOMAINS OF INSTRUCTION

We sometimes forget that we teach more than just content in the classroom. Values and attitudes are an important outcome of a student's education. Students also are bound by the physical abilities and skills that they bring with them to the classroom. Teachers need to be aware of the attitudes (the affective domain) and the physical skills (the psychomotor domain) that they teach as well as the intellectual (the cognitive domain).

(11-11) Complete the following chart showing the types of goals, levels of objectives and an original example for each of the domains. (pp. 558-562)

|  | Type of Goals | Levels of Objectives | Original Example |
|---|---|---|---|
| Cognitive Domain |  |  |  |
| Affective Domain |  |  |  |
| Psychomotor Domain |  |  |  |

(11-12) Classify the following activities as cognitive (C), affective (A), or psychomotor (P). (pp. 558-562)

_____ turning off the TV in order to read a book

_____ writing an essay about energy

_____ building a birdhouse using wood scraps and nails

_____ stretching before running or skiing

_____ translating a letter in English from a pen pal in Mexico

_____ contributing canned goods to a community food bank

_____ doing flash cards with a younger third grade sibling

_____ debating the pros and cons of freedom of speech

_____ learning to play ping pong

PLANNING: RESEARCH RESULTS

Because of its importance in the teaching process, planning has often been a topic of research, especially in the area of behavioral objectives.

(11-13) What are the main criticisms of behavioral objectives?  (p. 563)

_____

_____

_____

(11-14) Why are behavioral objectives still used and by whom?  (p. 563-565)

_____

_____

_____

(11-15) Give three reasons why veteran teachers don't usually write objectives and detailed plans.  (pp. 566-567)

_____

_____

_____

PLANNING:  IMPLICATIONS FOR TEACHER TRAINING AND PRACTICE

(11-16) If research reveals that veterans teachers don't write lesson plans, why should beginning teachers learn to do so?  (p. 568)

_____

_____

# CHAPTER ELEVEN
# PLANNING FOR INSTRUCTION

## APPLICATION EXERCISES

Exercise 11.1

Exercise 11.1 measures your understanding of topics covered on pages 545-561 of your text.

1. The objective in Mai Ling's lesson plan has elements of both Mager's and Gronlund's approaches to writing objectives. Identify these elements.

2. Laurie Zentz is an elementary teacher studying Native Americans from different regions of the country.

"At the beginning of the school year, I had decided that my students should have a better understanding and appreciation of other cultures. When I saw a chapter in the social studies book on Indians, I decided to focus on their culture and life-style.
"My major goal was to have the students see these different Native American tribes as people.
"When we're finished, they'll be able to tell me where these Indians lived when I describe their life-style," Laurie comments in describing her unit. "I show a couple of films that really do a good job of illustrating the characteristics of each tribe, and then we have 'Native American Day' when kids dress up in native costume and explain how the tribe they represent worked and lived,' she went on. "I also give them a solid test on the stuff. I have some drawings and descriptions of hypothetical groups, and they have to tell me where the groups would live based on the information I give.
"It's a lot of work," she comments finally. "We have to find a day when we can invite the other grades in to see our 'village,' and getting all the presentations scheduled is a mess. But it's worth it. They get a lot out of it, and they like it."

a. Identify each of the elements of the Tyler model in Laurie's description of her planning.

b. We identified three primary functions of planning in the section. Based on Laurie's comments, identify which was most important for her, and provide a rationale for your explanation. Is it likely that Laurie is a classroom rookie, or is she probably a veteran?

c. Identify an example of long-term, unit, and individual lesson planning in the description.

3. The following is an excerpt from a case study of a first-year English teacher in an inner city school attempting to teach students to write a five-paragraph essay. How might task analysis have helped?

We read how to select and narrow a topic, how to evolve a thesis statement, how to construct an outline, how to prepare a first draft, how to proofread and revise. . . . Then came the true test--the essay assignment. . . . Talking about essays had been so comfortable; now they had to write one. . . . When only about a third of the students in each class submitted outlines, I know disaster had struck. Even fewer essays materialized on the due date. Most were rambling, unfocused efforts in one or two poorly written paragraphs. Almost no one had successfully applied even the most basic concepts we had been studying for five entire weeks! (Shulman & Colbert, 1987, p. 7)

Exercise 11.2

Exercise 11.2 measures your understanding of topics covered on pages 561-577 of your text.

1. Look again at the objectives related to adjective on page 562 of your text. Classify each according to the levels of the cognitive taxonomy.

2. Charlie Jenks is working on a unit on folktales with his 10th grades. The following is the plan taken from his plan book:

> Folktales
> pp. 234-286
> Make folktales about them
> (F T abt Mrs. Marks)

"I start by showing them a couple of folktales that I wrote about teachers here at the school, and then we figure out what makes them folktales," Charlie commented in describing his unit. "Then I get them to compare what I wrote to stuff in their books, like 'Pecos Bill' and 'Paul Bunyan.' At the end of the unit, I give them some examples on a test and have them decide whether or not they're folktales.

I'm after two things," Charlie continued. "I think they need to understand what the characteristics of a folktale are, but in reality how important is it to their life, really? I used to emphasize the academic side of folktales. Some got it and some didn't. The ones that didn't were turned off to literature. So now my main concern is their attitude toward the unit. It went so well last year that some of them voluntarily wrote folktales. In fact, that's what I'm after for this year, and I'll just see how many of them do it. I'm going to tell them they can write a folktale about Mrs. Marks (the school principal) if they want to."

Complete the following on the basis of Charlie's description of his unit.

a.    Describe how the anecdote illustrates reflection on Charlie's part.

b.    Assume Charlie plans his unit as it's described in the conversation.
   • Discuss how he deviated from the Tyler model.
   • Describe how this practice is typical of veteran teachers.

c.    Identify Charlie's cognitive objective and its level.

d.    Identify Charlie's affective objective and its level.

# CHAPTER ELEVEN
# PLANNING FOR INSTRUCTION

SELF-HELP QUIZ _____

TRUE-FALSE QUESTIONS:  Write T in the blank if the statement is true or F if the statement is false.

_____ 1.  The amount of actual written planning done by teachers increases their tendency to stay focused on the topic being taught.

_____ 2.  According to Mager, a behavioral objective should state an observable behavior, the conditions under which the behavior will occur, and the materials necessary to perform the behavior.

_____ 3.  Gronlund feels that stating conditions and criteria in an objective is essential for regular classroom instruction.

_____ 4.  When a first grade teacher concludes that students must know how to write their numbers, count to ten, and count objects accurately before she teaches them simple addition, she has performed part of a task analysis.

_____ 5.  An example of a long-term plan for a junior high English teacher would be to cover short stories and poetry the first semester and to study novels and plays in the second.

_____ 6.  Objectives that require students to recall and comprehend knowledge are considered higher level objectives.

_____ 7.  Application, analysis, synthesis and evaluation level cognitive objectives and activities make up the major part of classroom questions, exercises, and tests.

_____ 8.  Staying after school throughout the winter to participate in extra band practices even though it means walking home in the dark is an example of a psychomotor outcome.

_____ 9.  The primary reason many states and school districts provide teachers with standardized behavioral objectives for specific subjects areas is to save teachers the time-consuming task of writing their own.

_____10.  Inexperienced teachers often use the Linear Rational Model while veterans usually only do so when required by their administrators.


MULTIPLE CHOICE QUESTIONS:  Circle the best answer for each question.

11.  When a teacher analyzes the effectiveness of an activity after it has been carried out to determine whether it needs adjusting for future use, what function of planning is being fulfilled?
   a.  Emotional security.
   b.  Organization.
   c.  Reflection.
   d.  None of the above.
   e.  All of the above.

12.  According to Mager, what is missing from the following objective?
   Given a mixed unlabelled list of familiar animals, the student will classify animals into the categories of vertebrate or invertebrate.
   a.  The objective is properly stated.
   b.  The condition is missing.
   c.  The observable behavior (performance) is missing.
      d.      The criteria is missing.

13. Which educator would have advocated the approach used to write the following objective?
    Goal: Understands mammals
    Specific behaviors:
        1. provides examples of mammals
        2. identifies mammals among other animals
        3. identifies characteristics of mammals

    a. Gronlund
    b. Bloom
    c. Mager
    d. Tyler

14. Which of the following is **NOT** a step in a task analysis?
    a. Ms. Gardner determines that her biology students need to be able to dissect a worm during a 45 minute lab class well enough to identify major organs and systems.
    b. She lists the material she will need: worms, dissecting instruments, disinfectant, labels, charts, and lab coats for day of the dissection.
    c. She knows from a previous quiz that some of her students will need to learn to identify some of the organs while others will need help with the fine motor skills required in the actual dissection process.
    d. Ms. Gardner makes a list of all the things that her students will need to know before the lab class in order to succeed at the activity planned.

15. Which phase of the Linear Rational Model is being planned when Ms. Gardner (in item 14) decides to ask her students to draw from memory a labelled diagram of their dissections the day following the lab class?
    a. Organizing learning activities.
    b. Designing evaluation procedures.
    c. Preparing learning activities.
    d. Specifying objectives.

16. At which level of Bloom's Taxonomy would the following activity be classified?

    After the teacher demonstrates the use of the formula for finding the area of a circle, $A = \pi r^2$, students are given new examples of circles for which to find the area on their own.
    a. Knowledge level.
    b. Evaluation level.
    c. Application level.
    d. Analysis level.

17. If students in item 16 were asked to draw and measure their own circles using compasses and rulers in addition to calculating the areas, in which domains of instruction would they be operating?
    a. Cognitive and affective.
    b. Cognitive and psychomotor.
    c. Affective and psychomotor.
    d. Cognitive, affective, and psychomotor.

18. Which of the following is a major criticism of behavioral objectives?
    a. Writing all the behavioral objectives for a course would be too time-consuming.
    b. There are no specific standards for the writing of behavioral objectives.
    c. Effective teaching can be accomplished without objectives, whether written or not.
    d. Curriculum experts cannot agree on which behavioral objectives are important and which are not.

19. Which of the following is NOT an explanation for why veterans teach without writing objectives and detailed plans?
   a. Veteran teachers can mentally store their plans in their heads and use only notes as reminders.
   b. Veteran teachers often start planning with a topic or an activity rather than an objective.
   c. Much of the subject matter taught by experienced teachers cannot be expressed in terms of objectives.
   d. Objectives for an activity are often implicit in the activity itself or embedded in criterion-referenced tests.

20. What can be concluded about the use of the Linear Rational Model in teacher training?
   a. New teachers should be trained to use the Linear Rational Model as it was written, because they will probably use it for their entire teaching careers.
   b. New teachers should not be trained to use the Linear Rational Model because it is outdated.
   c. Novice teachers, like veterans, can teach effectively by planning and carrying out lessons in their heads.
   d. The Linear Rational Model is a valuable conceptual tool to help beginning teachers thinking about their teaching and the planning process.

# CHAPTER TWELVE
# EFFECTIVE TEACHING

## CHAPTER OUTLINE

C. Phases of direct instruction
    1. Introduction and review
    2. Presentation
    3. Guided practice
    4. Independent practice
       a. Homework
D. Models of direct instruction
V. Beyond Effective Teaching: Helping Students Construct Knowledge
    A. Teaching from a Constructivist perspective: Misconceptions
    B. Teaching for understanding
VI. Teaching organized bodies of knowledge
    A. Organized bodies of knowledge
  B. The lecture
  C. Lecture-recitation
    1. Presenting information
    2. Comprehension monitoring
    3. Integration
VII. Discussions
    A. Characteristics of effective discussions
    1. Focus
    2. Student background knowledge
    3. Emphasis on understanding
    4. Student-student interaction
    B. Obstacles to effective discussions
VIII. Alternatives to Whole-Group Activities: Student Groupwork
    A. Groupwork: Promoting student involvement
    1. Planning and conducting groupwork activities
    2. Transitions to and from groupwork
    3. Working in pairs: Introducing groupwork
    4. Working with larger groups
    5. Groupwork with higher level tasks

## CHAPTER OBJECTIVES _____

- Describe the relationship between teachers' use of time and student learning
- Identify essential teaching skills in descriptions of teacher activities
- Identify the characteristics of effective teacher questioning
- Apply essential teaching skills to classroom practice
- Identify the common elements of different direct instruction models.
- Employ direct instruction in the teaching of procedural skills
- Identify the characteristics of instruction based on constructivism
- Describe the elements of the lecture-recitation method of teaching
- Identify the features of effective discussions
- Describe procedures for organizing and implementing student groupwork

## CHAPTER OVERVIEW

As you have moved through your text, your understanding of learning and the factors that impact it has gradually developed. You examined the characteristics of the people you will teach in chapters 2-5 and the nature of learning itself in chapters 6-8. The emphasis gradually shifted from the learner to the teacher in chapter 9, with the first part of the chapter devoted to different theoretical views of motivation and the second part focusing on the things teachers can do to promote motivation. The study of classroom management in chapter 10 continued the transition to teachers and teaching, demonstrating the positive effects of orderly classrooms on both motivation and achievement. In chapter 11 we began to focus on instruction and the need for careful planning.

We are now looking at instruction. We first consider effective teaching--the patterns of teacher behavior that increase learner achievement--and then we go beyond effective teaching to consider instruction from a constructivist perspective as well as alternatives to whole-group activities. As you study this chapter you will see that the content is closely related to the information you studied in chapters 9 and 10. That makes sense; expert teachers motivate their students and they are also effective managers.

One of the first things we notice about effective teachers is their efficient use of time. Allocated time is the amount designated for a particular content area or topic, such as elementary teachers designating an hour for math, or a middle school scheduling 50-minute periods.

Of the amount allocated, effective teachers spend little time on management factors such as taking roll, instead using most of the available time for instruction. In addition, they use teaching techniques that encourage students to stay on-task, or engaged, as much of the time as possible, and finally, they teach so that academic learning time--the amount of time students are engaged and successful is maximized.

Effective teachers, regardless of grade level, subject matter area, or topic, have personal characteristics and a repertoire of skills--called essential teaching skills--that increase student achievement. They have a positive approach to their teaching, they have high expectations for their students, they are good role models, and are caring and enthusiastic. (We also found in chapter 9 that these same characteristics promote student motivation.) Effective teachers are well organized; they start their classes on time, have materials prepared in advance, and minimize disruptions. They have well established classroom routines, all of which increase instructional time. This organization also promotes orderly classrooms, as we saw in chapter 10.

Effective teachers communicate clearly; they use precise language, their presentations are thematic and lead to a point, and they state specifically when one topic is ending and another is beginning. They appropriately emphasize important points.

Skilled teachers begin their lessons with attention getters, help maintain attention with something to look at, listen to, feel, taste, or smell, and they avoid the tendency to drift off the subject.

Students in effective teachers' classrooms are given prompt and specific feedback about their performance. The feedback is presented with a supportive manner, which helps maintain a safe learning environment for the students.

Effective teachers are responsive to students. They constantly monitor the students' verbal and nonverbal behaviors and they intervene at the first signs of uncertainty, confusion, or inattention.

As lessons near an ending, effective teachers lead students through a summary that helps them structure and organize the content in their own minds.

Skilled teachers maintain the flow of their lessons with questioning. They ask a large number of questions, call on volunteers and nonvolunteers equally, provide cues and prompts when students are unable to respond, and give students time to think about their answers. They ask an appropriate mix of high and low level questions.

Expert teachers adjust their instruction to best reach students with varying backgrounds. They learn about students' interaction patterns, maximize student involvement and success, and adjust their instruction to accommodate their students' individual differences.

When teachers teach procedural skills, such as adding fractions with unlike denominators or writing sentences with appropriate subject-verb agreement, direct instruction is a useful approach. Direct instruction exists in four steps: an introduction and review, presentation, guided practice, and independent practice. Effective direct instruction is conducted in a structured and supportive learning environment. Different direct instruction models exist, but they are all variations on the basic four steps.

The effective teaching literature provides a threshold, above which all teachers should be; expert teachers go beyond this threshold to help students develop understanding in depth, capitalize on the social nature of learning, and develop problem solving ability. It is based on the belief that learners construct their own understanding rather than have it delivered to them "prepackaged" by the teacher.

When teachers teach organized bodies of knowledge--combinations of facts, concepts, and generalizations--a lecture-recitation approach is practical. The lecture-recitation method combines short periods where teachers present information, which are followed by teacher questions that gauge students' understanding. As additional segments of teacher presentation and comprehension checks are added, teachers ask additional questions that encourage students to examine the relationships among the segments.

Student discussions are useful strategies for stimulating thinking, challenging attitudes, and developing interpersonal skills. Discussions require that students have an extensive knowledge base, so the development of student background always precedes discussions. Teachers help students maintain focus in the discussion, and they guide students as the students practice and develop their critical thinking skills.

Student groupwork provides an alternative to whole-group learning activities. Effective use of groupwork requires careful organization, routines that move students to and from groups quickly, and procedures, such as specific directions, a limited amount of time, and requiring a written product, to promote on-task behavior and student accountability.

# CHAPTER TWELVE
# EFFECTIVE TEACHING

## CHAPTER-AT-A-GLANCE _____

| MAIN TOPICS | KEY POINTS | KEY TERMS |
|---|---|---|
| Teacher Effectiveness Defining Teaching Quality | • Effective teachers have students who achieve more than they would be expected to achieve for their grade level and background.<br>• Effective teachers display different behaviors than teachers who are less effective. | • Teacher effectiveness, 588 |
| Time: A Tool for Analysis | • Teachers allocate larger amounts of time for content areas and topics, such as reading and math, that have high priority.<br>• Effective teachers spend as much of their allocated time as possible on instruction. They minimize time spent on activities such a taking roll, dealing with management problems, and making transitions from one activity to another.<br>• Skilled teachers keep their students involved in learning activities--they maximize engaged time--and they help students experience as much success as possible to promote academic learning time--the combination of engagement and success. | • Allocated time, 589<br>• Instructional time, 590<br>• Engaged time, 591<br>• Time-on-task, 591<br>• Academic learning time, 591 |

| Essential Teaching Skills | • Effective teachers at different grade levels and in different content areas display similarities, called essential teaching skills, in their behavior. These skills are demonstrated in teachers' attitudes, organization, communication, and presentation of content, their feedback and responsiveness to students, they way they summarize and close lessons, and their questioning skill.<br>• Effective teachers have high expectations for their students, genuinely care about them as individuals, serve as models, and are enthusiastic about their work.<br>• Skilled teachers are well organized. They have materials prepared in advance, they begin their lessons promptly and minimize disruptions to preserve as much instructional time as possible.<br>• Expert teachers communicate with precise language, their lessons follow a central theme, they signal transitions, and they emphasize important points.<br>• Competent teachers demonstrate a thorough understanding of the content they teach.<br>• Effective teachers plan their lesson beginnings to attract student attention and provide context for the content to follow, and they use visual displays to maintain student attention throughout the lesson.<br>• To aid learning, skilled teachers give students specific, immediate, informational feedback with a positive emotional tone.<br>• Effective teachers are aware of and responsive to their students; they constantly monitor students' verbal and nonverbal behavior for indications of inattentiveness or confusion.<br>• To help students encode information and reach equilibrium in their learning, good teachers end their lessons with clear summaries called closure.<br>• Questioning is an enormously important teaching skill. Effective teachers ask a large number of questions, call on all students equally, provide additional questions and cues when students are unable to answer, and give students time to think. | • Essential teaching skills, 592<br>• Active teaching, 593<br>• Managerial organization, 594<br>• Conceptual organization, 595<br>• Precise terminology, 595<br>• Mazes, 595<br>• Connected discourse, 596<br>• Transition signal, 596<br>• Emphasis, 597<br>• Focus, 597<br>• Introductory Focus, 598<br>• Sensory focus, 598<br>• Academic focus, 598<br>• Feedback, 599<br>• Monitoring, 600<br>• Review, 601<br>• Closure, 601<br>• Questioning frequency, 603<br>• Equitable distribution, 603<br>• Call-out, 603<br>• Prompt, 604<br>• Wait-time, 605 |
|---|---|---|

| | | |
|---|---|---|
| Interacting with Students: Accommodating Diversity | • Experimental programs that help teachers adjust their instruction to the interaction patterns of their students have proved successful in increasing the participation and success of cultural minorities.<br>• Teachers can learn about the interaction and speech patterns of their students by talking to them outside of class and participating in extracurricular activities.<br>• Effective teachers maximize the success and involvement of all their students. | |
| Direct Instruction | • Skills, such as finding the longitude and latitude of different locations, or solving algebraic equations, have specified procedures, they can be illustrated with many examples, and they are developed through practice; they are called procedural skills.<br>• Procedural skills are effectively taught with a direct instructional procedure--one that begins with an introduction and review, followed by presentation of new content, and completed with student practice, first under the guidance of the teacher and then independently. | • Direct instruction, 611<br>• Procedural skills, 611 |
| Beyond Effective Teaching: Helping Students Construct Knowledge | • All teachers should be able to demonstrate essential teaching skills; experts go beyond these skills to help students develop understanding in depth, put activities in the form of problems, and capitalize on the social nature of learning.  This is a constructivist view of instruction.<br>• Teaching from a constructivist orientation is very demanding for teachers; it requires clear goals and careful monitoring of student discussions. | |
| Teaching Organized Bodies of Knowledge | • Combinations of facts, concepts, and generalizations, called organized bodies of knowledge, are efficiently taught with a lecture-recitation procedure, which includes cycles of teacher presentation followed by checks where student understanding is assessed, and learners are helped to integrate new and old learning. | • Organized bodies of knowledge, 622<br>• Lecture-recitation, 623 |

| Discussions | • Discussions are useful for stimulating thinking, challenging attitudes, and developing human relations skills.<br>• For discussions to be worthwhile they must be focussed on a specific topic, and students must have extensive background knowledge.<br>• Discussions emphasize student-student interaction and the integration of ideas; they are not effective for initial learning. | • Discussions, 626 |
|---|---|---|
| Alternatives to Whole-Group Activities: Student Groupwork | • Groupwork provides an alternative to whole-class activities.<br>• Effective groupwork requires careful planning and monitoring by the teacher and a specific task, short time limit, and written product from the students. | Groupwork, 630 |

# CHAPTER TWELVE
## EFFECTIVE TEACHING

## GUIDED REVIEW _____

### TEACHER EFFECTIVENESS: DEFINING TEACHING QUALITY _____

Teacher effectiveness describes the patterns of teacher behavior that increase student learning.

(12-1) How did researchers arrive at the patterns of teacher behavior that are described as effective teaching? (p. 588)

_____

_____

(12-2) Briefly trace the history of research on teaching that led to the teacher effectiveness movement and beyond. (pp. 588-589)

_____

_____

_____

_____

_____

### TIME: A TOOL FOR ANALYSIS _____

Effective teachers use their time efficiently. Time can be described at four different levels, and each succeeding level correlates more strongly with learning.

(12-3) Describe allocated time. Describe its correlation with learning. (pp. 589-590)

_____

_____

(12-4) Identify at least three examples of common classroom activities that consume allocated time but are not considered part of instructional time. (pp. 590-591)

_____

_____

(12-5) Describe two differences between high and low achievers in terms of their time-on-task. (p. 591)

_____

_____

(12-6) Look at Figure 12.1 on page 589 of your text. There we see that academic learning time is the area of the smallest circle, and engaged time is the area of the next circle. What does the difference in the areas of the two circles represent? (pp. 591-592)

_____

_____

## ESSENTIAL TEACHING SKILLS

Essential teaching skills are the behaviors that maximize instructional time and promote student engagement and success. They are the behaviors we would expect to see in all teachers regardless of grade level, subject matter area, or topic.

(12-7) Imagine that you're sitting in the back of a classroom. Identify teacher behaviors that would indicate enthusiasm, high expectations, modeling and caring. (Hint: Think back to your study of motivation in chapter 9. What were some specific behaviors that indicate enthusiasm? What is one of the best indicators of teacher caring?) (p. 593).

_____

_____

_____

_____

(12-8) Identify each of the characteristics of effective managerial organization. Give two original examples of classroom routines. (p. 594)

_____

_____

_____

12-9) Describe the difference between managerial and conceptual organization. Give an example of conceptual organization. (pp. 594-595)

_____

_____

_____

(12-10) Give an example of imprecise language, and another example of scrambled discourse. How do they detract from learning? (pp. 595-596)

_____

_____

_____

(12-11) Give an example of a transition signal. (p. 596)

_____

_____

(12-12) Identify two different ways of emphasizing important information. Give an example of each. (p. 597)

_____

_____

_____

(12-13) Two teachers are teaching about the periodic table in chemistry. One has a very thorough background and the other's background is limited. What differences would we expect in the communication of the two teachers? (p. 597)

_____

_____

(12-14) Think again about the case study that introduced chapter 12 (pages 584-587 of your text). How did Shirley Barton provide for introductory focus, and what did she do for sensory focus in the lesson? (p. 598).

_____

_____

_____

_____

(12-15) Suppose we're sitting in a class, and we comment, "The teacher lost academic focus in this lesson." What does that statement mean? (p. 598)

_____

_____

(12-16) Describe each of the characteristics of effective feedback. Give an example of feedback that is immediate but not specific nor informational. (pp. 599-600)

_____

_____

_____

_____

(12-17) A teacher provides general praise as feedback for one student in a class but gives specific praise to another. Why would the teacher respond differently to the two students? (You might want to refer again to page 273 in chapter 6 to help you respond.) How does the different feedback demonstrate the teacher's skill at monitoring? (pp. 600-601)

_____

_____

_____

(12-18) Review that is designed to promote elaboration would occur at what point in a lesson, beginning, middle, or end? What is closure? (p. 601)

_____

_____

_____

(12-19) One teacher asks a large number of questions in her class, while another provides careful explanations. Which of the two is likely to have students who learn more? Explain. (p. 603)

_____

_____

_____

_____

(12-20) What does equitable distribution mean? Why is equitable distribution important? (pp. 603-604)

_____

_____

_____

(12-21) Look again at Shirley Barton's lesson (pages 584-587 of your text). Identify at least one example of prompting in the case study. Why is prompting important? (p. 604)

_____

_____

_____

(12-22) What is the length of typical teacher wait-times? As a rule of thumb, how long should teacher wait-times be? Should wait-times for drill and practice activities be longer or shorter than those requiring application of a rule or generalization? Explain. (p. 605)

_____

_____

_____

## INTERACTING WITH STUDENTS: ACCOMMODATING DIVERSITY

Effective teachers make an effort to understand their learners' social interaction patterns, they maximize student participation and success, and they adjust their instruction to accommodate individual differences.

(12-23) Identify two simple things teachers can do to learn about their students' speech patterns and conversational styles. (p. 610)

_____

_____

(12-24) Identify three different questioning skills that teachers can use to maximize student involvement and success. (pp. 610-611)

_____

_____

_____

## DIRECT INSTRUCTION

Procedural skills are types of content that have specific operations, can be illustrated with a wide variety of examples, and are developed through practice. Direct instruction is an effective procedure for teaching procedural skills.

(12-25) Identify at least two examples of procedural skills. (pp. 611-612)

_____

_____

_____

(12-26) State each of the phases of direct instruction. Identify each of the phases in Shirley Barton's lesson. (pp. 613-616)

_____

_____

_____

_____

## BEYOND EFFECTIVE TEACHING: HELPING STUDENTS CONSTRUCT KNOWLEDGE

Expert teachers go beyond basic teaching skills to help students develop understanding in depth, they put instructional activities in the form of problems for students to solve, and they capitalize on the social nature of learning.

(12-26) Look at the teaching episode illustrating the lesson on place value with third graders. Explain why the instruction in this episode is based on a behaviorist view of learning (Hint: From your study of chapter 6, think about reinforcement and its impact on behavior). (p. 618)

_____

_____

_____

(12-27) Identify two important differences between a constructivist and a behaviorist view of learning. (p. 619)

_____

_____

(12-28) Identify three features of Keisha Coleman's instruction that were important in helping students "construct knowledge." (pp. 618-619)

_____

_____

_____

_____

(12-29) Identify three misconceptions that can result from an incomplete understanding of instruction from a constructivist perspective. (pp. 620-621)

_____

_____

_____

_____

## TEACHING ORGANIZED BODIES OF KNOWLEDGE

Organized bodies of knowledge are combinations of facts, concepts, generalizations, and principles and the relationships among them.
Organized bodies of knowledge are closely related to declarative knowledge as it was discussed in chapters 7 and 8.

(12-30) How are organized bodies of knowledge different from facts, concepts, generalizations, and procedural skills? (p. 622)

_____

_____

_____

(12-31) Identify illustrations of presenting information, monitoring comprehension, and integration in Carrie Thompson's lesson on pages 623 and 624 of your text. (pp. 624-626)

_____

_____

_____

_____

## DISCUSSIONS

Discussions are instructional strategies designed to promote student thinking, challenge attitudes, and develop interpersonal skills. Discussions require careful teacher organization and extensive student background.

(12-32) Describe the four important features of effective discussions. Identify each of the features in Jean Levitt's lesson on page 627 of your text. (pp. 627-629)

_____

_____

_____

_____

## ALTERNATIVES TO WHOLE-GROUP ACTIVITIES: STUDENT GROUPWORK

Student groupwork involves students working together in groups small enough so that all members can participate on clearly defined tasks. Groupwork allows less aggressive students opportunities for involvement, and it allows all students to construct and defend conclusions and share them with others.

(12-33) Assume that you have trained your students in groupwork and they are able to move into and out of the groups quickly. Identify four other aspects of groupwork that are important. What is the primary reason for these aspects? (p. 630)

_____

_____

_____

_____

_____

_____

_____

# CHAPTER TWELVE
# EFFECTIVE TEACHING

## APPLICATION EXERCISES _____

EXERCISE 12.1

Exercise 12.1 measures your understanding of topics covered on pages 583-592 of your text.

1. Identify the amount of time allocated for science and social studies in Shirley Barton's class. What does this allocation suggest about her instructional priorities?

_____

_____

2. What percentage of Shirley's allocated time in math was actually devoted to instruction?

_____

3. Consider students' engaged time in Shirley's class. Based on your analysis of the lesson, was it equal to, slightly less than, or significantly less than her instructional time? Provide the basis for your answer with information from the lesson.

_____

_____

_____

4. Using at least one example from the lesson, explain how Shirley maximized her students' academic learning time.

_____

_____

_____

EXERCISE 12.2

Exercise 12.2 measures your understanding of topics covered on pages 592-608 of your text.

1. Identify at least two specific behaviors in Shirley Barton's teaching in the case study that demonstrated enthusiasm and two others that indicated warmth and empathy.

_____

_____

_____

_____

2. Identify at least one specific behavior in Shirley's lesson that demonstrated her understanding of the importance of modeling.

_____

_____

3. Four managerial functions of organization were described in this section. Identify an example of each in Shirley's lesson.

_____

_____

_____

_____

4. Identify an example in Shirley's lesson where she demonstrated effective communication through clear transition signals.

_____

_____

_____

5. Examine Shirley's questioning behavior. Based on information in the case study, explain how she combined her monitoring and verbal feedback skills to effectively interact with Jon, Tim, Gayle, and Karen.

_____

_____

_____

_____

6. Explain how Shirley's interaction with Ken was a mechanism for maximizing academic learning time.

_____

_____

EXERCISE 12.3

Exercise 12.3 measures your understanding of topics covered on pages 608-617 of your text.

1. Examine the following list of skills and concepts.

When adding _ing_ to a word ending in a consonant, simply add _ing_ if the final consonant is preceded by a long vowel sound or another consonant, but double the consonant if it's preceded by a short vowel sound.

When simplifying an arithmetic expression, first complete the operations in parentheses, then multiply and divide left to right, and finally add and subtract left to right.

The concept _adverb._

The amount of work done on an object is equal to the force exerted on it times the distance it moves.

Select one of the topics and describe how it would be taught using the basic direct instruction model. Include specific examples and a description of each of the four steps in the model.

_____

_____

_____

_____

_____

_____

_____

2. A second-grade teacher has her students working on the procedure for subtracting with regrouping. During the guided practice phase of the direct instructional model, she puts a problem on the chalkboard and has them work the problem on a small chalkboard at their desks. When they're finished, they hold the board over their heads until she looks at the problem. What feature of the Hunter model is being demonstrated here?

_____

_____

```
┌──────────────────────────────────────────────────────────────┐
│ ┌──────────────────────────────────────────────────────────┐ │
│ └──────────────────────────────────────────────────────────┘ │
└──────────────────────────────────────────────────────────────┘
```

EXERCISE 12.4

Exercise 12.4 measures your understanding of topics covered on pages 617-626 of your text.

1. Look again at Shirley Barton's lesson. Assess the extent to which her lesson was constructivist. What aspects of her lesson were behaviorist? Cite specific information from the case study for your answer in each case.

_____

_____

_____

_____

_____

_____

_____

2. Analyze Carrie Thompson's lesson. Identify as many examples of the essential teaching skills as you can find in her teaching. Cite specific examples from the lesson to illustrate each skill.

_____

_____

_____

_____

_____

_____

_____

_____

EXERCISE 12.5

Exercise 12.5 measures your understanding of topics covered on pages 626-631 of your text.

1. Focus is one of the important features of effective discussions. Explain how Jean Levitt, in leading the discussion of the Revolutionary War, did or did not demonstrate each of the three components of focus as an essential teaching skill.

_____

_____

_____

2. Identify an example from Jean's lesson where she encouraged thinking skills.

_____

_____

_____

3. What did Jean do to encourage interaction in her class?

_____

_____

_____

_____

# CHAPTER TWELVE
# EFFECTIVE TEACHING

## SELF-HELP QUIZ _____

TRUE/FALSE QUESTIONS. Write T in the blank if the statement is true, and write F if it is false.

_____ 1.  A teacher trait is another term for a teacher effectiveness behavior.

_____ 2.  The correlation between instructional time and learning is higher than the correlation between engaged time and learning.

_____ 3.  Teacher enthusiasm is positively correlated with student motivation, but it isn't correlated with student achievement.

_____ 4.  If teachers maintains academic focus, their discourse will automatically be connected.

_____ 5.  An example that is used for introductory focus could also be used to provide sensory focus.

_____ 6.  According to research, teachers should avoid giving young children negative feedback (statements that tell students that answers are incorrect).

_____ 7.  According to research, in question and answer sessions teachers typically direct questions to individual students rather than letting anyone answer who wishes to do so.

_____ 8.  The primary value of increasing teacher wait-time is that it makes students feel safe in trying to answer.

_____ 9.  Teachers who present careful (well-organized) lectures generally have students who learn more than teachers who ask a large number of questions.

_____ 10.  In comparing teacher lectures to discussions, discussions are superior for increasing student motivation, but discussions are inferior for promoting student retention of information.

MULTIPLE CHOICE:  Circle the best response in each case.

11.  Look at Figure 12.1 in your text.  Consider the band between the outside edge of the circle representing engaged time and the outside edge of the circle representing instructional time. Of the following, the best description of this band is:

    a.  the amount of time teachers spend on activities, such as taking roll, passing out papers, and making Announcements.

    b.  the amount of time the students are off-task during instruction.

    c.  the amount of time students are on-task and successful.

    d.  the amount of time students are on-task but not successful.

12.  Third period in Bartram Middle school begins at 10:00 a.m. and ends at 10:50.  Kristy Williams, one of the teachers, typically starts her math class at 10:02.  Her friend, Kevin Anderson, typically gets started about 10:04. Of the following, the best conclusion we can make based on this information is:

    a.  Kristy is a more effective teacher than is Kevin.

    b.  Kristy's students are on task more than are Kevin's.

    c.  Kristy has more allocated time than does Kevin.

    d.  Kristy is better organized than is Kevin.

13. Of the following, teachers' understanding of the content they teach is most strongly related to:

    a.  high expectations.

    b.  organization.

    c.  precise language.

    d.  academic focus.

14. A teacher in a discussion of the Northern and Southern Colonies prior to the Civil War says, "We've looked at the economic conditions in the North in the middle 1800's. Now we're going to shift and look at the economy in the South during this same period." Of the following, the teacher's comment best illustrates:
   a. effective lesson organization.
   b. ineffective lesson organization.
   c. effective communication.
   d. ineffective communication.
   e. ineffective lesson focus.

15. A teacher displays the following sentence on the board:

   Studying is important if you want to be successful.

   She then asks, "How is the word 'studying' used in the sentence? Ed?"
   ". . . It's a verb," Ed answers.
   She responds, "Not quite. Help him out, . . . Kathy?"

Of the following, the best assessment of the teacher's response to Ed's answer is:
   a. effective lesson organization.
   b. effective communication
   c. ineffective communication.
   d. ineffective sensory focus.
   e. ineffective feedback.

16. A teacher displays the following problem on the overhead.

   To make it more attractive, we want to cover our bulletin board with colored paper.  How much paper will we need?

   She continues, "What do we need to do first to solve our problem? Jan?"
   ". . . I'm not sure," Jan answers.

Which of the following is the best teacher response to Jan's answer?
   a. "Come on now, Jan. Think about it for a moment."
   b. "What is the problem asking us for, Jan?"
   c. "Can someone help Jan out with this problem?"
   d. "Look, Jan. The first thing we need is the area of the bulletin board. Right?"

17. Of the following, the best example of a procedural skill is:
   a. Solving an algebraic equation for the value of x.
   b. Understanding the concept of equivalent fractions.
   c. Knowing that in the number 236, the 2 represents 2 hundreds, the 3 represents 3 tens, and the 6 represents 5 ones.
   d. Identifying adjectives and adverbs in sentences.

18. Which of the following goals is most appropriately taught with the lecture-recitation model.
   a. Finding equivalent fractions.
   b. Applying Newton's Law of Inertia to everyday examples.
   c. Using figurative language to make writing more attractive.
   d. Identifying the impact of Columbus's discovery of the New World.

19.  Effective discussions strongly emphasize the development of critical thinking in students.  Of the following, the factor that most impacts the students' ability to think critically is:
    a.  a lesson that remains focused on the question or problem being discussed.
    b.  students' extensive knowledge base.
    c.  high levels of interaction among the students.
    d.  a facilitative teacher.

20.  "Computers can be effectively used when other forms of illustration are difficult to accomplish." Which of the following best represents that statement?
    a.  Identifying parts of speech in sentences.
    b.  Practicing on multiplication facts.
    c.  Identifying the similarities in the Jamestown and Plymouth Colonies.
    d.  Calculating the distance a dropped object falls every second.

# CHAPTER THIRTEEN
# CLASSROOM ASSESSMENT

## CHAPTER OUTLINE _____

I. Classroom assessment
   A. The functions of classroom assessment
      1. Increased learning
      2. Increased motivation
   B. Measurement and evaluation
      1. Formal and informal measurement
      2. The need for systematic assessment
   C. Validity
   D. Reliability
   E. Norm-referenced and criterion-reference evaluations
II. Teacher-made tests
   A. Teachers' assessment patterns
      1. Teacher beliefs about assessment
      2. Assessment practices of elementary teachers
      2. Assessment patterns in the middle and secondary schools
   B. Assessment patterns: Implications for teachers
   C. Preparing test items
      1. Multiple-choice items
         a. The stem
         b. Distracters
            c. Measuring higher level learning
      2. True-false items
   3. Matching items
      4. Completion items
      5. Essay items
      6. Performance measures
   D. Using commercially-prepared test items
      1. Implications for teachers
III. Alternative Assessment
   A. Curricular alignment: Goals, instruction, and assessment
   B. Portfolio assessment
   C. Setting criteria
      1. Checklists and rating scales
IV. Effective testing
   A. Designing tests
      1. Tables of specifications
   B. Preparing students for tests
      1. Teaching test-taking skills
      2. Test anxiety
      3. Specific test-preparation procedures
   C. Administering tests
   D. Analyzing results
   E. Preparing students for alternative assessments
IV. Grading and reporting: The total Assessment System

A. Designing a grading system
   1. Tests and quizzes
   2. Alternative assessments
   3. Seatwork and homework
B. Assigning grades
   1. Formative and summative evaluation
   2. Raw points or percentage?
V. Computers in the Assessment System
   A. Planning and constructing tests
   B. Scoring and interpreting tests
   C. Maintaining student records
VI. Standardized Testing
   A. Standardized testing with alternative formats
   B. Descriptive statistics
      1. Frequency distributions
      2. Measures of central tendency
  3. Measures of variability
      4. The normal distribution
   C. Types of scores
      1. Raw scores
      2. Percentiles
      3. Stanines
      4. Grade equivalents
      5. Standard scores
      6. Standard error of measurement
   C. Types of standardized tests
      1. Achievement tests
      2. Diagnostic tests
      3. Intelligence tests
         a. A short history of intelligence tests
         b. The Stanford-Binet
         c. The Wechsler scales
         d. Individual versus group intelligence tests
      4. Intelligence testing and placement
      5. Aptitude tests
VII. Issues in Classroom Assessment
   A. Minimum competency testing
   B. The future of testing
VIII. Student Diversity and Assessment
   A. Bias in measurement
      1. Bias in content
      2. Bias in testing procedures
      3. Bias in test use
   B. Assessment responses to student diversity
      1. Reducing bias in the testing process
         a. Prepare students for tests
         b. Use familiar problem stems
         c. Make provisions for non-native English speakers
         d. Accommodate diversity in scoring
         e. Discuss results
      2. Alternative tests
         a. System of Multicultural Assessment (SOMPA)
         a. Kaufman Assessment Battery for Children (KABC)
      3. Clinical approaches

# CHAPTER OBJECTIVES _____

- Identify examples of basic assessment concepts
- Describe classroom teachers' assessment patterns
- Identify characteristics in specific test items that detract from their validity
- Construct test items using a variety of formats
- Construct alternative assessments to meet learning goals
- Prepare portfolio assessments
- Recognize effective testing procedures in classrooms
- Identify ways that technology can help improve teacher assessment
- Describe characteristics of standardized tests
- Explain issues in standardized testing

# CHAPTER OVERVIEW _____

Your study of this text is nearing completion. To this point you have examined the nature of learning and the influence that student characteristics, motivation, classroom management, and effective instruction all have on the amount students achieve. We now turn to the process of assessment, which is an effort to answer the question, "How much have the students learned?" You can say very little about learning and the factors that impact it until you are able to answer that question, so assessment is a critical component of the entire teaching-learning cycle.

Assessment includes all the processes teachers use to determine the amount their students are learning. Assessment includes tests and quizzes, seatwork and homework, answers to questions, and "alternative assessments" such as portfolios of student work. Assessment also includes decisions about grading, reteaching and supplementary instruction. Well crafted assessments increase both learning and motivation.

When teachers make decisions, such as grading, they are using the process of evaluation, and the information they use as a basis for the decisions are called measurements. Formal measurements, such as tests and quizzes, are attempts to systematically gather information, while informal measurements occur incidentally, such as listening to a student's response to a question.

Valid measurements are consistent with stated goals. Decisions about achievement based on personality, responsiveness in class or any factor other than the extent to which the learner reaches a lesson's goal are invalid. Reliable measurements are consistent. Unreliable measurements cannot be valid. One of the strengths of objective test formats, such as multiple-choice, is their high reliability. Essay tests are notoriously unreliable,

In a norm-referenced system, decisions about students are based on their performance compared to other students. With criterion-referenced systems teachers made decisions by comparing student performance to a pre-established standard.

Teachers at different grade levels vary in their assessment patterns. Teachers in the elementary grades use performance measures, such as portfolios of students' work, and they rely on informal measures and commercially prepared tests to a greater extent than do teachers of older students. They also place a greater emphasis on affective goals, such as "gets along well with others." The tests middle and secondary school teachers prepare most commonly use completion and matching formats, and they are composed of mostly knowledge/recall items. The teachers rarely revise the items once they're prepared.

The multiple-choice format is effective for preparing valid items. Much of the effectiveness of an item depends on writing convincing distracters. They should be similar in length, grammatical style, and technicality of language. The correct choice should be varied randomly. Negative wording should be emphasized the choice "all of the above" should be avoided. Higher order thinking can be measured by giving students information, for which only one choice is the best interpretation.

As with multiple-choice, the true-false format can be used effectively as an interpretive exercise. The matching format is effective when the same alternatives are used for a series of items, such as classifying a series of statements as different types of figurative language. The completion format is one of the "weakest" and should generally be avoided. When the essay format is used, specific criteria for scoring the items should be prepared in advance.

Alternative assessments ask students to demonstrate skills similar to those required in real-world settings, such as writing business letters, designing and setting up an experiment in a science lab, or "trouble shooting" a stalled engine. Portfolios of student work, systematic observations of students, and interviews are examples of alternative assessments. Checklists or rating scales are commonly used to establish the dimensions and criteria for alternative assessments.

Commercially prepared test items--those included with publishers' textbooks--are often of poor quality. Teachers should use them with care.

Effective teachers prepare their students for tests by specifying precisely what will be on the tests, giving students a chance to practice responding to items under testlike conditions, and establishing positive expectations for student performance. This process improves students' test-taking skills and reduces test anxiety. During tests, effective teachers prepare a comfortable physical environment, give precise directions about taking the test, and monitor the students the entire time they take the test. They score and return tests promptly, discuss areas of misconception, and comment positively about the results. They also make plans for revising misleading or confusing items.

Decisions about the relative weight of tests, quizzes, homework, and performance measures are left up to individual teachers. They must also make decisions about making up missed work and reporting affective dimensions of student performance. These factors together with the processes of preparing students for tests and administering them make up the teacher's total assessment system. Computers can help in preparing and storing items, scoring and interpreting tests, and maintaining student records.

All students take standardized tests. These tests are given to large groups under uniform conditions, and they are scored with uniform procedures. An individual's performance is then compared to comparable people who have taken the test. Standardized testing is extremely important and somewhat controversial. The calls for national reform in teaching are virtually all based on the fact that American students perform less well on standardized tests than do their counterparts in other industrialized countries.

Experts use statistical methods to cope with the vast amount of information gathered on standardized tests. Measures of central tendency--the mean, median, and mode--describe a group's performance as a whole, and the standard deviation gives an indication of the variability in the scores.

For large samples, standardized test scores tend to approximate a normal distribution. In normal distributions, the mean, median, and mode are the same score, about 68% of all scores are within one standard deviation from the mean, and about 98% of the scores lie within two standard deviations from the mean.

Student's performances on a standardized tests are commonly reported in terms of percentiles (a ranking compared to all others who have taken the test); stanines, which describes scores in bands distributed from the mean; grade equivalents, that compare students to average scores for a particular age group; or standard scores, that describe scores in standardized deviation units from the mean. The standard error on a test gives a range of scores into which the students true score is likely to fall.

Achievement tests measure student learning in different content areas, diagnostic tests give detailed descriptions of students' strengths and weaknesses in particular skill areas, intelligence tests attempt to measure the ability to think in the abstract, solve problems, and an individual's capacity to acquire knowledge.

The Stanford-Binet and the Wechsler Scales are the two most common individually administered intelligence tests. Both have a verbal and a performance section, and they have a similar view of intelligence.

Intelligence tests should be used cautiously for purposes of placing students into ability groups, because labeling students has a powerful effect on the way students are treated in schools.

Minimum competency testing is a controversial issue in standardized testing. Minimum competency tests are used as a basis for decisions about promotion and graduation.

As our student populations become more diverse, the issue of bias in testing has become increasingly controversial. Critics believe that many standardized tests reflect white, middle-class values, which discriminate against other cultures and socioeconomic groups. Teachers can reduce bias in testing by carefully preparing students for tests, using familiar problem stems, making provisions for students with limited English skills, and discussing test results.

The System of Multicultural Assessment and the Kaufman Assessment Battery for Children, two alternative tests designed for use with students from different cultures and socioeconomic backgrounds, provide a more comprehensive picture of intelligence, and they have generated considerable interest in the educational community.

Clinical approaches to assessment combine standardized test data with other information, such as grades, student work samples, and teacher input for making decisions about student progress.

# CHAPTER THIRTEEN
## CLASSROOM ASSESSMENT

### CHAPTER-AT-A-GLANCE _____

| MAIN TOPICS | KEY POINTS | KEY TERMS |
|---|---|---|
| Classroom Assessment | • The information teachers gather about their students together with the decisions they make based on the information are all a part of classroom assessment.<br>• Effective assessment increases both student achievement and student motivation.<br>• Measurement is the process of gathering information about students, and the decisions teachers make based on the information are called evaluations.<br>• When assessments are congruent with stated goals they are valid; when they measure attainment of the goals consistently, they are reliable. Assessments must be reliable to be valid.<br>• When teachers make decisions about students based on their performance compared to peers, a norm-referenced system is used; when their performance is compared to a pre-set standard, the system is criterion-referenced. | • Classroom assessment, 645<br>• Measurement, 646<br>• Evaluation, 646<br>• Informal measurement, 646<br>• Formal measurement, 646<br>• Validity, 647<br>• Reliability, 648<br>• Norm-referencing, 649<br>• Criterion-referencing, 649 |
| Teacher-Made Tests | • Elementary teachers tend to rely on performance measures--such as the ability of students to write complete sentences--informal measurements, and commercially prepared tests to a greater extend than do middle and secondary teachers. They also focus more on affective goals than do teachers of older students.<br>• When middle and secondary school teachers prepare test items, they most commonly use the completion and matching formats. More than three fourths of all teacher prepared items measure knowledge and recall of facts.<br>• The quality of teacher prepared test items can be improved if simple guidelines are followed.<br>• Commercially prepared test items are often of low quality, the goals they measure may not be consistent with teachers' goals; they should be used with caution. | • Multiple-choice items, 653<br>• True-false format, 657<br>• Matching format, 658<br>• Completion items, 659<br>• Essay items, 660 |

| | | |
|---|---|---|
| Alternative Assessment | • Alternative assessments ask students to perform tasks similar to those they will face outside of school.<br>• Alternative assessments require students to do something, they tap higher level thinking and problem-solving skills, and they involve real-world applications. They are consistent with constructivist views of learning.<br>• Curricular alignment means that goals, learning activities and assessments are congruent with each other.<br>• Portfolios--collections of student work that are judged against preset criteria--are commonly associated with alternative assessment.<br>• Checklists and rating scales are often used as methods of setting criteria for alternative assessments. | • Alternative assessments, 663<br>• Curricular alignment, 664<br>• Portfolios, 666<br>• Checklists, 667<br>• Rating scales, 667 |
| Grading and Reporting: The Total Assessment System | • In designing an assessment system teachers make decisions about the number and weight of tests and quizzes, the incorporation of alternative assessments, homework, making up work, affective aspects of student performance, and the way the final assessment will be reported.<br>• Assessments used for information and feedback are called formative evaluations, while those used to make grading decisions are called summative evaluations. | • Formative evaluation, 680<br>• Summative evaluation, 680 |
| Computers in the Assessment System | • Teachers can increase their efficiency in the assessment process by sing them to create, store, and access items, score and interpret tests, and maintain student records. | |

| Standardized Testing | • Standardized tests are given to large groups of students under uniform testing conditions, and they are scored according to uniform procedures. | |
|---|---|---|
| | • As alternative assessments are used for standardized testing, issues such as goals and criteria, logistics, and validity must be resolved. | |
| | • To summarize the large amount of information obtained from standardized tests, experts use descriptive statistics--the mean, mode, and median to determine how the group did as a whole, and the standard deviation to determine the spread of scores. | |
| | • Results from standardized tests approximate a normal distribution, in which the mean, median, mode fall on the same score and approximately 68% of all scores lie within one standard deviation from the mean. | |
| | • Summaries of a student's performance on a standardized test often include the raw score, or number of items answered correctly, the percentile--a ranking of the student's performance compared to all other who have taken the test--and stanine, which is a range of scores based on the normal distribution. | |
| | • Standardized tests will sometimes report grade equivalents, which compare an individual's score to the average score of a particular age group, or standard scores, which describe scores in terms of standard deviation units. | |
| | • Different types of standardized tests are designed to perform different functions; achievement test measure how much students have learned in a particular content area, diagnostic tests make detailed measurements of students' mastery of specific skills, intelligence tests attempt to measure students' ability to learn, think in the abstract, and solve problems. | |
| | • The Stanford-Binet, and the Wechsler are the two most popular, individually administered intelligence test that exist. Each is composed of a verbal and a performance section, and their views of intelligence are very similar. | |
| | • Intelligence tests should be used cautiously for placing students in ability-grouped classes, because labeling students has a powerful effect on the way they're treated in schools. | |
| | • Aptitude tests attempt to measure students' potential for further learning. | |

| | | |
|---|---|---|
| Issues in Classroom Assessment | • Minimum competency testing is a controversial issue in assessment.<br>• Minimum competency tests are used to assess students' mastery of basic academic skills, and the results are used as a basis for making decisions about student promotion and graduation. | |
| Student Diversity and | • Test bias occurs when content on the test, testing procedures, or interpretation of test results favor one culture or economic group more than another.<br>• Teachers can help reduce possible test bias by preparing students for tests, using familiar problem stems, making provisions for non-native English speakers, accommodating diversity in scoring, and discussing test results with students. | • Multiple-trait scoring, 704 |

# CHAPTER THIRTEEN
## CLASSROOM ASSESSMENT

### GUIDED REVIEW

### CLASSROOM ASSESSMENT

Classroom assessment includes all the information teachers gather about student performance together with the decisions they make based on the information gathered.

(13-1) Give two examples of informal measurements, two examples of formal measurements and two examples of evaluations. (p. 646)

_____

_____

_____

_____

(13-2) Give specific examples of at least two assessment decisions that would not be valid. (pp. 647-648)

_____

_____

(13-3) Explain why multiple-choice is a more reliable format than is essay. Which are likely to be more reliable, informal or formal measurements? Explain. (pp. 648-649)

_____

_____

_____

(13-4) Many school districts have policy that describes grading criteria, such as 93-100 - A; 85-92 - B; etc.. Is this system more closely related to norm-referenced evaluation or criterion-referenced evaluation? Explain. (p. 649)

_____

_____

_____

The primary way teachers gather assessment information is through testing, and particularly for middle and secondary school teachers, teacher-made tests are the most commonly used.

(13-5) Identify three ways in which the assessment patterns differ between teachers of elementary students and teachers of older learners. (pp. 650-652)

_____

_____

_____

(13-6) Look at the stems of the first two items in Figure 13.1 on page 654 of your text. Describe the weakness in each of these stems. (p. 654)

_____

_____

_____

(13-7) Look at each of the items in Figure 13.2 on page 655 of your text. Describe the problem with the distracters for each of these items. (pp. 655-656)

_____

_____

_____

_____

_____

_____

(13-8) Look at the item in Figure 13.3 on page 656 of your text. Identify the features of this item (other than the quality of the distracters) that make it different from the examples in Figure 13.2. (p. 656)

_____

_____

_____

(13-9) Look at the items in Figure 13.4 on page 657 of your text. Identify a weakness in each of the items. (p. 657)

_____

_____

_____

_____

(13-10) Based on the guidelines in your text, identify two topics that would be appropriate for a matching format. (pp. 658-659)

_____

_____

(13-11) Because of two important weaknesses in the completion format, experts suggest that it should be used sparingly. What are these weaknesses? (pp. 659-660)

_____

_____

_____

(13-12) Create an essay item based on the guidelines in Table 13.7 on page 661 of your text, and specify criteria for scoring the item based on the guidelines in Table 13.8 on the same page. (pp. 660-661)

_____

_____

_____

_____

ALTERNATIVE ASSESSMENT

Alternative assessments ask students to perform tasks similar to those they'll face in the real world. They ask students to perform, create, or produce something, they focus on higher level thinking and problem solving, and they involve real-world applications.

(13-13) Give a specific example of a goal, learning activity, and assessment are "aligned," and give an other example where they are out of "alignment." (p. 464-466)

_____

_____

_____

(13-14) You are a fifth grade teacher, and you want to use portfolios as a basis for assessing your students in math. Identify at least three types of products that would go into the portfolio. (p. 666)

_____

_____

_____

(13-15) Create a rating scale to measure a teacher's demonstration of the essential teaching skills discussed in chapter 12. Be sure the rating scale includes the four elements of well-defined criteria specified on page 667 of your text. (pp. 666-668)

_____

_____

_____

_____

_____

_____

_____

EFFECTIVE TESTING
_____

Effective testing includes the designing of the actual test, specifically preparing students for the test, administering it, scoring and analyzing the results, and discussing the results with the students.

(13-16) Look at the section discussing descriptive statistics on pages 686-690 of your text. Prepare a brief list of objectives for this section and a simple table of specifications that could be used in designing a test for this section. (pp. 669-671)

_____

_____

_____

_____

(13-17) Describe five things you can do to help reduce text anxiety in your students. (p. 673)

_____

_____

_____

_____

_____

_____

(13-18) Describe three things you should do in specifically preparing your students for tests, three more that you should do when administering the test, and an additional three you should do after the test has been given. (pp. 674-677)

- Preparing students

_____

_____

_____

- Administering the test

_____

_____

_____

- Analyzing results

_____

_____

_____

## GRADING AND REPORTING: THE TOTAL ASSESSMENT SYSTEM

Teachers must make a number of decisions in designing an assessment system that works for them.  A criterion for determining the validity of the system might be, "Could I defend this system to a parent if necessary?"

(13-19) Identify at least five questions you must answer as you design an assessment system for your classes (pp. 677-678)

_____

_____

_____

_____

_____

(13-19) Describe the difference between formative and summative evaluation. (p. 680)

_____

_____

_____

## COMPUTERS IN THE ASSESSMENT PROCESS

Computers can be a powerful aid in making the assessment process easier and more efficient.

(13-20) Describe at least three ways in which computers can be used to make the assessment process more efficient. (pp. 681-684)

_____

_____

_____

_____

## STANDARDIZED TESTING

Learners of all ages take standardized tests. They are tests given to large groups of students under uniform conditions, and they are scored with reliable procedures. Many of the policies and concerns related to education are the result of student performance on standardized tests.

Because of the large number of students taking standardized tests, statistical methods are used to summarize the results.

(13-21) Look at the scores in Table 13.14 on page 687 of your text. Confirm the mean, median, and standard deviation for the distributions by calculating them. (pp. 686-688)

_____

_____

_____

_____

_____

(13-22) Look at the frequency distribution in Figure 13.9 on page 689 of your text. Give two reasons why this distribution is not "normal." (pp. 689-690)

_____

_____

_____

(13-23) Look at the sample achievement test report on page 691 of your text. We see that Jessie's percentile rank for vocabulary is approximately 80. Describe what this rank means. (p. 690)

_____

_____

_____

(13-24) Suppose a student scores a 59 on a test with a mean of 50 and a standard deviation of 6. In what stanine would this student be? (pp. 690-692). What would the student's z-score and T-score be? (pp. 692-693)

_____

_____

_____

(13-25) Describe the differences between achievement, diagnostic, intelligence, and aptitude tests. (pp. 693-698)

_____

_____

_____

_____

_____

## ISSUES IN CLASSROOM ASSESSMENT

Concern is now being raised over the widespread use of standardized testing as a basis for making decisions about students. Minimum competency testing is one of the prominent issues.

(13-26) Identify an argument for and another argument against minimum competency testing. (pp. 698-699)

_____

_____

_____

_____

The issue of cultural bias is one of the most controversial in all of testing. Critics argue that many standardized tests are invalid for students who aren't white or middle class. However, sensitive teachers can do much to help reduce the Bias can exist in measurement, content, testing procedures, and test use. for non-white, non-middle-class student values, which discriminate against other cultures and socioeconomic groups. Teachers can reduce bias in testing by carefully preparing students for tests, using familiar problem stems, making provisions for students with limited English skills, and discussing test results.

(13-27) Give an example of each of the following: 1) bias in content, 2) bias in testing procedures, and 3) bias in test use. (pp. 701-702)

_____

_____

_____

_____

(13-28) Identify five ways teachers can reduce possible bias in testing. (pp. 703-705)

_____

_____

_____

_____

_____

# CHAPTER THIRTEEN
# CLASSROOM ASSESSMENT

## APPLICATION EXERCISES _____

EXERCISE 13.1

Exercise 13.1 measures your understanding of topics covered on pages 643-649 of your text.

Answer items 1-4 on the basis of the following case study.

> Ginger Kelly's second graders have finished subtraction of one-digit from two-digit numbers without regrouping and are now working on subtraction of one-digit from two-digit numbers with regrouping. Her goal is for them to be skilled at identifying and solving problems that both do and do not require regrouping. She has four students working problems at the board while the others do the same problems at their seats.
>  "Now let's try one more," she directs, seeing that the four students have gotten the problem right. She then gives the class another problem.
>  As they work, she notices Erin gazing out the window instead of working. She goes to Erin's desk and, to her delight, finds that Erin has already correctly finished the problem.
>  "Good work, Erin!" she exclaims after seeing Erin's paper.
>  "They've got it," she says to herself, seeing that the students at the board have again done the problem correctly.
>  Ginger then tells her students they will have a quiz the next day on problems similar to these.
>  The next day, Ginger gives her students a 10-problem quiz involving subtraction of one-digit from two-digit numbers, 7 of which require regrouping. The students are told to show all their work on the work sheet.

1. Identify at least two examples of informal measurement and at least one example of formal measurement in the case study.

_____

_____

_____

2. Ginger concluded, "They've got it," as she watched the students work. Based on the information in the case study, assess the extent to which the conclusion was valid at that point in her instruction. Give reasons for your assessment.

_____

_____

_____

3. Based on the information in the case study, assess the extent to which Ginger's quiz was valid and how likely it was to be reliable. Give reasons for your answer.

_____

_____

_____

4. Suppose that in Ginger's grading system 94% to 100% was an A, and 86% to 93% was a B. Suppose further that six students got an A on the quiz because they got all the problems right, and eight more got a B because they missed only one problem. Is Ginger's system norm-referenced or criterion-referenced? Explain why.

_____

_____

_____

5. What is the primary advantage of informal measurement? What is the primary danger in using informal measurements?

_____

_____

_____

6. What is the primary function of formal measurement?

_____

_____

EXERCISE 13.2

Exercise 13.2 measures your understanding of topics covered on pages 649-657 of your text.

Examine each of the following items and analyze them according to the criteria specified in Table 13.4 on page 654 of your text. An item may be effective according to the criteria, or it may be inconsistent with <u>one</u> or <u>more than one</u> of the guidelines.

1. Of the following, the best explanation for why the South lost the Civil War is
   a.   the North had better military leadership.
   b.   there were more big cities in the north.
 *c.   the North had more industry that could support an army, whereas the South was mostly agricultural.
   d.   it was too hot in the South.
2. Which of the following is a characteristic of young, rugged mountains?
   a.   They always have U-shaped valleys.
   b.   They have gently flowing streams.
 *c.   They have rugged, rocky peaks that extend above the tree line.
   d.   All of the above.
3. Which of the following best illustrates an omnivore?
 *a.   Ben is an animal of the forest. He spends most of his time in the winter in a long sleep. He roams around searching for the berries he loves to eat. When he is near a stream, he will also sometimes catch fish.
   b.   Billy is a high mountain animal. He has a thick coat to protect him from the cold. He has to scrape and scratch through the snow to get to the tender mosses that make up most of his diet.
   c.   Sylvia lives in a nest near the top of a huge tree. She spends much of her time soaring through the air searching with her keen eyes for the rabbits and rodents that she brings back for her young.
   d.   Sally spends most of her time in the water in the far north. On warm days, she lies near the water to sun herself before diving for the fish that make up her diet.

EXERCISE 13.3

Exercise 13.3 measures your understanding of topics covered on pages 657-649 of your text.

Look at the sample items taken from the commercially prepared test on p. 662 of your text and analyze them according to the criteria specified in this section of the chapter. In cases of inconsistency, describe specifically how the items fail to meet the criterion.

a. The completion items

_____

_____

_____

_____

b. The alternative response items

_____

_____

_____

_____

```
┌─────────────────────────────────────────────────┐
│┌───────────────────────────────────────────────┐│
│└───────────────────────────────────────────────┘│
└─────────────────────────────────────────────────┘
```

EXERCISE 13.4

Exercise 13.4 measures your understanding of topics covered on pages 668-677 of your text.

1. Your students are taking a test, and the intercom breaks in saying, "Ms. . . , a parent, is on the phone. She needs to talk to you. She says it's important. Can you come to the office for a moment?" Using the information in this section as a basis, describe the most appropriate response to the request.

_____

_____

_____

_____

2. You have worked harder than you thought possible to get your students ready for an important test. "They have to be ready," you say to yourself. "Nobody could do a better job of teaching than I did here." To your chagrin, most of the class do very poorly on the test, and many of the responses seem to indicate a lack of effort on the part of the students. Based on the information in this section, which of the following is the best response to the students? (Provide a rationale for your decision.)
   a.   We did a good job on the test. Now let's try and keep it up.
   b.   We did okay on the test. I believe if we work a little harder we can do better yet.
   c.   We didn't do as well as I had hoped considering that we prepared so much. Let's try and redouble our efforts for the next test.
   d.   I'm quite disappointed in the test results. Considering how hard I worked to get you ready, it doesn't look like some of you studied as much as you could have.

_____

_____

_____

EXERCISE 13.5

Exercise 13.5 measures your understanding of topics covered on pages 677-684 of your text.

Examine items 7, 10, and 15 in the distribution of scores presented in Table 13.13 on page 683 of your text. Put yourself in the role of the teacher who has given the test.

1. What does the distribution reveal that would cause you to question the items?

_____

_____

_____

2. What are two possibilities that might explain the results?

_____

_____

_____

3. What would you do in response to these possibilities?

_____

_____

_____

4. Criticize item 1 in the distribution of scores. If the item is used, why is it appropriately placed?

_____

_____

_____

5. Using the criteria for effective preparation of multiple-choice items, examine and criticize the distribution of correct answers for the quiz.

_____

_____

_____

_____

## EXERCISE 13.6

Exercise 13.6 measures your understanding of topics covered on pages 685-706 of your text.

Tamara scores in the 50th percentile, Joey scores in the 70th, and Helen scores in the 90th.

1. Identify the stanine for each student.

_____

_____

2. Identify the approximate z-score and T-score for each student.

_____

_____

3. What is each student's IQ according to the Wechsler scales?

_____

_____

_____

4. Maria takes the Scholastic Aptitude Test and finds that she scored an 1100, 600 in math and 500 in English. What is her approximate percentile rank in math and English?

_____

_____

_____

5. Rhonda scores a 62 on a test with a mean of 50 and a standard deviation of 8. If the test results approximate a normal distribution, what is Rhonda's:

a. Approximate percentile rank?

_____

b. Stanine?

_____

c. z-score?

_____

6. A test is given with a mean of 60, a median of 60, a mode of 60 and a standard deviation of 5. Approximately half the group of students who took the test scored from 55 to 65 on the test. Of the following, which is the best conclusion?
a. The scores fit a normal distribution.
b. The scores do not fit a normal distribution.
c. We don't have enough information to determine whether or not the scores fit a normal distribution.
Explain your answer.

_____

_____

_____

_____

_____

7. Joanne scores a 45, Franklin scores a 40, and Monica scores a 35 on a test with a standard error of 3. Which of the following statements are true? (More than one answer may be true.)

   a.      Joanne's true score is higher than both Franklin's and Monica's.

   b.      Franklin's true score is higher than both Joanne's and Monica's.

   c.      Franklin's true score might be higher than both Joanne's and Monica's.

   d.      Monica's true score might be higher than both Joanne's and Franklin's.

   e.      Joanne's true score is higher than Monica's and might be higher than Franklin's.

Explain your answer in each case.

_____

_____

_____

8. You carefully followed the procedures suggested for preparing your students for tests, which were outlined in your text. You then give your class the test and you find that Jaramillo, one of your students of Hispanic descent, missed over half of the items on a 20-item test, while only one of your white students missed more than 5 items. Jaramillo is a recent immigrant to the United States, but his background in English is good. Which of the following is the most accurate statement?

a. The test is biased against students of Hispanic background.

b. The test is not biased against students of Hispanic background.

c. We don't have enough information to evaluate the test for bias.

Explain your choice.

_____

_____

_____

_____

265

# CHAPTER THIRTEEN
# CLASSROOM ASSESSMENT

## SELF-HELP QUIZ _____

TRUE-FALSE QUESTIONS:  Mark T in the blank for a true statement and mark F for a false statement.

_____ 1. A test item could be invalid and still be reliable.

_____ 2. A test item could be unreliable and still be valid.

_____ 3. Teachers should give fewer tests in low achieving classes than in higher achieving classes.

_____ 4. Formal measurements are usually less reliable than are informal measurements.

_____ 5. If students understand a topic, and they respond incorrectly to a test item measuring the topic, the test item is invalid.

_____ 6. Norm-referenced evaluations discourage low achieving students more than do criterion-referenced evaluations.

_____ 7. Middle and secondary school teachers use "weak" formats most commonly in their preparation of test items.

_____ 8. Specifying for students exactly what will be on a test tends to detract from the test's validity.

_____ 9. Teachers who give frequent tests and quizzes tend to have students with higher test anxiety than those who test less frequently.

_____ 10.      Standardized tests tend to be less reliable than are teacher-made tests.

MULTIPLE-CHOICE QUESTIONS: Circle the best choice in each case.

Look at the following four descriptions, and use the information for items 11 and 12.

1.      A teacher gives a 20 item quiz on flower plants.
2.      A teacher sees a student squint as she looks at the chalkboard.
3.      A teacher calls on a student.
4.      A teacher marks B+ on a student's essay.

11. The evaluation(s) is/are:
a.  1,2,3,4
b.  1,3,4
c.  1,4
d.  3,4
e.  4

12. The informal measurement(s) is/are:
a.  1,2,3
b.  2,3
c.  1,3
d.  2
e.  3

13. Two teachers independently score a student response on a essay. One teacher judges the response to be worth a B, and the other judges it to be worth a C. The question to which the student responded was consistent with stated objectives. Based on this information, which of the following is the most accurate response?
   a. The assessment is valid but not reliable.
   b. The assessment is reliable but not valid.
   c. The assessment is both reliable and valid.
   d. The assessment is neither reliable nor valid.

Use the following information for items 14-17.

A goal for the 10th grade English department at Geneva Lakes high School is for all the students in the 10th grade to be able to make and defend an argument. Different teachers approach measurement of the goal differently.

After discussing arguments and supporting evidence and giving a series of examples, Mrs. Baldwin gives the students in her class five written essays and asks the students to decide which essay best makes and defends an argument and which essay makes and defends an argument least well.

Mr. Brannan has each student in his class write an essay in which they make and defend an argument.

Mrs. Duncan has a class discussion in which individual students take a position. Some of the other students defend the position, while others take issue with the position. In all cases the individuals must provide evidence when they defend or take issue with the position. Mrs. Duncan then evaluates the students based on their responses in the discussion.

Mr. Combs describes the process of making and defending an argument. He then gives some examples of arguments and asks the students to write a series of statements that supports the argument.

14. The teacher whose measurements are most valid is:
   a. Mrs. Baldwin
   b. Mr. Brannan
   c. Mrs. Duncan
   d. Mr. Combs

15. The teacher whose measurements are most reliable is:
   a. Mrs. Baldwin
   b. Mr. Brannan
   c. Mrs. Duncan
   d. Mr. Combs

16. The teacher whose measurements are least reliable is:
   a. Mrs. Baldwin
   b. Mr. Brannan
   c. Mrs. Duncan
   d. Mr. Combs

17. The height of a normal distribution at any particular point represents which of the following?
   a. The raw score on a test.
   b. The number of people who attained a particular score on a test.
   c. The mean score of the people who took the test.
   d. The standard deviation of the scores on the test.

Use the following information for items 18-20.

A student takes a 60-item subtest of a standardized test. The subtest has a mean of 48 with a standard deviation of 6. The student gets a 54 on the subtest.

18. The 54 on the subtest is best described as the:
a. raw score.
b. standard error.
c. standard score.
d. stanine score.

19. Of the following, the best estimate of the student's percentile ranking is:
a. 96
b. 90
c. 84
d. 50

20. Of the following, the best estimate of the student's stanine ranking is:
a. 5
b. 6
c. 7
d. 8
e. 9

# FEEDBACK FOR APPLICATION EXERCISES

## CHAPTER 2: STUDENT DEVELOPMENT

Exercise 2.1

1.     Andre has a "multiplying fractions" schema.  Rather than accommodating the schema to allow the formation of a division of fractions schema, he incorrectly assimilated the problem into his already existing schema, which prevented any disruption of his equilibrium.

2.     Susan's unpredictable behavior disrupts Celena's equilibrium, which makes her uneasy and uncomfortable.  Her "Susan schema" does not allow her to understand or predict Susan's behavior.

3.     Kathy is demonstrating adaptation through the process of accommodation.  She has a "making and defending a position" schema, and she now is accommodating the schema to form a "persuasive argument" schema.  Her writing is developing as  a result.

4.     This example illustrates year-long development, and as a result, Malavai now has schemata that he didn't have earlier.

Exercise 2.2

1. Karen is formal operational.  She is able to simultaneously consider two variables.  Further, she appears to comfortably deal with abstract concepts, such as nationalism.  It is important to note that merely because she is at least 12-13, and therefore chronologically fits formal operations, doesn't mean that her thinking is necessarily formal operational. Without prerequisite experience learners' thinking might be concrete operational at best.

2. Cher is preoperational.  Knowing that the word horse represents the category horses is a form of symbolic thought.

3. Tim is formal operational.  He is applying an abstract concept (negative numbers) in an even more abstract way by referring to "negative time."

4. Susan is concrete operational.  She could handle the concept of fulcrum when shown the concrete materials.

5. Luis is at the sensorimotor stage.  The example suggests he hasn't acquired the concept of object permanence.

6. Ann is concrete operational.  She was able to perform a logical operation when she has concrete materials to manipulate.

Exercise 2.3

1. The words were presented only in the abstract, so the students merely memorized the brief definitions.  As a result they performed poorly on the antonym exercise, which is a form of application.  Karin needed to develop the words beginning in the concrete, much as Carol Barnhart had done earlier in the chapter.

269

2. While James has discussed air and air pressure with the students and has also had them read about it, there is no indication in the case study that James has provided any concrete experiences for the children. As a result, they remain dominated by their perception, and perceptually they see water pouring on the can and the can collapsing. Given the students' limited experience, their conclusion is not surprising.

Exercise 2.4

1. Stage 3. The focus is on the individual's reputation, or the opinion of others. Although there is an element of the self involved, since it is his or her reputation, the primary focus is on others, making it Conventional Ethics.

2. Stage 4. The concern is for the general orderliness of society.

3. Stage 2. The focus here is on the self. The individual is not getting in return what the cost requires. No concern for others or principled ethic is indicated in the example.

4. Stage 1. The concern is strictly related to punishment.

5. Stage 3. The person's concern is for the feelings of family.

6. Stage 3. This example isn't as obvious as the others, but the individual is basing the decision on the ethical example of others. There is no evidence of fear of punishment, and no exchange, as in Stage 2, is implied.

7. Stage 1. Grounding is a form of punishment.

8. Stage 5. A principle is being stated. It could be argued that the statement exists in the form of a general principle, and is therefore more appropriately Stage 6, but as indicated in the text of the chapter, the description of Stage 6 isn't completely clear.

9. Stage 1. Being in trouble with parents is an expression of concern for the self. No evidence of concern for others' feelings or example is demonstrated.

10. Stage 2. Again the concern is for the self, but by contrast with item 9, the concern isn't for being punished, rather the individual is simply not getting anything from the experience. It answers the question, "What's in it for me?"

11. Stage 5. An ethical principle is being stated.

12. Stage 3. The concern is for her parents' feelings.

13. Stage 4. She is strictly obeying a rule.

14. Stage 3. She is adhering to behavior as demonstrated by a peer group. Her ethic is based on the example of others.

Exercise 2.5

1. Carmella is in the identity-confusion stage. Her concern for her appearance and what others think of her is typical of this stage.

2. Deon is in the industry-inferiority stage. While he isn't a strong student, he is developing a sense of accomplishment and competence through his success in sports, and through them should positively resolve the crisis.

3. Kathy is in the initiative-guilt stage of development. She is past doing things on her own and has taken the initiative to make the pictures for her father. Her parents supportive attitude in the face of a potentially aggravating experience should help her positively resolve the crisis.

4. Mr. Thomas is in the generativity-stagnation stage. His concern for the next generation is an indicator of a positive resolution of the stage.

5. Tom is in the intimacy-isolation stage. His superficial relationships and his inability to feel strongly about someone indicates that he is having difficulty with the crisis, which at this point is not being positively resolved.

6. Mike is in the identity-confusion stage. He is experiencing the normal feelings of an adolescent boy beginning his search for identity as he moves toward manhood.

7. The case study indicates that Emmitt has a problem with initiative indicating that he didn't fully resolve the initiative-guilt crisis, which in turn left him with this problem. On the other hand, he appears to be resolving the identity-confusion crisis acceptably as indicated by him being a typical "normal" youngster for his age. The best the teacher can do is to provide him with opportunities to take initiative and then strongly reward any activities that result. Also, make it a point to encourage initiative in all his work and then be careful not to penalize him in any way for taking it.

# FEEDBACK FOR APPLICATION EXERCISES

## CHAPTER 3: STUDENT DEVELOPMENT: APPLICATIONS

Exercise 3.1

1. This parent was using social learning theory to teach language. She used modeling and reinforcement to elicit more adult-like speech from her daughter.

2. This dad applied behavioral views of language acquisition to improve his daughter's vocabulary. When the child correctly identified an animal she was given the toy as reinforcement. When wrong, the child was corrected and provided with the correct answer.

3. Psycholinguists believe that children acquire language by being exposed to it in its varied forms. They advocate talking to children at very young ages and holding conversations with them as soon as they are ready.

---

Exercise 3.2

1a. (E) This is an example of past irregular which usually occurs around the age of 2.

1b. (E/L) The ability to ask questions (reordered sentences) usually occurs around age 3.

1c. (L) This is a very complex sentence structure expressing cause and effect relationships. These usually appear around first grade.

1d. (E) One and two utterances are the first stage of language acquisition.

1e. (L) Embedded sentences (i.e. The car was skidding. The car slid off the road) are usually found in pre-school and kindergarten children.

2a. Pablo attends a transitional program. In transitional programs the first language (Spanish) is used until English proficiency is reached. Then it is used as an aid or supplement to English to help students when they have problems with English instruction.

2b. Jacinta's class is a maintenance program, designed to develop expertise in both Spanish and English.

2c. Abdul's fourth period class is a pull-out ESL program designed to supplement his regular instruction.

3. The most effective strategy is to build on the students' experiences. One way to begin would be to label several objects in the room in both Spanish and English as Tina Wharton did in the example on page 99 of your text. Then describe the objects, writing the descriptions on the board, and discussing the descriptions in detail. In the discussion, point out that each of these describing words are adjectives. Then, follow a similar procedure with adverbs. Have the students describe the action of something, such as the way you walk across the floor. Again, write the description on the board and discuss is thoroughly, pointing out that the description of the action is an adverb in each case.

---

Exercise 3.3

1a. <u>Authoritarian</u>. The teacher failed to mention or explain the rule on fighting. Before we judge her too harshly we should also know past history and the context of the argument.

1b. <u>Authoritative</u>. She encouraged students to think about the problem and work it out themselves. Hopefully this would lead to future problem-solving skills.

2a. <u>Permissive</u>. If there are topics that need to be learned, the teacher's responsibility is to teach these.

2b. <u>Authoritative</u>. By acknowledging that some topics are more interesting than others but that interest alone should not dictate what is learned, the teacher is helping students understand the process of learning.

3a. <u>Authoritarian</u>. A verbal reprimand without explanation would be considered authoritarian. The next response in 3b offers an alternative.

3b. <u>Authoritative</u>. Reminding the student of the reasons for and consequences of the action helps him understand the importance of rules.

4a. <u>Permissive</u>. Grading is an aspect of instructional decision-making that should be <u>shared</u> with but not totally given to students. Grades not only influence motivation and students' study behaviors but also have an impact on the teacher's workload.

4b. <u>Authoritative</u>. While the teacher seeks student input into this instructional decision and shares with the class her perspective she still communicates that the decision is hers.

A final note: While the ideal might be to act totally in the authoritative mode and never in the permissive or authoritarian, the reality is that we all lapse into these others. The goal is to realize when we do and to strive to make our classrooms a place where students can grow as people.

Exercise 3.4

A direct instruction approach would specifically target the concepts and skills being taught. It would begin by pretesting specific concepts like "more" and "left" as well as operations such as subtraction. Instruction would specifically target these concepts and skills and would use practice with feedback to ensure that these were learned.

A developmental approach would integrate this information into larger, more meaningful social tasks. For example, the teacher might use pieces of candy or cookies at treat time to talk about numbers and how they are useful. Or, the teacher might use cooking to show how math relates to the real world.

Exercise 3.5

Elementary children need concrete experiences to make abstract concepts meaningful. One way to do this would be to bring in real bones that students could touch and feel. These might be borrowed from a high school health teacher or might be bones from a chicken, cow or pig that the local butcher has provided. Another option would be to bring in a skeleton, such as those used in life science and biology classes. As you're discussing the different bones it would be good to have students compare their size and function and have them "find" the bones on themselves.

Exercise 3.6

1a. This statement reflects on Margaret Mead's findings that the transitions of adolescence are influenced by culture. The opportunities and options of American culture make the decision-making process more complex.

1b. Hall described adolescence as an inevitable period of confusion and tension. Though descriptive on one level this view fails to place this period of development in a large perspective.

1c. Erikson's view of teenage turmoil is similar to Hall's but framed in a much more healthy, developmental perspective. Yes, teenagers are confused but they'll figure it out, and the process of wrestling with these questions is a healthy one.

2. Sandy's statement, "I'm going to play it by ear for a while," suggests identity moratorium. Identity moratorium occurs when students pause in their development to take a look around and evaluate their option's.

    Ramon's comments suggest identity foreclosure. He has adapted the values of his parents without serious consideration of how they fit him.

    Nancy's comments, by contrast, suggest identity diffusion. Her interests are scattered, and she hasn't taken a serious look at what she wants to be or become.

    Taylor's comments approximate identity achievement. It appears that he has taken a realistic look at his strengths and weaknesses and is choosing a career path that is realistic.

# FEEDBACK FOR APPLICATION EXERCISES

## CHAPTER FOUR: INDIVIDUAL DIFFERENCES

Exercise 4.1

Some positive practices identified in the episode included:

a. Flexible grouping. Tony was in one math group and moved up to another in the middle of the year.

b. Different groupings for different subjects. Students are often good in different subjects and having alternate grouping arrangements for different content volumes allows teachers to match instruction to student needs.

c. Heterogeneous homeroom grouping. This was only implied in the episode, but the fact that Tony stayed in his homeroom in the afternoon suggested that subjects like science, social studies, art and health were taught in diverse groups. This minimizes some of the negative affective consequences of grouping.

d. Positive expectations. No matter what group students are in they should be made to feel that they can and will succeed. Mrs. Lemar did a nice job of communicating this at the beginning of her math class.

---

Exercise 4.2

First, you must establish a climate where all students feel accepted and valued. One way to accomplish this is to carefully practice equitable treatment of your students. This means call on all the students in your class approximately equally, prompt each one when they're unable to answer, give each similar feedback, and use the same body language with each.

Second, use a constructivist approach to your instruction, and use open-ended questions liberally.

Third, keep all performance records private, and tell the students to avoid sharing their grades with anyone else in the class. This is designed to take the pressure off the students who want to perform well, but feel peer pressure to avoid doing so.

Finally, you may even tell them to not raise their hands in class, (again to keep some students from "standing out" in front of their peers). Then be sure to call on all students equally, and be certain that you give them enough support to be certain that each is able to answer.

---

Exercise 4.2

1. Research indicates that female students take fewer elective and fewer advanced science classes. Probably the strongest explanation is cultural; female students don't perceive science as an appropriate field for them to major in nor do they view science-related careers as positively as do male students.

2. In the short term she should do everything she can to make the females in her class comfortable, modeling her interest in science and communicating positive expectations for them in the class. Long term solutions might include recruiting in lower level classes, working with other science teachers to make sure the science curriculum is gender friendly and actively talking with parents and counselors about careers in science.

---

Exercise 4.4

Field dependent students are more likely to enjoy and participate in small group activities requiring cooperation and group goals. Field independent students, by contrast, typically prefer working alone on individual projects. Students' different reactions to the small group project may be attributable to differences in field dependence-independence.

Exercise 4.5

a. Greater Structure and Support: Students had assignments written on the board when they entered the room and expectations during the lesson were clearly laid out.

b. Active Teaching: The teacher was actively involved in explaining and modeling the new content.

c. Instructional Strategies Emphasizing Student Engagement: All the students in the class actively practiced all the problems.

d. More Frequent Feedback: Students received feedback after each problem as well as after they completed their seatwork.

e. Smaller Steps with More Redundancy: The teacher did this in several ways. First, the board assignment reviewed content from the previous day. Second, she provided ample opportunities for students to practice with feedback. Finally, seatwork provided additional opportunities for practice and feedback.

f. Higher Success Rates: The teacher ensured that group success rates were high (90%) before proceeding to individual practice. Even then she spent additional time with students still having problems.

# FEEDBACK FOR APPLICATION EXERCISES

## CHAPTER 5: TEACHING STUDENTS WITH EXCEPTIONALITIES

Exercise 5.1

1. Teaching. Often minor adjustments are all that are needed in the classroom to help exceptional students learn in the regular classroom. Different seating arrangements, more explicit directions, teacher follow-through, and encouragement are little things that can make a big difference.

2. Identification. Teachers are often in the best position to identify learning problems because they observe students as they interact with learning materials and peers. Toni's observation of Marisse suggested that something was getting in the way of her success in the classroom.

3. Acceptance. A major obstacle to acceptance is ignorance. When students understand how exceptional students are different, this knowledge can often serve as the foundation for acceptance.

Exercise 5.2

1. Due Process: Pablo's parents were consulted from the beginning and their approval for testing was obtained. If they hadn't given their approval, the process would have stopped there. In addition, their input was further solicited in the development of the I.E.P., and the decision to keep him in the regular classroom but require resource help. If they had not approved of these decisions, they had the right to an external independent review of the process.

2. Protection Against Discrimination in Testing: This is an especially critical component of P.L. 94-142 because of the growing number of non-English speaking students in our schools. Because of this problem, and in response to a court case (Diana v. State of Education, 1970), one state, California, agreed to test all children whose primary language was not English in both their primary language and English (Salvia & Ysseldyke, 1988). Because of the close interrelationship between language and intelligence testing, this provision is probably essential to accurate testing.

3. Least Restrictive Environment: The general thrust of this provision is to keep children, as much as educationally possible, in the regular classroom. Research suggests that mainstreaming students like Pablo in the regular classroom has both academic and social advantages.

Exercise 5.3

G    1. Problems functioning in regular classrooms. (These problems require special, supplementary help for these students.)

MR    2. Below average performance on intelligence tests. (This is a distinguishing characteristic of the mentally retarded.)

LD  3. Problems often involving language. (Students with learning disabilities often have trouble with reading and listening.)

LD,BD 4. Management problems often interfering with learning. (Management problems can be a factor with all of these students but is most characteristic of students with learning disabilities and behavior disorders.)

LD  5. Discrepancies between two measures of achievement. (This discrepancy often helps identify the specific type of learning disability.)

BD  6. Students sometimes withdrawn and extremely shy. (Though this could be found in all mildly handicapped students, it is characteristic of one type of behavioral disorder.)

G  7. Failure and frustration often interfering with learning. (All mildly handicapped students experience these and they do interfere with learning.)

# FEEDBACK FOR APPLICATION EXERCISES

## CHAPTER 6: BEHAVIORAL VIEWS OF LEARNING

Exercise 6.1

1. Cathy jerking her head back in response to the bursting balloon is an example of a reflex, and therefore is not a learned behavior.

2. Ronnie's crying is a learned behavior, based on previous negative experiences with needles or other experiences associated with needles. (People are not instinctively or reflexively afraid of needles.)

3. Donnell's increased speed is primarily the result of his improved strength and physical conditioning rather than the result of learning.

4a. The unconditioned stimulus is the situation that caused the embarrassing experience. This situation is a combination of being called on, being stared at, and the boys giggling. We can't be sure of the exact combination of the factors. It could be any one of them, two of them, or all three.

4b. The unconditioned response was Duranna's stomach clenching and her face turning red. (This is a reflexive response to the situation.)

4c. The conditioned stimulus is an environment where students are being questioned. It has become associated with the initial embarrassing situation.

4d. Duranna's uneasiness is the conditioned response. Notice that uneasiness is a response that is similar to the unconditioned response--stomach clenching and face turning red.

Notice that the conditioned and unconditioned stimuli are not necessarily related in any inherent way (just as Pavlov's assistants and the meat powder are not inherently related), but they become associated. The conditioned and unconditioned stimuli are similar or identical (similar in Duranna's case; identical for Pavlov's dogs).

4e. Her uneasiness has now generalized to geometry because the environment there is similar to the environment in American History.

4f. Duranna discriminates between Spanish, where the questioning is patterned, and American History and geometry, where the process has been anxiety inducing.

5. Mr. Harkness needs to call on Duranna in a situation where he is certain that she is not taken by surprise. After Duranna is called on several times without incident (the conditioned stimulus occurring repeatedly in the absence of the unconditioned stimulus), her uneasiness should begin to disappear. He also needs to make and enforce a rule that forbids students from laughing at each other's embarrassment.

---

Exercise 6.2

1. Miguel is being punished for speaking out in class, which is evidenced by the decreasing incidence of question-asking behavior. This is a form of presentation punishment, since an undesired consequence is being given, rather than something desirable being taken away.

2. Mr. Orr's behavior is being negatively reinforced. Miguel's questions make him uncomfortable since he can't always answer them. His sarcasm stops Miguel's behavior which removes an undesirable situation (being asked questions he may not be able to answer). As a result we see his sarcasm increasing.

3. For this statement to be true, the students would have to prefer doing map work rather than longitude and latitude problems. The map work (the preferred activity) could then be used as a reinforcer for the less preferred activity (doing longitude and latitude problems).

---

Exercise 6.3

1. The concept is continuous reinforcement, and this case study illustrates the rapid reduction in behavior after a continuous reinforcement schedule. Normally, the door opens every time (continuous reinforcement) as evidenced by Mrs. Thornton's comment, "That's never happened before." The door opening each time is a reinforcer for putting the key in and attempting to open the door. This time when it didn't open, Mrs. Thornton quickly gave up, which is characteristic of behavior when a continuous reinforcement schedule is used and the reinforcers are removed. If the door had been "balky," meaning she had to struggle to get it open (an intermittent schedule) she would have persevered longer.

2. The concept being demonstrated in this example is discrimination. Mary is discriminating between the spider and the other animals, which are insects.

3. The example illustrates extinction as a result of lack of reinforcement. Ken is getting no reinforcement for his effort, and as a result the effort is disappearing.

4. Mrs. Howe is making an effort to shape her students' behavior by reinforcing behaviors that are successive approximations of the desired behavior.

5. The case study is an example of satiation. Mrs. Starke has apparently sent too many positive notes home to the point that they've lost their potency as reinforcers.

6. Mr. Weiss was applying a fixed-interval form of reinforcement to his classroom. While this can have disadvantages, as discussed in the text of the chapter, his giving a problem every day kept the interval short, so student effort remained high. This is not an example of continuous reinforcement, because not every studying behavior is reinforced. The students are reinforced on the interval of one day.

---

Exercise 6.4

1. The story is a form of symbolic modeling. When the two lazy little pigs get eaten, the readers are vicariously punished; the readers observe the consequences of the little pigs actions, and perhaps adjust their own behavior accordingly. When the conscientious little pig outwits the wolf, the readers are vicariously reinforced. The most likely modeling outcome is to facilitate existing behaviors. The students know how to be conscientious, and the combination of the symbolic modeling of the conscientious little pig and vicarious reinforcement could result in increased conscientiousness.

2. Readers are caught in a dilemma between vicarious reinforcement and vicarious punishment. They are vicariously reinforced through the Sidney Carton's noble act, but they are vicariously punished through the fact that he gave his life under the guillotine. It is a form of symbolic modeling.

3a. Attention is illustrated in 1-4 of the case study. Mrs. Holmes pulled down a map, referred the students to it and has them find themselves on it. She then asked for another city.

3b. She promoted retention by modeling the process of finding the location of longitude and latitude (beginning at 5). She continued the process through 8 of the case study.

3c. Reproduction began at 9 when she asked Joanie to locate the longitude of Chicago. This continued through the locations of each city.

3d. Motivation was illustrated in several places. She began the lesson by explaining that the skill was an important one, used throughout the course. During the course of the lesson she reinforced with comments like, "Good", and "Excellent." Finally, students received points for completing their homework.

4a. Joe imitated the behavior he saw in his colleagues by sitting back down and working when he saw them sitting working.

4b. His smile in response to the question "as he always did in response to a question" is an example of contiguity.

4c. Joe is being positively reinforced for coming late. He is not in an aversive situation prior to demonstrating the behavior (going to the meeting), so nothing undesirable is being removed. It is therefore not negative reinforcement. We know his lateness is being reinforced because he is coming later and later (His behavior is increasing, not decreasing.)

# FEEDBACK FOR APPLICATION EXERCISES

## CHAPTER 7: COGNITIVE VIEWS OF LEARNING

Exercise 7.1

1. The teacher posed the question, "What are we going to do first to simplify this expression?" and before the students had a chance to answer, she posed a second question, "What is important to remember whenever we simplify something like this?" Because information is quickly lost from the sensory registers if processing doesn't begin (through attention), one of two things is likely to happen: The students will attend to the first question and lose the second one from their sensory registers, or their attention to the first question will be disrupted by the second question, so their attention to the first one will be incomplete. Either situation has a negative impact on learning.

2. She should ask the first question, wait for a response from a student, and then asked the second question.

3. Working memory has only limited capacity. You have introduced a great deal of information in the lesson-- religion, exploitation, indignation, overpopulation, scarce natural resources, and how all the details of these factors led to the Japanese attack on the United States. Since the students seemed attentive, it is likely that their working memories were overloaded, and rather than being able to encode the information into long-term memory, it was lost from their working memories.

4. Because of working memory's limited capacity and the rate at which information is transferred into long-term memory, it is likely that students "miss" some of the presentation. A textbook can then be used to "fill in the gaps."

5. Too much working memory space is taken up by the algebraic manipulations involved in the problems, leaving inadequate space for the actual physics involved. The algebra skills must become automatic, thereby reducing the amount of working memory space they occupy, so more of this space can be devoted to focusing on the physics in the problems.

6a. Declarative
6b. Procedural
6c. Declarative
6d. Procedural

7. A propositional network could appear as follows:

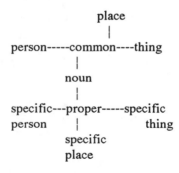

We must keep in mind, however, that propositional networks are individual and idiosyncratic, meaning the network for one learner can be different from that of another. An improperly constructed network is a source of learner misconceptions.

---

Exercise 7.2

1. You could begin the lesson by asking the students what they would do if they met a new friend and they wanted to tell the friend exactly where they live. How might they describe their location for their friend.

As second could be to bring in a globe, have the students describe its characteristics, and then ask the students how we might describe a location on it.

2. Present the students with a paragraph in which the rules are embedded. Then ask the students why words such as boy's, girls', and children's are punctuated the way they are.

A second option would be to have the students describe some things that belong to one or more of them. Write their descriptions on the board properly punctuating the possessives. Then ask them why different words are punctuated the way they are.

3. Bring in a model skeleton and have the students describe it. Then tell them that the class needs to explain why the skeleton exists the way it does, e.g., closed skull, curved ribs, large upper leg bone, etc.

Have the students feel their own skeletons and describe them. Then ask them to explain why their skeletons exist the way they do.

4. An ideal question would be, "Describe what you see in this sentence." The students' answers would give you insight into their understanding.

5. The case study illustrates the impact that expectations have on the perception of an event. The two teachers went into the experience with very different expectations, and as a result they interpreted their experience very differently.

---

Exercise 7.3

1. Nikki was using elaboration. She had a "force and acceleration problems without friction" schema, which together with the sample problem served as the foundation from which elaboration could take place.

2. Tanya's matrix was a form of organization which would make the information more meaningful, thereby aiding its coding into long term memory.

3. Meg's flash cards are a form of rehearsal.

4. Juan's nonsense word "Pmat" is a mnemonic device.

5. These conceptions are meaningful for the students, even though they're invalid. Meaningfulness means that associations exist. Associating mammal with four legs, warmth, and land is meaningful, as is associating fish and water. Students can easily come to these conclusions, because many examples are consistent with the ideas; for example, the majority of the animals in water *are* fish.

6. A matrix in which, for example, the geography, climate, economics and people's lifestyle in the south is compared to that in the north would be an excellent way to organize the information. Table 7.3 on page 332 of your text illustrates a matrix comparing two immigrant groups.

7. You could begin by reviewing finding areas of squares, rectangles, and triangles, then "cutting" parallelograms and trapezoids into rectangles and triangles, adding the areas to find to total area of each, and finally combining the formulas to derive a formula for finding the area for each.

---

Exercise 7.4

1a. When Joan's understanding of natural fibers helped her better understand synthetic fibers when they were later studied, proactive facilitation was taking place.

1b. Diane's earlier work with base two confused her understanding of base three which came later. This is a form of proactive interference.

1c. When Jill's teacher made her presentation, Romeo and Juliet, which she had studied earlier began to make sense. For Jill, retroactive facilitation was taking place.

1d. Steve's later learning impaired earlier understanding. This is a form of retroactive interference.

2. Embedding examples of rules in a paragraph would the best way to capitalize on context.

3. Jaun's propositional network for the solar system was complete and interconnected than was Randy's. Because there were more links in his network, retrieval would be easier for him. (Look again at Figures 7.5 and 7.6 on page 315 of your text for a visual comparison the two students' networks.

---

Exercise 7.5

1. Marissa is demonstrating metacommunication. She realizes that she may not have understood what Mrs. Jensen was saying, and she demonstrated control over her communication (listening) by asking Mrs. Jensen to repeat the question.

2. Steve is demonstrating meta-attention. He is aware that he is attending to the radio instead of his homework, and he controls his behavior by turning off the radio.

3. Billy is demonstrating metacommunication. He is aware that he may not be communicating clearly, and he governs his behavior by asking for questions.

4. Claudia is demonstrating metamemory. She realizes that she doesn't remember the difference between neap and spring tide, and she adopts a strategy to help her remember.

5. The student is demonstrating meta-attention--awareness that she would have difficulty attending and control over her attention.

# FEEDBACK FOR APPLICATION EXERCISES

## CHAPTER 8: COGNITIVE VIEWS OF LEARNING: APPLICATIONS

Exercise 8.1

1. This lesson focused on declarative knowledge. Often in science, social studies, literature, and health, we want students to remember not isolated facts or concepts, but large, cohesive integrated bodies of information. Mary Jo Fernandez attempted this by providing a structured overview at the beginning of the lesson and a comprehensive review with a chart at the end of the unit.

2. Bill Stanton was teaching his students a generalization that related the concepts <u>color</u> and <u>depth perspective</u>. He accomplished this with his examples (the paintings) that illustrated the relationship. Illustrating the relationship is critical when a generalization is being taught.

3. Dan Shafer was teaching the concept <u>inference</u>. He gave the students a definition and a series of examples, which were embedded in the context of a paragraph. He then reinforced the concept by having the students identify examples of inference in another paragraph.

4. Juanita Kennedy was teaching her students declarative knowledge. Her unit involved a combination of facts, such as the names of the animals, concepts--the animals themselves--and generalizations, such as what different animal groups eat and the products they give us.

5. Kathy Connor's students were learning the <u>rule</u> for simplifying arithmetic expressions. She demonstrated the rule with examples and she had the students apply the rule with several more examples.

6a. The concept being taught was "dogie." Note how the teacher helped her students use context clues to teach the concept. This is a helpful and widely applicable concept learning strategy for use with printed material.

6b. The superordinate concept could be either cows (cattle) or calves in general. Both are larger, more inclusive concepts in which the target concept is embedded.

6c. A coordinate concept would be calves <u>with</u> mothers.

6d. The essential characteristic mentioned in the episode was "motherless." From student responses we could infer that other characteristics like "four-legged, nurses from mother" were present in students' schema for calf, but these are not the essential characteristics.

6e. The teacher used the picture of a cattle drive to present a positive example of the concept. This is an essential component of concept learning, but one that is often by-passed because examples for some concepts are hard to find or create.

This concept would be easy to learn, because it only had one essential characteristic, and the characteristic is very concrete.

Exercise 8.2

The different problem solving stages occurred as follows:

**Understanding The Problem:**

Bill Watson encouraged this when students drew a diagram of the problem and broke it down into what was given and what the students needed to know.

**Devising a Plan:**

This stage occurred when Shanda broke the problem down into a circle problem minus one quarter and when Kerry remembered the formula for the area of a circle.

**Implementing the Plan:**

Students implemented the plan when they used their hand calculators to solve the equation.

**Evaluating the Results:**

The teacher encouraged this in several ways. First, he asked them to estimate whether their answer was "about right." Then he asked them to use the correct units. Finally he encouraged them to check their answers against earlier notes and diagrams. Each of these makes their problem solving more thoughtful and less impulsive.

Exercise 8.3

1. The criteria for effective transfer are <u>quality</u>, <u>variety</u>, and <u>context</u>. We have little evidence about the context in any of the three episodes. The quality of Mrs. Jung's examples wasn't good, since she only used verbal descriptions. The quality of Mr. Hume's examples was a bit better, since he used a picture of a sea turtle. Mrs. McManus clearly had the best quality examples, and even though Mr. Hume had the added variety of the sea turtle, Mrs. McManus's quality would more than make up for this deficit, so the likelihood of transfer would be the greatest in her case. The poor quality examples in Mrs. Jung's case would make transfer least likely for her students.

2. In addition to neglecting <u>context</u>, none of the teachers used any <u>nonexamples</u>.

3a. Two advanced organizers used in the lesson were:

The parts of the blood are like a baseball team. Each has a job to do. Their job is to carry different materials in the blood.

Red blood cells are our body's oxygen railroad.

Both of the advance organizers were in the form of analogies.

3b. The lesson started with the advance organizer which compared the parts of the blood to a baseball team. It progressed to the parts of the blood, and then the specific role of the red blood cells was described. The most general ideas were presented first, and they were followed by increasingly specific ideas.

3c. Ann elicited horizontal associations when she asked the students how the parts of the blood were different from each other. Vertical associations are formed when information on one level is linked to information on a higher level. Ann elicited a vertical association when she referred Tamara back to the advance organizer, and a second case occurred when Ann asked Kim, "How does this relate to our first statement of yesterday.?"

4a. The abstraction being taught was the concept "triangle."

4b. The data that Jill used to teach the concept were the positive (triangles) and the negative (squares, circles, etc.) examples that she placed on the felt board.

4c. Jill presented her examples out of context.

4d. A deductive lesson focusing on the same concept might begin with the teacher defining the concept; "A triangle is a shape with three sides and straight lines," move to an explanation of the essential characteristics--the three sides and straight lines--and finally progress to determining of other shapes were triangles or not.

# FEEDBACK FOR APPLICATION EXERCISES

## CHAPTER 9: INCREASING STUDENT MOTIVATION

Exercise 9.1

1. The increase in Jim's motivation can best be explained on the basis of cognitive theories of motivation. His comment, "It's sort of interesting the way Brewster's always telling us about the way we are 'cause of something that happened a zillion years ago," best indicates a response to a need to understand the way the world works. We have some inferential evidence for Kathy's enthusiasm and modeling, but this evidence is more conjectural than the evidence for a need to understand.

2. The impact of teacher expectations are best explained on the basis of social learning theories of motivation. Learner makes inferences about the teacher's perception of their ability based on the teacher's behavior. For example, when a student tries to answer a question, but is unable to do so, and the teacher exhorts and prompts the student, the student concludes that the teacher thinks he or she is capable of answering. This can result in an increased sense of self-efficacy, which in turn increases motivation.

3. Knowing that they will be allowed to respond without fear of interruption (or ridicule) increases a student's sense of safety, which is part of Maslow's Hierarchy of needs. Maslow's work best fits humanistic views of motivation.

4a. Cognitive theorists would suggest that Kathy's statement describing a relationship between a thousand years ago and the present appeals to learners' instinctive need for order, predictability, and how the world works.

4b. Humanistic theorists would suggest that the description of the relationship appeals to Maslow's level of "Intellectual Achievement."

5. David's comment to Kelly was a response to Kathy's enthusiasm. The motivating effects of enthusiasm are best explained modeling, which is consistent with social learning views of motivation.

---

Exercise 9.2

1. One way to promote arousal is to begin a lesson with a question or problem. For example, the teacher might write a pair of sentences on the board, such as the following:

> Steve sketched Conchita a picture of his new house.

> Mom gave Sen a ride to school.

She could then ask the question, "What do Conchita and Sen have in common in the two sentences?" The students' search for the commonality would promote arousal.

2. Kathy was attempting to meet a need for belonging when she pulled Jennifer's desk into the middle of the row, and she was attempting to meet Nikki's need for safety when she admonished Joe for interrupting.

3. She helped meet a need for control and self-determination when she gave them the option of group presentations on the Renaissance or writing a paper on the Middle Ages. She also allowed them to decide the group order.

4. Kathy attempted to focus on a need for achievement by emphasizing that the quality of a student's paper depended on the quality of their argument, not a cut-and-dried answer. Second, she emphasized the long-range need for developing the skill of making and defending an argument, and finally, she allowed the students to revise the paragraphs based on the day's discussion.

5. Attribution theorists would recommend the statement. The teacher's statement puts students in a "win-win" situation. If they do well, they have the pride of accomplishment on a difficult task. If they do poorly, they can attribute the results to task difficulty rather than lack of ability or effort.

6. This statement would not be recommended. By contrast with item 5, this statement forces Tommy to attribute his success to an external source (ease of the task) thereby reducing his pride in the accomplishment.

7. This is not a recommended statement. The teacher is unwittingly inducing an attribution of low ability for Billy's poor performance which is precisely what teachers are encouraged to avoid.

8. This statement is recommended. The teacher is encouraging Susan to attribute her success to effort, which is the attribution most encouraged.

9. According to attribution theorists, this is an unlikely statement. The student attributes past success to ability which is a stable cause, leading to the expectation of similar results in the future.

10. The theory would suggest that this is a likely statement. The student attributes failure to a stable cause (ability), which, as in item 9 leads to the expectation of similar results.

11. This is a likely statement. Success on the last test was attributed to luck, which is unstable, leading to the expectation of different results in the future.

---

Exercise 9.3

1. When Susan encouraged Jim to hurry to class because, ". . . you know how Brewster is about this class. She thinks it's sooo important," she was responding to Kathy's modeling.

2. David's comment, "Brewster loves this stuff," was a response to Kathy's enthusiasm and her modeling of the importance of what they were studying.

3. This comment best indicates Kathy's expectations for the students.

4. Kathy's admonishment of Joe for interrupting Nikki, helped meed Nikki's need for safety.

5. Kathy prompted Kim when Kim didn't respond to Kathy's question, "Now, how did we start? . . . Kim?"

Kathy used an example of a crusade with her suggestions that they would be going on a "crusade" to change people's minds about eliminating extracurricular activities.

Kathy provided for teacher-aided practice by leading the discussion of whether or not the Crusades were a success.

Kathy provided for independent practice by first having the students write their paragraphs and then allowing them to revise their paragraphs based on the class discussion.

Exercise 9.4

1. When Kathy began her unit, she brought into class pictures of the crusaders. This provided an eye-catching introduction.

2. She personalized the activity by drawing an analogy between the Crusades and them "crusading" to change the leaders' minds about extracurricular activities in Lincoln High School.

3. She promoted involvement by calling on a variety of students and using their products as the basis for providing feedback.

4. Steve got a B for the first 9 weeks, so his base score was 80. He got a 78 on the quiz giving him 10 improvement points.

Karen had a B+ for an 85, and she got a 90 on the quiz giving her 20 improvement points.

Joe had a C- for a 65, and he got a 75 on the quiz giving him 30 improvement points.

Georgette got a D for the first grading period, giving her a 60. She got a 65 on the quiz resulting in 20 improvement points.

The 80 improvement points for the four students results in a team average of 20.

*FEEDBACK FOR APPLICATION EXERCISES*

## CHAPTER 10: MANAGING STUDENT BEHAVIOR

Exercise 10.1

1. Her class was too crowded.  There was nothing that she could do about this, since they were assigned to her.  The second factor was the possibility of distraction from outside the classroom through the window.  She could have arranged the desks so that the students were facing away from the window or at least facing at a diagonal from the window.

2. Andrea is a junior high teacher, and students at this age tend to pick at each other, making remarks and putting their classmates down.  By contrast, Joe's fifth graders are less inclined to demonstrate those behaviors, and as a result, a rule such as Andrea's second one is less necessary.

3. Andrea's first three rules are stated negatively:  "Do not . . ."

4. Her fourth rule is not specific.  "Be prepared and ready. . ." has an uncertain meaning.

5. "Laying it on them" doesn't allow any student input.

6. "Working on it all the time" is merely another way of indicating that she is carefully monitoring her rules and procedures.

7. This comment indicates that she provided a rationale for the rules that she is using.

Exercise 10.2

1. Donnell had her handouts prepared in advance and had them ready to go when her class started.  She then began immediately as the bell rang.  Vicki was still organizing her handouts as the students came into the room, and she didn't get started on time.

2. First, Judy's class was extremely orderly, and the limits for behavior were very clearly established.  Second, Judy provided leadership in the way she conducted her class.  Her goals were clear, she carefully guided the learning, and she accomplished this while maintaining order.  Third, her learning activity began when she asked the students to find the longitude and latitude of the cities.  As a result, when she went over the answers, each had an investment in them because of already having worked the problems.  She also promoted a sense of belonging by calling on individual students to respond, and in this way promoted involvement.

3. Judy demonstrated withitness in the following ways.  First, she "caught the right one" by responding to Kevin rather than Alison, since Kevin is the one who "started it." Second, she responded instantly to Kevin's misbehavior rather than waiting until it became more disruptive, and finally, she first responded to Kevin and Alison before she moved to Sondra, since Kevin's behavior had the potential to be the more disruptive.
    Judy demonstrated overlapping when she moved next to Kevin, and stopped his misbehavior while at the same time maintaining the flow of her lesson.

4. First, Judy's verbal and nonverbal behavior were congruent. Her nonverbal behavior communicated that she meant it in reinforcing the words. Second, she used an "I-message" in dealing with Sondra, and third, her general pattern was assertive rather than either hostile or passive.

5. Mr. Adam's was overdwelling on the students' behavior. A simple directive to get back on task would have been more effective.

6. Isabelle demonstrated both withitness and overlapping. At the same time that she was helping Vicki, she was monitoring the rest of the class (overlapping), and she moved immediately to Lance and Ken when they began their horseplay.

7. In the following responses note how they: 1) address the behavior, 2) describe the behavior in terms of its effect on the teacher, and 3) describe the teacher's feelings generated by the behavior.

7a. You must get your assignments in on time. When you don't, I have to give you make-up work, which takes up my time and frustrates me.

7b. Felicia, blurting out the answers is against the rules. This makes it difficult for me to try to give everyone a chance to answer, and it bothers me when I can't give everyone an equal chance.

7c. Sean, when you turn around to talk, you can't listen to me. I need to have everyone's attention. I get worn out and irritable when I have to repeat directions.

---

Exercise 10.3

1. Alberto demonstrated several characteristics of effective intervention. First, he kept his encounter with Heather very brief and he didn't get in an argument with her. He followed through by seeing her after class and explaining the consequences. While Heather protested to the contrary, Alberto was consistent in his dealing with her and Susan. He didn't force Heather into any admission of guilt, thereby forcing a power struggle. His consequences for misbehavior were clear and he administered them.

2. First, Alberto had clearly stated rules for which rationales were provided. This occurred in the planning phase. Second, he was firm in his dealings with Heather. Third, he communicated clearly, addressing the behavior, used "I-messages," and was assertive in his response.

# FEEDBACK FOR APPLICATION EXERCISES

## CHAPTER 11: PLANNING FOR INSTRUCTION

Exercise 11.1

1. Both of Mai's objectives have an observable behavior in them. This is characteristic of both Mager's and Gronlund's approaches to writing objectives.

In addition, both Mai's objectives have a goal statement: "Students will know how to convert fractions to decimals." This is a feature of Gronlund's approach to preparing objectives.

Both of Mai's objectives include a condition: "when given different fractions" and when given a series of fraction to decimal problems," as well as a criterion: "each correctly." ("Solve" is the observable behavior.) Stating a condition and criteria are characteristic of Mager's approach to writing objectives.

2a. Laurie's objective is stated near the beginning of the case study: ". . . they'll be able to tell me where these Indians live when I describe their lifestyle for them."

As an illustration of the second phase of the model Laurie selected the films and designed "Indian Day" which included dressing in native costumes and explaining their tribe to others.

Her organization of learning activities occurred when she chose to sequence the films first, followed by the presentations to the other students. Her scheduling of presentations was part of the organization process.

Laurie's evaluation was the test she gave.

2b. Organization was probably the most important function for Laurie. Much of the information in the case study describes her organizational efforts. She appears secure, and we have little evidence one way or the other about her reflection.

She is likely a veteran, since she appears quite sure of herself. In addition, the learning activities she developed were complex and sophisticated. It is unlikely that a rookie would "take them on" initially.

2c. Long-term planning occurred when Laurie decided that appreciation of others' cultures should be a year-long goal. Her focus on Native American cultures was at the unit level. Daily lessons included the movies as well as "Native American Day."

3. The unit's major problem is that it failed to break down a complex task into teachable (and learnable) parts. Students needed opportunities to practice and receive feedback on all of the subskills (e.g. writing a sentence, punctuation, organizing a single paragraph) before attempting the larger skill. This also provides valuable feedback to the teacher about how well the unit is going. A clear indicator for the need for task analysis occurs when only a small percentage of students reach the final goal.

Exercise 11.2

1.        The objectives would be classified as follows:

        Define adjectives -  Knowledge
                To list examples -  Comprehension.  However, if the examples listed are merely ones recalled
                from class discussion, the level is simple knowledge.

        Identify examples in sentences - Comprehension

        To make writing attractive with creative use of adjectives - Synthesis

2a. The final paragraph of the case study illustrates reflection on Charlie's part when he first describes his goals
and then concludes that the students' attitudes are the most important outcome of his unit.  Analyzing last year's
success with the unit is also evidence of reflection.

2b. Typical of veteran teachers, Charlie described the learning activities and their organization first, and later in
the process described his goal for the unit.  Also typical of veteran teachers, he didn't specify any evaluation at the
outset.

2c. "Understanding the characteristics of folk tales" is a comprehension level goal.  When the students write their
own, they can be working at the application or synthesis level depending on the degree of creativity.  Note that,
"understanding . . . ." wasn't an explicit objective for Charlie.  (It should also be noted that most experts would
say that Charlie had a goal for his unit rather than an objective since "understanding" is not observable, but instead
must be inferred from some other observable behavior.

2d. His affective objective is for the students to voluntarily write folk tales.  This is at the "Valuing" level.  Students
who write the folk tales are doing more than "Responding."  The writing requires commitment and extended
involvement.

# FEEDBACK FOR APPLICATION EXERCISES

## CHAPTER 12: EFFECTIVE TEACHING

Exercise 12.1

1. A half hour each was allocated for science and social studies. Compared to the hour allocated for math and the hour and a half each for reading and language arts, this suggests a lower priority placed on these subjects.

2. Shirley got her math lesson started at 10:01, she lost about a minute to the intercom interruption, and she finished at 10:52. As a result, she lost 5 minutes of instructional time, or 9% of her allocated time. This represents a much more efficient use of allocated time than is typical in most classrooms.

3. While we can't be certain about the attentiveness of each class member based on a written case study, the evidence we have indicates that her engaged time was very high, although slightly less than her instructional time, e.g. Jimmy and Karen were whispering, suggesting that they probably were off-task.

4. Academic learning time is the combination of success and engagement. As we saw in Question 3, high engagement rates are difficult to infer from a written anecdote, but we can see that Shirley made an attempt to actively involve students in the lesson. Active involvement strongly correlates with high engagement rates. In terms of success rates, most of Shirley's questions led to correct answers, and when they were initially unable to answer, Shirley prompted them.

Exercise 12.2

1. Shirley demonstrated several of the behaviors associated with enthusiasm. For instance, she "strode vigorously across the room," changed her vocal inflection, such as her response, "Excellent, Jon!" and tapped her knuckle on the chalkboard. Her general manner in the lesson suggested energy and a positive, vigorous approach to her teaching.

She also exhibited a concern for students and their well being. She had an encouraging smile, she gave the students time to think when she asked them a question, she stayed with Karen when she was initially unable to answer, and in spite of her task orientation, she took a few seconds to ask Nikki how she felt.

2. She directly modeled the algorithm for finding equivalent fractions. As she began, she said, "Watch what I do here," and then carefully demonstrated the procedure.

3. Shirley demonstrated excellent organizational skills: 1) she started her math lesson within a minute of the time it was scheduled to begin; 2) she prepared her illustrations of equivalent fractions the night before and had them at her fingertips when she needed them; 3) her routines were well established as evidenced by the children passing their papers forward without being told her transition from reading to math took only a total of three minutes; and 4) she was able to get the students back on task within a minute of the time the intercom interrupted her, and she minimized the disruption with Jimmy and Karen, stopping their whispering without saying a word.

4. Shirley simply signaled a transition by saying, "We're going to shift gears now where we want to add fractions when the denominators are not alike." This communicated to the students that they were on a topic that was new but related.

5. Shirley was alert and careful to react to individual student's answers in the questioning process. For example she said, "OK, fine," to Tim, "Good," to Gayle, and "Excellent," to Jon in response to each as they answered with confidence. In contrast, when Karen gave an uncertain answer, Shirley responded, "Yes, good, Karen. I saw you actually counting them." Monitoring allowed her to match feedback to students' responses.

6. When Shirley asked Ken how he knew that 2/3 and 4/6 are the same, Ken was able to respond. Shirley than supplied enough prompts to be certain that Ken was successful in answering. He was obviously involved, and the combination of success and involvement is characteristic of academic learning time.

Exercise 12.3

1. In each case the lesson would begin with a review of the previous day's work. In the case of the rule about adding the "ing" suffix, the teacher would review consonants, long vowel sounds, short vowel sounds, single and double consonants, and two different consonants at the end of words.

The math teacher would review each of the operations as well as operations combined with parentheses.

In teaching the concept of adverb, the teacher would review adjectives, nouns, and pronouns including examples of adjectives describing the other two parts of speech.

The teacher would review and illustrate force and movement.

In the second (presentation) phase the language arts teacher might include examples such as:

run     running jump  jumping     speed  speeding
get     getting  talk  talking     go     going

(Ideally these examples would be embedded in the context of a written passage.)

An example for the math teacher could be:     $4 + 5(2 + 6) - 8/4$

(As with the language example on suffixes, embedding the skill in the context of a problem would be more meaningful than presenting it in the abstract.)

The English teacher would use examples such as:

> The boy quickly ran up the stairs.
> The children were talking loudly.

(As in the two previous cases, embedding the examples in context is better than presenting them in isolation.)

The science teacher could use examples such as pulling a student sitting in a chair across the room. This could be contrasted with pushing on the wall showing force without movement.

In each case the teacher would give students an assignment. In the first case, students would have to form words where the suffix was added; in the second students would have to simplify a series of expressions; in the third they would have to identify adverbs in sentences; and in the fourth the students would have to determine if work was being done or not. During the guided practice phase, the teacher would have the students work an example and would then discuss it with the class. She would repeat the process - probably once or twice - until she was satisfied that students could work the rest of the problems on their own.

In the independent practice phase, students would work the remainder of the exercises on their own under the supervision of the teacher.

2. This is a technique for "checking for understanding."

Exercise 12.4

1. Shirley's overall orientation toward her lesson was constructivist. She began her lesson with the problem of adding 1/2 of one cake to 1/3 of another, and she guided the students as they developed their own understanding of equivalent fractions rather than merely presenting them with an algorithm. The most specific example of constructivist oriented teaching occurred when she asked the class to prove that adding the top numbers was the way to add fractions, which was followed by Natasha's explanation and the discussion between Natasha and Adam. This teacher-student, and student-student interaction captures the essence of instruction based on constructivism.

   The most behaviorally oriented aspect of the lesson occurred when she modeled the algorithm for finding equivalent fractions and then expected similar performance from the students. We don't have evidence of the students' understanding of the algorithm.

2. While other instances may exist as well, the following are some of the most prominent examples of essential teaching skills.

Carrie displayed energy and enthusiasm in her presentation and interaction with the students. For instance she "[moved] quickly to the center of the room," "punctuated alternately holding up one picture and then the other," responded, "Yes, very good!" and "Excellent observation, Ann!"

   She was well organized, having her pictures ready and waiting on her desk as she began the lesson.

   Her communication was clear and precise, vague terms and mazes being completely absent. Her lesson remained focused on the topic, indications of both connected discourse and academic focus.

   She provided introductory focus with her pictures and initial question and maintained sensory focus with the pictures and map.
   She provided feedback in the form of praise with comments such as, "Yes, very good!" "Yes indeed," "Excellent observation, Ann!" and "Good thought, Adam." A particularly good example of feedback was her comment to Donna, "Yes! Good thinking, Donna. We said at the beginning of the lesson that the Spanish and Portuguese views of colonialization were quite different." Since Donna's response was hesitant, Carrie embellished the feedback with added information. Noticing Donna's hesitation and responding the way she did is also evidence of Carrie's skill at monitoring, and monitoring was further indicated by her noticing that Donna had "drifted off" and calling on her to induce her back into the lesson.

   While closure was not illustrated in the lesson, Carrie's comprehension-monitoring and exploring relationships were both forms of review.

   Carrie's skill with questioning was also illustrated. She called on a different student for each question, asked the question first and specified the student's name second, prompted Donna rather than turning to someone else when Donna was inattentive, and gave the students time to answer. Each of the features of effective questioning was illustrated in her teaching.

Exercise 12.5

1. Jean Levitt demonstrated both the skills of <u>introductory focus</u> and <u>academic focus</u> very well. <u>Sensory focus</u> was less well demonstrated. Introductory focus was created by her statement, "The British advantages during the Revolutionary War should have ensured victory." Academic focus was clearly demonstrated with she reminded Ed and Joan that they were dealing with an irrelevant issue and refocused the group on the original question. Since there was no sensory stimuli, such as something to see, hear, or touch, sensory focus was less well demonstrated.

2. While thinking skills can be demonstrated in a number of ways, one of the best is encouraging students to support conjectures, opinions, and inferences with facts or observations. Jean did this when she asked Hank to support his conjecture about numerical advantage not being necessarily important.

3. Jean encouraged participation by directly calling on students to respond. She demonstrated a form of equitable distribution by calling on the students individually and by name.

# FEEDBACK FOR APPLICATION EXERCISES

## CHAPTER 13:  CLASSROOM ASSESSMENT

Exercise 13.1

1.  Ginger was making informal measurements when she watched the students doing the practice problems at the board.  While they might appear to be formal measurements, she wasn't getting the same information from all the students under the same conditions, so they were informal.  She was also making an informal measurement when she noticed that Erin was gazing out the window rather than working.  The quiz was an example of a formal measurement.

2. At that point in the lesson, Ginger's conclusion was not valid. Her conclusion was based only on the performance of the four students at the board (and Erin). She didn't have any information about the performance of the other students.

3. Ginger's quiz was both valid and reliable. Her goal was for the students to identify and solve problems that require regrouping, and 7 of the problems she gave required regrouping while 3 did not. (The only uncertainty in the relationship between the goal and assessment is that technically the students are not solving problems. They're merely applying an algorithm.) Reliability would be dependent upon scoring consistency as well as the length and the appropriate difficulty of the quiz.

4.  Ginger's system is criterion-referenced.  Getting all the problems right is a 100%, and missing one is a 90% (9 out of 10 correct).  The students are evaluated according to a pre-set standard and are not compared to each other.

5.  Informal measurements are valuable in making routine decisions, such as whom to call on and when, how long to conduct an activity, how much review is needed, and when to intervene if students are off-task.  Since informal measurements are not always reliable, grading decisions based on them may not be valid, and teachers must be careful to include measurements for grading purposes that are formal and systematic.

6.  Formal measurements are used for important decisions, such as when to move on to a new topic or assigning grades.

Exercise 13.2

1. Item 1 can be criticized on the basis of the following criteria:
    a)  Choice D is an implausible, and putting an implausible distracter at choice D is particularly unwise since test-wise students are unlikely to choose it anyway.
    b)  Choice C is the answer.  Having some of the answers as choice C is appropriate, of course, but it is often overused.
    c)  The correct answer is longer than the other distracters.

2. Item 2 can be criticized on the basis of the following criteria:
    a)  It uses "all of the above" as a distracter.
    b)  The absolute term "always" appears in choice A.
    c)  The right answer is again choice C.
    d)  The right answer is longer than the other distracters.
    e)  The term "rugged" appears in both the stem and the right answer.

3. Other than the fact that each distracter is lengthy and requires that students are capable readers, Item 3 meets the criteria. It is particularly effective in that the characteristics of omnivore are illustrated rather than merely giving the names of animals. For instance, suppose the item were written as follows:

Which of the following best illustrates an omnivore?
   a. Bear
   b. Mountain goat
   c. Eagle
   d. Seal

As written, it requires students to know the diet of each animal. They could understand the concept of omnivore but not know that a bear is one, and miss the item for that reason. That would make the item invalid.

Exercise 13.3

A. The Completion Items: While the blanks are of equal length, two of the three items have the blank in the body of the sentence. Items 2 and 3 are not clearly phrased so that only one possible answer is correct.

B. Alternative Response Items: Numbers 2 and 3 are "give aways" for a test-wise student. Students with only a vague understanding of mountains would likely choose "high" over "low," even if they had no idea of what "relief" meant. The notion of "crust" being the outer layer can be determined from experiences, such as the "crust" of a piece of bread.

Exercise 13.4

1. While there is no single "correct" response, teachers should remain in the classroom and carefully monitor their tests. On this basis an appropriate response would be, "My students are taking a test and I can't leave them. Please take a message, and I'll call Mrs. _____ as soon as I can." In the case of an extreme emergency, either the principal should handle it, or s(he) should come down to your classroom to monitor your students while you go to the front office.

2. As with item 2, there is no answer that is no absolute right or wrong answer. However, based on the background material and the information in the item, choice B is preferred.

The rationale is as follows:

Choice A is misleading and could even be called dishonest. In order to maintain credibility the teacher must remain "real."
Choice C is not a "bad" response. The only advantage in choice B by comparison is that it is stated in positive terms.

Choice D is undesirable. The implication is that "I" worked hard, but "you" didn't come through. Even if this is true, it doesn't help student performance, and may even detract from effort on subsequent tests.

Exercise 13.5

1. The distribution indicates that more students chose a particular distracter than the correct answer in each case. For instance, in Item 7, 11 people chose the correct answer--C-- while 13 selected choice D. In Item 10, 11 people chose C--the correct answer--while 19 chose B. Item 15 is particularly questionable, since only 3 people chose the correct answer, while 17 chose D.

2. Either an important misconception exists in the minds of the students, or the items were somehow misleading.

3. The teacher should look at the items, go over them with the students to find out why they chose the particular distracter and respond accordingly. Some appropriate responses would be the following:

   If important misconceptions exist, the content should be retaught, emphasizing the correction to the misconception, and the students' understanding should be measured again on the next test.

   If the items were written in a misleading way, they should be revised.

   If, in the teacher's judgement, the items are invalid, they should be "thrown out" of the test, and the total reduced by the number eliminated.

4. The distracters for Item 1 didn't "work," since only one person chose an answer other than the correct answer. This is a good item at the beginning of a test, since it allowed nearly all the students to begin the quiz successfully. In general, the least demanding items should be placed at the beginning of a test or quiz.

5. An examination reveals the following distribution of correct answers.  A - 2, B - 0, C - 8, D - 4, E - 1.  This definite overuse of choice C as a correct response is typical of teachers. (Not having B as the correct choice for any items, however, is atypical).  Efforts should be made to randomly distribute the correct answer among the four or five choices used.

---

Exercise 13.6

1. Tamara is in stanine 5, Joey in stanine 6, and Helen in stanine 8.

2. Tamara has a z-score of 0 and a T-score of 50, Joey a z-score of approximately .5 and a T-score of 55, and Helen a z-score of approximately 1.4 and a T-score of 64.

3. Tamara's IQ is 100, Joey's is approximately 107, and Helen's approximately 120.

4. Maria's approximate percentile rank in math is 84, and her approximate percentile rank in English is 50.

5. Rhonda's score indicates that she is 1.5 standard deviations above the mean. On this basis her approximate percentile rank would be 92, she would be in stanine 8, and her z-score would be 1.5.

6. The best conclusion is that the scores do not approximate a normal distribution. While the mean, median, and mode are all the same, a normal distribution has approximately 68% of all scores falling from one standard deviation below the mean to one standard deviation above the mean. This distribution has half the scores falling from one standard deviation below to one standard deviation above the mean.

7. Because the standard error is 3, Joanne's true score is between 42 and 48, Franklin's is between 37 and 43, and Monica's is between 32 and 38.

This means choices c and e are true.

8. We don't have enough information to make a conclusion about test bias. First, we don't know why Jaramillo missed the items. Second, we don't know about the performance of other students of Hispanic descent. We can't make any conclusions about test bias until we have more information about the test content.

# ANSWER KEYS TO SELF-CHECK QUIZZES

**Chapter 1: Teaching in the Real World**

TRUE/FALSE: 1.F  2.F  3.F  4.F  5.F

MULTIPLE CHOICE: 6.d  7.b  8.d  9.a  10.c


**Chapter 2: Student Development**

TRUE/FALSE: 1.F  2.T  3.T  4.F  5.F  6.T  7.T  8.F  9.F  10.T

MULTIPLE-CHOICE: 11.b  12.d  13.a  14.d  15.d  16.b  17.c  18.d  19.a  20.a


**Chapter 3: Student Development: Applications**

TRUE/FALSE: 1.F  2.T  3.F  4.F  5.T  6.F  7.T  8.T  9.F  10.F

MULTIPLE-CHOICE: 11.b  12.d  13.a  14.c  15.a  16.d  17.b  18.d  19.c  20.d


**Chapter 4: Individual Differences**

TRUE/FALSE: 1.T  2.F  3.F  4.T  5.F  6.T  7.F  8.F  9.F  10.F

MULTIPLE-CHOICE: 11.b  12.c  13.a  14.b  15.d  16.d  17.b  18.b  19.a  20.d


**Chapter 5: Teaching Students with Exceptionalities**

TRUE/FALSE: 1.T  2.F  3.F  4.F  5.T  6.T  7.F  8.F  9.F  10.T

MULTIPLE-CHOICE: 11.a  12.c  13.a  14.b  15.d  16.b  17.c  18.a  19.b  20.a


**Chapter 6: Behavioral Views of Learning**

TRUE/FALSE: 1.F  2.F  3.F  4.T  5.F  6.T  7.F  8.T  9.F  10.T

MULTIPLE-CHOICE: 11.a  12.d  13.a  14.c  15.a  16.b  17.c  18.c  19.b  20.c


**Chapter 7: Cognitive Views of Learning**

TRUE/FALSE: 1.F  2.F  3.F  4.F  5.F  6.F  7.T  8.F  9.F  10.T

MULTIPLE-CHOICE: 11.d  12.c  13.b  14.b  15.d  16.d  17.d  18.d  19.a  20.b

**Chapter 8: Cognitive Views of Learning: Applications**

TRUE/FALSE: 1.F  2.F  3.T  4.F  5.F  6.T  7.F  8.F  9.T  10.T

MULTIPLE-CHOICE: 11.b  12.d  13.a  14.d  15.d  16.c  17.c  18.c  19.d  20.b

**Chapter 9: Increasing Student Motivation**

TRUE/FALSE: 1.F  2.F  3.T  4.F  5.T  6.F  7.F  8.F  9.T  10.T

MULTIPLE-CHOICE: 11.a  12.d  13.b  14.b  15.a  16.b  17.c  18.c  19.d  20.b

**Chapter 10: Managing Student Behavior**

TRUE/FALSE: 1.F  2.T  3.F  4.F  5.F  6.T  7.F  8.F  9.F  10.T

MULTIPLE-CHOICE: 11.b  12.b  13.a  14.c  15.b  16.b  17.a  18.d  19.d  20.d

**Chapter 11: Planning for Instruction**

TRUE/FALSE: 1.T  2.F  3.F  4.T  5.T  6.F  7.F  8.F  9.F  10.T

MULTIPLE-CHOICE: 11.c  12.d  13.a  14.b  15.b  16.c  17.b  18.a  19.c  20.d

**Chapter 12: Effective Teaching**

TRUE/FALSE: 1.F  2.F  3.F  4.F  5.T  6.F  7.F  8.F  9.F  10.F

MULTIPLE-CHOICE: 11.b  12.d  13.c  14.c  15.e  16.b  17.a  18.d  19.b  20.d

**Chapter 13: Classroom Assessment**

TRUE/FALSE: 1.T  2.F  3.F  4.F  5.T  6.T  7.T  8.F  9.F  10.F

MULTIPLE-CHOICE: 11.d  12.d  13.d  14.b  15.a  16.c  17.b  18.a  19.c  20.c